High-Performance DIESEL Builder's Guide

JOE PETTITT

CarTech®

CarTech®
CarTech,® Inc.
39966 Grand Avenue
North Branch, MN 55056
Phone: 651-277-1200 or 800-551-4754
Fax: 651-277-1203
www.cartechbooks.com

© 2007 by Joe Pettitt

All rights reserved. All text and photographs in this publication are the property of the author, unless otherwise noted or credited. It is unlawful to reproduce – or copy in any way – resell, or redistribute this information without the express written permission of the publisher.

All text, photographs, drawings, and other artwork (hereafter referred to as information) contained in this publication is sold without any warranty as to its usability or performance. In all cases, original manufacturer's recommendations, procedures, and instructions supersede and take precedence over descriptions herein. Specific component design and mechanical procedures – and the qualifications of individual readers – are beyond the control of the publisher, therefore the publisher disclaims all liability, either expressed or implied, for use of the information in this publication. All risk for its use is entirely assumed by the purchaser/user. In no event will CarTech®, Inc., or the author, be liable for any indirect, special, or consequential damages, including but not limited to personal injury or any other damages, arising out of the use or misuse of any information in this publication.

This book is an independent publication, and the author(s) and/or publisher thereof are not in any way associated with, and are not authorized to act on behalf of, any of the manufacturers included in this book. All registered trademarks are the property of their owners. The publisher reserves the right to revise this publication or change its content from time to time without obligation to notify any persons of such revisions or changes.

Edited by: Travis Thompson

ISBN 978-1-61325-062-4
Item No. SA129P

Printed in USA

Title Page:
Diesel trucks are just as at home at the strip as they are pulling the race car. The guys at Bully Dog built this truck and beat a gas powered pickup on the show Pinks. (Photo courtesy of Bully Dog)

Back Cover Photos

Top Left:
The later version of Ford's 6.0L Power Stroke diesel generates 570 ft-lbs of torque, which is great for spinning the tires. The new 6.4L makes even more horsepower and torque, plus it runs cleaner and quieter.(Photo courtesy of DHRA)

Top Right:
Towing is almost as demanding on the driveline as drag racing. If you're wheelin' a heavyweight rig, you'll need to enhance your transmission, and sometimes even your driveshaft and rear end. Bully Dog offers a turnkey performance built Allison 1000 with upgraded C1 through C4 clutch packs plus the main pressure and backflow valves. It also offers a super strong converter that uses dual-discs for the lock-up clutch. (Photo courtesy of Bully Dog)

Middle Left:
Here you can see the total diesel performance package coming together. Add increased airflow (upgraded turbos), improved air density (massive intercooler), and the proper fuel and tuning to match (upgraded injectors, fuel pump, and tuning). Now you just have to worry about the drivetrain holding up! (Photo courtesy of BD Diesel Performance)

Middle Right:
Improving the efficiency of the airflow path, from the intake through the tailpipe, is a key aspect to improving diesel performance. You need to get air into and out of the engine to make power; then you just need to worry about getting enough fuel. (Photo courtesy of BD Diesel Performance)

Bottom Left:
Gale Banks is designing components and devising the techniques to allow direct injection diesels to make power at high RPM. This intake runner design, running nearly straight from the plenum to the valve, is part of the puzzle. A low-restriction, torque-producing balance tube manages the pressure waves in the plenum.

Bottom Right:
A more efficient turbocharger builds boost without introducing as much heat into the intake charge. This helps keep your intake change dense and the power up. This BD Diesel Performance Super B Special turbo is rated to make 525 hp. (Photo courtesy of BD Diesel Performance)

TABLE OF CONTENTS

About the Author 4
Acknowledgments 4
Introduction 5

Chapter 1: Diesel Theory 8
Diesel vs. Gas Engines 10
How Diesel Engines Work 10
Thermodynamics 11
Work Done During
Volume Change 12
Throttling Process 13
Types of Diesel Engines 15
Common Rail Injection 17
Engine and Exhaust Brakes 18

**Chapter 2: Introduction to
Diesel Performance 19**
The Diesel Power Stroke 19
Gale Banks on Mass Flow 21
The Turbocharger was
Invented for Diesel 25
Defining the Limits 27
Combustion Basics 29
Electronic Engine Controls 30
Factory Derating Tactics 32
Summary 33

**Chapter 3: Induction and
Combustion 34**
Tuning the Airflow Path 34
Volumetric Efficiency 35
Laminar Airflow 36
Swirl and Flow 37
Gale Banks on Airflow and
Combustion 39
Airflow After the Compressor 42
Cummins and Duramax
Intake Manifolds 44
Air Distribution and
Power Balancing 44
Porting for Flow and Swirl 46
Camshafts and Valvetrain 47

Chapter 4: The Turbocharger 50
The Basics 51
The Gas Law 51
Heat and Adiabatic Efficiency 52
The Air Density Ratio 53
Choosing a Turbo 53
Compressor Maps 55
Estimate Mass Flow at
Torque Peak 59
Blow-Off and Bypass Valves 60
Intercooling Theory 61
Turbine Basics 62
Wastegates 64
Housing Aspect Ratio 65
Turbine Tech: How it Works 65
Turbine Maps 67
EGTs: What's too Hot? 68

Chapter 5: The Fuel System 69
Diesel Fuel 69
Diesel Fuel Contamination 70
Biodiesel 71
Cetane Number 72
Flash Point 73
Injection Systems 73
Electronically Controlled
Common Rail Injection 75
Talking Fuel Injection with
Bosch 77
Gale Banks on Fuel System
Tech 80
Tuning the Fuel Injection
Cycle 84

Chapter 6: Exhaust 86
Exhaust Manifolds 88
After the Turbo 91
Exhaust Brakes 93

Chapter 7: Nitrous and Propane 95
Nitrous Oxide 95
Nitrous and Diesel 98
Jetting Nitrous for Diesel 99
Tuning Tactics 99
Fuel, Air and Nitrous
Mass Flow 101
Nitrous System Components 102
Propane:
Is it worth the effort? 103

Chapter 8: Driveline 106
Manual Transmissions 107
Automatic Transmissions 110
Sensing Slip 112
Gearing 112
Fluid Cooling 117
Driveline Alignment and
Balance 118

Advice from Around the Industry 119

Chapter 9: GM Diesel Engines 124
1982–2000: 6.2- and
6.5L Turbo Diesel 124
2001–2004: Duramax LB7 125
2004–2006: Duramax LLY 126
2006–Mid-'07: Duramax LBZ 127
Mid-'07–On: Duramax LMM 131

Chapter 10: Ford Diesel Engines 132
1983–1994: 6.9/7.3L IDI 132
1994–2003: 7.3L Power Stroke 132
2003–2006: 6.0L Power Stroke 134
2008–On: 6.4L 137

**Chapter 11: Dodge Cummins
Diesel Engines 138**
1989–1993: First Generation 138
1994–1998: Second Generation 140
1998.5–2002: ISB Upgrade 140
2003–2007: Common Rail
Era 142
2007.5–On: 6.7L 143
Source Guide 144

ABOUT THE AUTHOR

Joe Pettitt is a freelance automotive journalist. He's written hundreds of articles for the performance press including *Hot Rod*, *Sport Compact Car*, *Drag Racer*, *Car Craft*, *Circle Track*, and *Motor Trend*. His adventures as a high-performance journalist include piloting IROC cars around the famous ovals of Daytona and Talladega, road racing a vintage Sunbeam Tiger, participating in the Pikes Peak Hill Climb, and strapping into the world's fastest open-road race record holder as a journalist/passenger. This mind-warping experience offered 27 minutes of sheer terror at over 220 miles per hour while making the 90-mile Silver State Challenge run from Ely, Nevada, to Lund, Nevada, with an average speed of over 194 mph. He also wrote for *Autotronics* magazine where he indulged his passion for great cars and great music. He's held Vintage Racing and FIA competition licenses. Joe Pettitt resides in Southern California with wife Patricia and daughters Vanessa and Jordan.

Gale Banks Engineering has pioneered domestic truck diesel performance. The man's performance approach is always about the combination. Diesels need air—lots of it, and the denser the better. If you can feed it more air mass then you can feed it more fuel, which makes for powerful combinations. (Photo courtesy of Gale Banks Engineering)

ACKNOWLEDGMENTS

I would like to thank Gale Banks and everyone else at Gale Banks Engineering, Joseph Donnelly, Ron Knoch at the DHRA, Keith Lockliear at Diesel Dynamics, JB Hinrichs at Edge Products, Chris Endres at MSD, Mark Chapple and Annette at TST Products, David Fetherston at Flowmaster, Justin McCarthy at Bully Dog, Max Lagod of Hypermax Engineering, Jim McFarland at Hypertech, Matt Bozarth of ATS Diesel, Bill Tichenor at Holly/NOS, and Brian Roth at BD Power.

INTRODUCTION

More than 100 years have passed since Rudolf Diesel received patent #608,845 in 1898 for an internal combustion engine that used pressure to ignite fuel. Of course the development of the engine started much earlier. Rudolf Diesel demonstrated his first engine, a 10-foot-tall cylinder with a nearly water-wheel-sized flywheel in Augsburg, Germany, on August 10, 1893. It used compressed air to force powdered coal into the combustion chamber. It subsequently exploded, nearly killing Diesel. He continued to develop the engine and demonstrated a second version that burned peanut oil in 1896. This second engine had a theoretical efficiency of 75 percent, which compared to the steam engine's efficiency of 10 percent, was truly a marvel.

The marvelous efficiency of the engine was embraced immediately by the economic interests of the day, even before Diesel had the patent. Times have certainly changed. By the time he was awarded his patent, Rudolf Diesel was a wealthy man and his engine design had become the prime mover of the industrial revolution.

Today's diesel engines, while not 75-percent efficient, are far more efficient than their gasoline burning, spark-ignited siblings. In addition, with the advent of common-rail injection, efficient turbochargers, and electronic engine management, diesels are poised to rival gasoline engine as the automotive performance powerplant of choice. This book may even help accelerate that process.

Diesel engines are already powering half the automotive fleet in Europe, and in the United States, diesel versions of Ford's F-series, GM's Silverado and Sierra, and the Dodge Ram are a growing market segment of light heavy-duty trucks.

This cutaway action shot of the inner workings of Jaguar's V-6 turbo diesel is an example of the more performance-oriented diesels available in Europe. The intake and exhaust runner angles are usually seen on high-performance dual overhead cam (DOHC) gasoline engines. (Photo courtesy of Bosch)

Diesels are powerful, they make tremendous torque and power at low RPM, they have great fuel efficiency, and with turbocharging and electronic engine management, it's relatively easy to enhance their performance.

Diesels are Different

Diesel engines operate much differently than gasoline-fueled, spark-ignited engines. So, even though you

INTRODUCTION

MAN was the first vehicle manufacturer to use Bosch diesel pumps in 1927. In 1932, the company used Bosch diesel injection to produce what was then the most powerful diesel truck in the world. (Photo courtesy of DiamlerChrysler)

This two-cylinder Benz was the world's first diesel engine installed in a vehicle. That was back in 1922. (Photo courtesy of DaimlerChrysler)

may have a good grasp of tuning a four-stroke gasoline motor, you need to know from the start that diesels are different—hence the need for the book you are now reading.

I've started at the beginning to highlight these fundamental differences. In the case of heat engines that means a short discussion on thermodynamics. Starting a performance book with a theory-heavy chapter on thermodynamics is admittedly going against the grain, but if you take the time to understand how an internal combustion engine works from a thermodynamic perspective, you'll be amazed how many previously unclear concepts of a performance engine (either diesel or gasoline) suddenly clear up.

After familiarizing you with the thermodynamics of a diesel engine, I provide an overview of current thinking on how to tune and build a hot rod diesel. After that, I discuss engines according to their major mass flow systems. I'll also discuss building bottom-end strength in a technical feature on the Gale Banks Engineering GMC Type R Duramax road-race truck. That machine is one of the three most sophisticated diesel engines on the planet. It has all the tricks you can do to the bottom end, as well as the oiling system, heads, valvetrain, and turbochargers. Okay, it isn't using sequential turbocharging, but if it'll produce quicker laps, the crew at Banks will do it.

Introducing Gale Banks

This is really special. Gale Banks was kind enough to sit down with me for several hours and explain much of what he's learned after many years of performance diesel tuning. Gale Banks has been a diesel performance enthusiast since way before it was cool. I recall interviewing him for a turbocharger story for *Hot Rod* in the late '80s. However, the conversation drifted to diesels. Gale's passion for diesel engines is tangible. The depth and breadth of his knowledge impressed me then, and I'm sure you'll be equally impressed with the diesel performance know-how he's been kind enough to share.

In our interviews, Gale had advice about just about every aspect of diesel technology. His experience and that of his team of engineers proved invaluable in packing this book with useful information and insights that haven't been available to the general public until now.

With the exception of Gale Banks Engineering, BD Diesel Performance, Hypertech, Bully Dog, ATS Diesel Performance, and Edge, just to rattle off a few, the aftermarket performance industry hasn't been working with diesel performance that long. And if you ask them, they'd say they're just starting to understand how to tease more power and torque from diesel engines. Piston design, fuel injection timing and pressures, faster computers, more boost, staged turbos ... it's getting really interesting.

By 1923, the OB 2 diesel engine from Benz & Cie. was the first commercial vehicle diesel engine in production. Of course, it came in a truck. (Photo courtesy of DiamlerChrysler)

HIGH-PERFORMANCE DIESEL BUILDER'S GUIDE

INTRODUCTION

The dyno puts the engine under load and measures every parameter that can influence performance and reliability. From intake air quantity, fuel quantity, exhaust gas temperature (EGT), backpressure, manifold temperature and pressure, cylinder pressure, and intercooling temperature.

The dyno operator at Gale Banks Engineering (GBE) readies his instrument. Careful measurement of an engine's performance is really only possible on a dynamometer. GBE uses the latest equipment to test and develop its engine components and electronic tuning products.

With that, I want to thank you for buying this book. I've put hundreds of hours into it to help you improve your machine safely and more effectively. I've called the people who know how to get the straight answers on diesel performance in order to further your understanding of your machine. Keep reading and I'll tell you how to tune your diesel more effectively and make informed purchases of performance parts because you know why you need them—not just buy something because everyone else did. I hope you find it all useful.

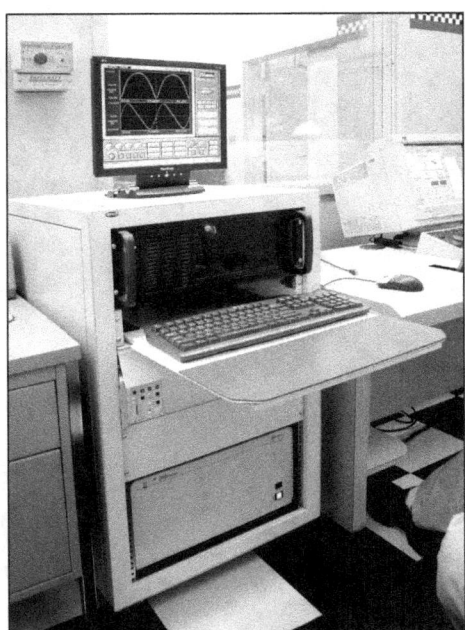

One of the key measurements in developing an engine is cylinder pressure. Not just raw average pressure, but its behavior throughout the RPM range. GBE uses a system that measures the cylinder pressure 1,444 times per revolution. This allows them to measure and analyze the energy released by the fuel and imparted into the piston every quarter of a degree.

You can see the manifold pressure port on the Banks Big Hoss manifold, as well as the layout of the common rail components on the Duramax. The plenum is located just on the other side of the valve cover, the fuel lines feed into the side of the injectors. The electrical connections are at the top of the injectors.

HIGH-PERFORMANCE DIESEL BUILDER'S GUIDE

CHAPTER 1

DIESEL THEORY

Much of the interest in diesel engines as an alternative to gasoline engines centers on the design's raw torque output and efficiency. And although today's diesel engines are extremely advanced and much more powerful and efficient than the engines available just a few years ago, it's interesting to note that diesels are not a new technology. Rudolf Diesel, in fact, obtained the German patent for diesel engines in the late nineteenth century. Gasoline engines of that time were very inefficient, and Rudolf intended to produce a more economical combustion engine.

As you might guess, it took a while for engineers to develop diesel technology to the point where it became the prime mover of maritime shipping and commercial vehicles and electric power generation. Of course, today's advanced diesels are even more efficient, as indicated by the following list of benefits that are attracting diesel customers as identified in a DaimlerChrysler report:

- 30-percent improvement in fuel economy

Rudolf Diesel's second version of his engine, demonstrated in 1896, was a success, burning peanut oil with a theoretical efficiency of 75 percent. Compared to the steam engine's efficiency of 10 percent, it was truly a marvel. (Photo courtesy of DiamlerChrysler)

DIESEL THEORY

- 20-percent reduction in greenhouse gas emissions
- Extended driving range between fueling stops
- Powerful low-end torque that makes the vehicles fun to drive
- Enhanced towing capacity

The report also says there are challenges to be met if diesel vehicles are to capture a significant share of the passenger vehicle market in North America, and the industry is working hard to meet those challenges. Most of those challenges are related to the particulate and NOx emissions output of the diesel engine. NOx is an abbreviation for Oxides of Nitrogen, a chemical brew that is a significant contributor to photochemical smog. As we'll see later in the book, most of the issues have solutions that do not have a serious impact on the power output and efficiency of the engine.

Since most readers are probably more familiar with gasoline engines, let's highlight some of the differences and similarities between gas and diesel engines.

To create combustion in either a diesel or gasoline engine you need three elements: heat (pressure), fuel, and oxygen. When you consider four-stroke gasoline engines, air and fuel are drawn into a cylinder through the intake valve during a piston down stroke, the piston compresses the charge during an up stroke, there's an explosion ignited by the spark plug that pushes the piston down, and the spent gases escape through the exhaust valve on the next up stroke of the piston. A diesel engine works much the same, except that there is no spark to ignite the air/fuel charge. It takes in just air, compresses it, and then injects fuel into the compressed air. The heat of the compressed air ignites the air/fuel mixture and off

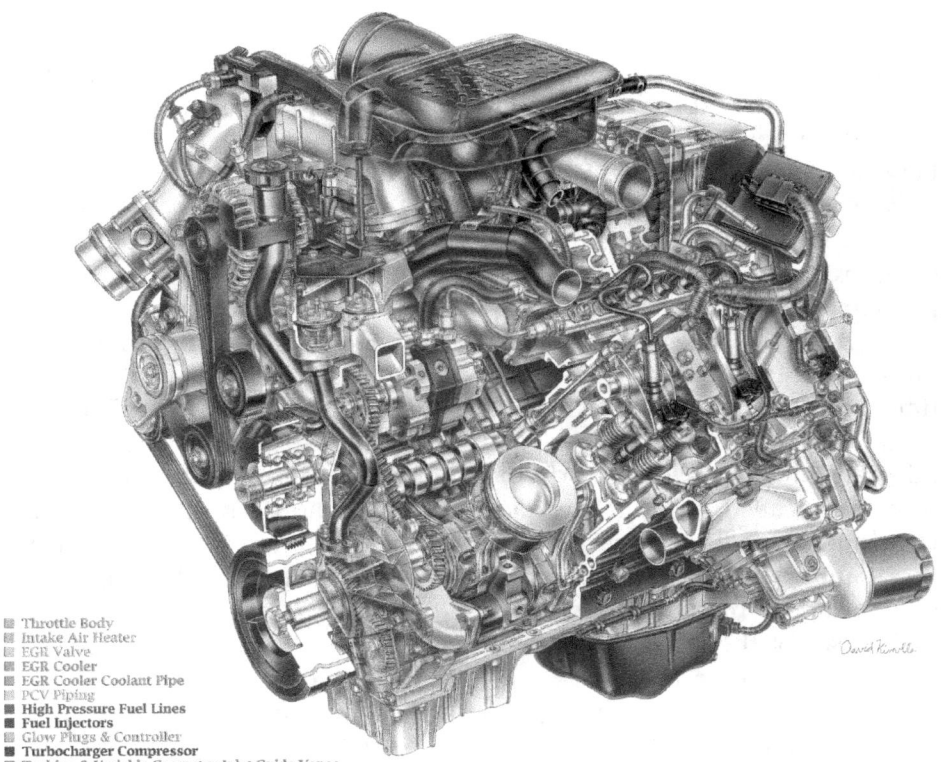

This cutaway drawing of a 2007 Duramax engine provides a glimpse of the heavy-duty construction of the engine compared to a gas engine. (Photo courtesy of General Motors)

Gas engines are designed to manage airflow (intake velocity) and to contain and use pressure in the cylinders differently than a diesel engine. And, of course, diesel engines don't have throttle blades. (Photo courtesy of General Motors)

you go.

Most street-driven gasoline engines have compression ratios between 8:1 and 12:1, while diesel engine compression ratios are between 14:1 and 25:1. The higher compression ratio of the diesel engine leads to better efficiency and power.

Diesel fuel is heavier and evaporates much more slowly than gasoline, as its boiling point is higher than water. Diesel also has good lubricant qualities, which is why it's sometimes called fuel oil. This quality is put to good use lubricating the fuel pumps and injectors, which operate at very high pressures. Diesel fuel is part of the answer to the fuel economy puzzle because it contains more energy per gallon than gasoline. On average, one gallon (3.8 L) of diesel fuel contains approximately 147,000 Btu, while one gallon of gasoline contains 125,000 Btu.

Because diesel fuel is far denser than gasoline, it gets very thick in cold weather. As a result, some diesel engines require glow plugs in cold-start circumstances when the air/fuel charge cannot be brought up to combustion temperatures. A glow plug works like a heated wire, raising the air temperature inside the cylinder for cold starting, after which it turns off.

Most modern gasoline engines use port fuel injection, where the fuel is injected into the intake manifold just outside the cylinder. Diesel engines utilize direct injection, where the fuel is introduced directly into the cylinder itself.

Diesel vs. Gas Engines

Diesel engines use heavier-duty components compared to gasoline engines because they operate at higher pressures and at lower engine speeds. Compared to gas engines, diesels operate more efficiently because of their higher compression, how they inject fuel, the slow burn of the fuel, and reduced pumping losses because of the un-throttled intake.

Diesel engines are typically built differently as well. The bottom end is the same crankshaft, connecting rod, and piston arrangement common to all reciprocating internal combustion engines. The diesel is much heavier-duty and features a longer stroke. The stroke needs to be longer because of the higher compression ratio. The pistons are also much different, featuring a dished negative space in the top and a longer skirt. The piston pin is also larger in diameter, in keeping with the heavy-duty theme.

Diesel engine block castings are designed to handle extreme forces. The walls of the block surrounding the cylinder bores and water jackets are thicker and stronger to handle the increased pressures in stride. You'll also see this heavy-duty construction in the cylinder heads and associated hardware.

Intake wise, virtually all modern diesels have turbochargers, while most gas engines are naturally aspirated. Gas engines are throttled using the intake (throttle body) and are designed to flow lots of air at atmospheric pressure, using the high velocity to fill the cylinders. The diesel is designed to flow the pressurized charge from the turbo. Power is controlled by the pressurized intake charge and the amount of fuel added via the injector. The injector is positioned just before the intake valve, with fuel injected in a fine spray in the direction of the airflow. Therefore, the diesel's power is controlled by increasing the density of the intake charge and by adding fuel into the chamber.

With common rail injection, the diesel injector, located in the center of the head, is fed by a constant pressure reservoir of fuel at around 1,600 bar (on second generation common rail diesels). It injects fuel in a series of pulses depending on the demands of the engine. The glow plug is a device positioned at an angle in the head to heat the air under cold-start conditions.

How Diesel Engines Work

The basic operation of a four-stroke diesel engine involves intake, compression, expansion (power), and exhaust strokes—the ol' suck, squish, bang, blow. The intake stroke starts with the piston at Top Dead Center (TDC) and the intake valve beginning to open. The piston then moves down the cylinder and fresh air is inducted into the cylinder. The intake valve closes as the piston nears Bottom Dead Center (BDC), thus starting the compression stroke. As the piston rises back up through the cylinder, the air is compressed and negative work, i.e., energy, is put into the compressed air. Fuel is added as the piston nears TDC. Because there is a finite combustion time, peak pressure occurs just after TDC, producing maximum work. Ignition delay (the time between fuel injection and when the fuel starts burning) is the reason for the fuel to be injected before TDC. The power stroke creates positive net work due to the high-pressure gases pushing the piston down. Combustion ends during the power stroke as the piston nears BDC, the exhaust valve opens, and the piston moves back up the cylinder, expelling the hot burned gases into the exhaust system (the exhaust stroke).

While diesel engines share the four-cycle process with gasoline engines, the manner in which fuel is introduced and regulated for speed

DIESEL THEORY

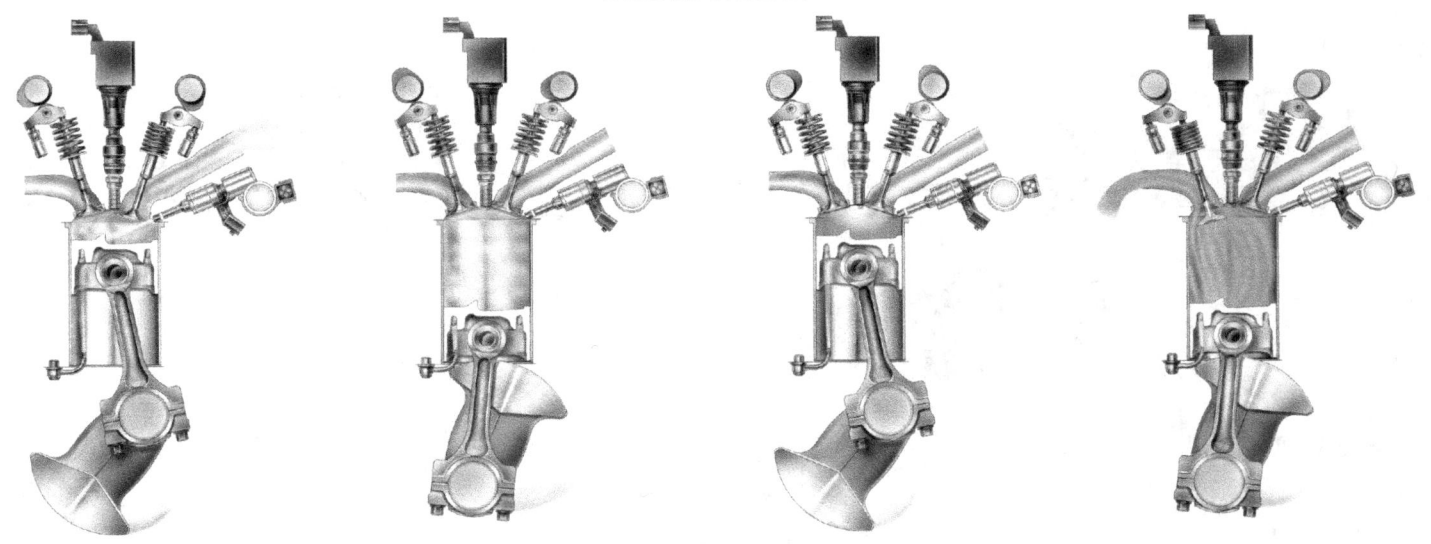

Intake   Compression   Power   Exhaust

Gasoline and diesel engines share the four-stroke cycle of (1) intake, (2) compression, (3) ignition/power, and (4) exhaust. Diesel engines use the introduction of fuel into the chamber as the mechanism to ignite the charge, as opposed to spark-ignited gas engines. There are two-stroke diesels, but they're becoming quite rare because in spite of their better power-to-weight ratio, it's difficult to control their emissions. (Photo courtesy of General Motors)

A direct-injection diesel forces diesel fuel through small orifices at very high pressure to atomize the fuel. As the diesel is injected into the air, it is heated by the compression of the piston rising in the bore until it ignites. (Photo courtesy of Bosch)

and load is very different. Speed and load control (changing the air to fuel ratio) is done only by controlling the fuel delivery, not by throttling the amount of air ingested by the engine. Increasing the amount of fuel injected into the cylinder increases the amount of energy put into the system, and proportionally, the amount of work the engine can do.

Diesel engineers refer to the calibrating of the air to fuel ratio as changing the equivalence ratio. The equivalence ratio is the stoichiometric air to fuel ratio divided by the actual air to fuel ratio. So an equivalence ratio less than one is "fuel lean," and one greater than one is "fuel rich." Stoichiometric is the point where all the fuel burns with all the oxygen. For diesel, stoichiometric is 14.4:1.

Because the intake air is not throttled (not restricted by a throttle blade) on a diesel engine, the fuel efficiency at part load is better than with a gasoline engine, which chokes the air entering the engine under small loads. Diesel engines always run lean, sometimes extremely lean, at part throttle.

Another important feature for diesel engines is that they only compress air during the compression stroke. Gas engines compress air and fuel, and it's possible for the fuel to ignite before the desired time if the pressure and temperature get too high. This means that diesel engines can run safer with higher compression ratios than gas engines, resulting in increased thermal efficiency.

Thermodynamics

The aforementioned is just a brief overview of how the diesel engine works, but to get a full understanding of how it all happens and how best to modify your engine for increased power output, we need to understand the concept of the heat engine. "Heat engine" is the term that describes the basic class of mechanical devices that use heat to generate power that can be harnessed to do work. Steam, turbine, spark-ignition internal combustion (gas), and compression-ignition (diesel) engines are all heat engines. A branch of physics called thermodynamics best explains the forces at work within a heat engine.

The first law of thermodynamics is the law of conservation of energy. A system has a definite amount of internal energy. This energy can be kinetic, potential, chemical, or nuclear. Not considering the type or mix of energy, a system changes state in only two ways: first, heat energy can flow into or out

CHAPTER 1

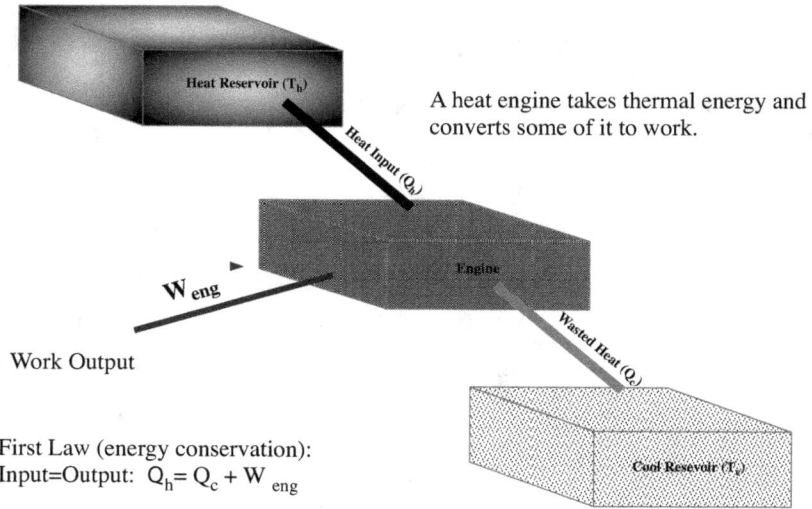

A heat engine takes thermal energy and converts some of it to work.

Work Output

First Law (energy conservation):
Input=Output: $Q_h = Q_c + W_{eng}$

A heat engine requires a temperature difference to function.

Heat energy can only flow from hot to cold unless you do work on the system, such as with an air conditioning system. In a diesel engine, the heat in the combustion chamber has to have a cool reservoir to flow to. Otherwise, the heat energy (and the vehicle) doesn't move. More simply, if the atmosphere at the end of the tailpipe was as hot and pressurized as the combustion chamber you'd have no pressure differential and nothing would move.

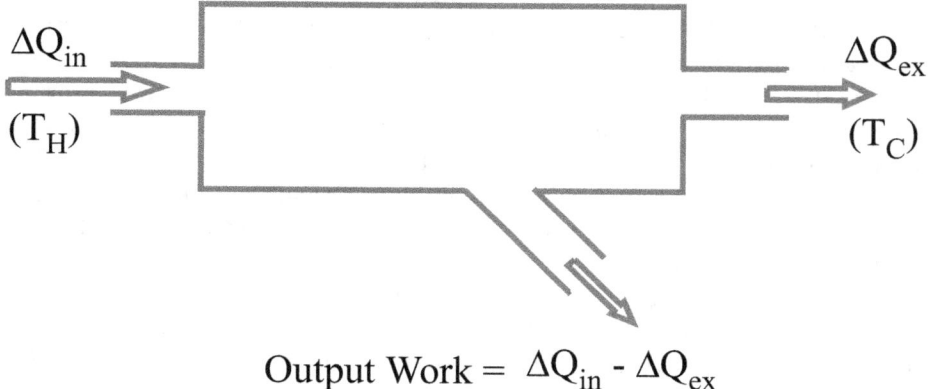

Output Work = $\Delta Q_{in} - \Delta Q_{ex}$

One of the interesting things about the first law of thermodynamics, the conservation of energy, is that all the heat units have to go somewhere. In a typical engine some of the heat (left) is turned to work (Output Work), but most just blows right on out the tailpipe (right).

of a system is equal to the heat injected into the system minus any work done. In that regard, it also describes the conservation of energy in that all energy is accounted for. Energy flowing into the system is either transformed into work, or it increases the energy content of the system.

During the compression stroke, work is done on the air when it's compressed. The air heats up as it's compressed, raising its heat energy content. When the fuel is injected, it burns, further raising the heat energy content and pressure. As the pressure pushes the piston back down the bore, some of the heat energy is converted to work. The air cools as the piston drops (expanding the size of the cylinder), lowering the pressure of the system. When the exhaust valve opens during the exhaust cycle, the heat is allowed to flow out into the cool, low-pressure atmosphere.

So, what does this mean for a diesel performance enthusiast? If you want to do more work (aka, make more power), you need more heat. To make heat, you need to burn more fuel, which requires more air. The more air and fuel you burn (the more energy you add into the system), the more power you make and the more work you can do.

Work Done During Volume Change

Thermodynamically speaking, work done in piston engines is accomplished by a volume change (the piston moving in the bore). With that said, it's important to know how work and volume change are related.

Fundamentally, the power from a piston-type engine comes from expanding gas putting pres-

of the system; and second, the system can do work of some kind against external forces.

The equation form of the first law of thermodynamics involves defining the variables:

ΔU = increase in internal energy

of the system
ΔQ = heat flowing into system
ΔW = work done by system

Resulting in: **$\Delta U = \Delta Q - \Delta W$**

Essentially, the first law states that a change in the internal energy

DIESEL THEORY

sure on the piston top and forcing it down the bore. The force exerted on the piston by the gas is given by the definition of pressure:

$$P = F/A \text{ or } F = PA$$

Where:

- A = Area of the piston top
- F = Force
- P = Pressure

Work occurs during the displacement of the piston and is defined as:

$$\Delta W = (\text{force} \times \text{distance})(\cos\emptyset)$$
$$(PA)(\Delta y)(1) = P(A\,\Delta y)$$

Since $A\,\Delta y$ is the increase in volume of the gas (ΔV) we can simplify the equation:

$$\Delta W = P\Delta V$$

Δ = delta, or a change, so this equations says that the change in work is equal to the pressure multiplied by the change in volume.

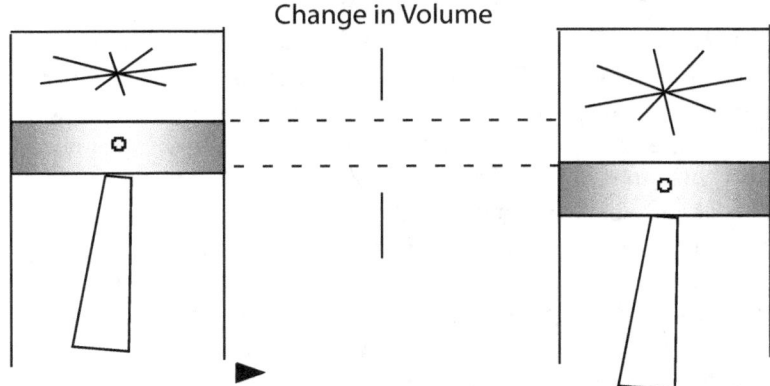

Work Done During Volume Change

Change in Volume

The heat energy in the chamber raises the pressure of the gases, which do work on the piston when they force it down the bore. In doing such work, some of the heat energy causing the pressure is converted to work and the temperature of the charge cools based on the amount of work done.

This equation applies to systems where the pressure is essentially constant during the volume change. As a practical matter we can use the average pressure to calculate the work done by the gas on the piston. Still, the key concept is that work is done by the pressure on the piston as the gas expands.

Throttling Process

The throttling process is one important difference between gasoline engines and diesel engines. A throttle controlling the intake of air in a gas engine is one of the reasons a throttle-less diesel engine is more fuel

---

Defining Work

Depending on which area of the physical sciences you're working in, "work" will have different definitions, or more accurately different dimensional units, i.e., foot-pound, Newton-meter, etc. This comes about mainly from the area of study. Large subjects like cars and trucks tend to have the forces working on them and through them measured in these larger units of value. Work itself is a way to measure and to accurately describe the one aspect of a body moving in a steady direction, and acted on by a force parallel to that direction. Thus the definition of work is given by the formula:

$W = F \times S$ where F is the force and S is the distance traveled by the object.

So a basic definition of Work is: a force acting on an object through a given distance.

In thermodynamics, Work is still a two dimensional unit (force and distance), but in this case, the force is the pressure and the distance is the displacement.

CHAPTER 1

Audi R10 TDI: Diesel History in the Making

The diesel revolution is underway. On this side of the world of light-heavy pickups and heavy-duty work in commercial and construction power units. That's changing. In fact, the choice sports trucks of today are diesel powered. With the explosive growth of diesel drag racing and the diesel pickup segment in the states, can it be long before the sports car and hot rodders get wise?

After Audi's dominating performance in the 2006 racing season and the great passenger car diesel engines in Europe, it won't be long until the diesel engine will be the preferred high-performance powerplant in cars, trucks, and SUVs here in the states. Audi kick started the turbo-diesel revolution with 18,600 miles of testing and approximately 1,500 hours on the engine dynamometers, a win at the car's debut race in the 12-hours of Sebring, and a win at the ultimate motorsport test: an overall victory at the legendary 24 Hours of Le Mans.

In April 2006 Audi's Rinaldo Capello, Tom Kristensen, and Alan McNish dominated the 54th running of the Mobil 12 Hours of Sebring. They started on the pole and never looked back, winning the race by four laps, an impressive margin for the new Audi R10 TDI Power racer. The winning team made 349 laps of the 3.7-mile airport course in 12 hours, 12 seconds.

Head of Audi Motorsport, Dr. Wolfgang Ullrich, wants the team to continue this winning streak. However, the challenge this time around is bigger than ever before, since TDI technology has never been pushed to its limits in motorsport. Audi is the first automobile manufacturer to face this challenge. In addition, the Audi R10 is the first sports car with a diesel engine to be developed in accordance with the new ACO (Automobile Club de l'Ouest) LM P1 regulations. Therefore, the Audi Sport technicians did not only have to prepare themselves for the peculiarities of TDI technology, but also to exploit the specifications dictated by the new regulations in order to set new benchmarks with TDI Power.

The aluminum V-12 power unit in the R10 TDI produces 650 hp. Even more remarkable is the maximum torque of over 810 ft-lbs. Tires, clutch, and gearbox must come to terms, just like the drivers, with these enormous forces for a 24-hour period.

The Audi R10's diesel engine is the first to be developed in accordance with the new ACO (Automobile Club de l'Ouest) LM P1 regulations, the most technologically interesting motorsport category found around the globe today. The aluminum V-12 in the R10 TDI produces 650 hp and over 810 ft-lbs of torque. (Photo courtesy of Audi)

In its debut race, the Audi R10 TDI won the 54th Mobil 12 Hours of Sebring by four laps making 349 laps of the 3.7-mile airport course in 12 hours, 12 seconds. Is this the start of a high-performance diesel revolution in racing? (Photo courtesy of Audi)

DIESEL THEORY

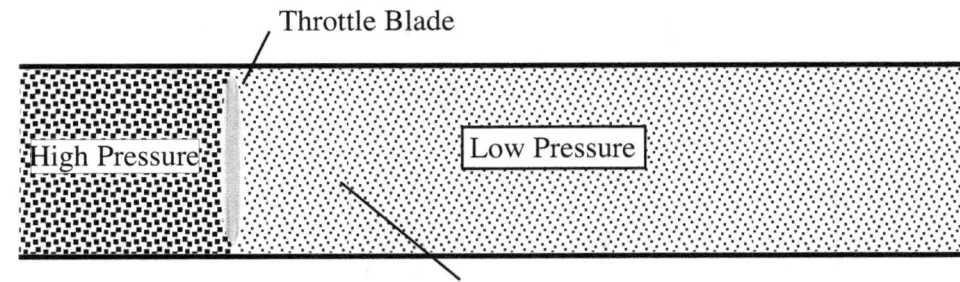

Throttling the intake air is a source of inefficiency of gas engines. Diesel engines control engine speed and power output by adjusting fuel flow, not by restricting intake air, which makes them more efficient.

efficient at part throttle operation.

The source of the inefficiency of throttled intake is the work from the engine required to produce the pressure drop across the throttle blade. Negative work is being done on the intake air on the piston side of the throttle (it is restricted from flowing freely). So in a reverse of the process that raises the internal energy of the intake air as it is compressed in the cylinder, the air is subjected to an instant pressure drop, thus reducing its internal energy and therefore temperature and pressure.

The negative work done on the intake air to reduce internal energy, pressure, and temperature shows up as increased fuel consumption. A throttle-controlled engine consumes more fuel at part throttle per unit of mass flow compared to a throttle-less engine because fuel is required to do the work to reduce the pressure on the cylinder side of the throttle blade.

Types of Diesel Engines

Although the basic diesel cycle is common to all diesels, how the fuel is delivered has varied over the years, making it a handy way to discriminate between different diesel engines. The fundamental division is the way the fuel is injected into the cylinder: directly or indirectly. Direct injection is the latest design and uses high injection pressures to mix the fuel efficiently with the charge air by injecting the fuel directly into the chamber. Indirect injection injects fuel into a small combustion chamber in the head, which ignites and injects a mix of combusting fuel into the main chamber. The eruption from the pre-combustion chamber provides the turbulence to atomize the fuel. Indirect-injection engines are less efficient than direct-injection engines because the pre-combustion chamber rejects heat into the cooling system, as does the main combustion chamber. In addition, indirect designs require systems for preheating for cold starts.

With each injection strategy, engineers have come up with several fuel delivery tactics.

Mechanical Injection Types

Multiple Unit Injection consists of a fuel supply pump, fuel filter, multiple unit injection pump, and one injector for each cylinder. The fuel supply pump and the fuel filter provide a low-pressure supply of fuel to the injection pump. The multiple unit injection pump contains an individual injection pump for each engine cylinder. Fuel is delivered from the multiple unit injection pump to the injectors at each cylinder in a timed sequence and a regulated amount, based on accelerator pedal position and engine speed.

Wobble Plate Pump Variation is basically the same as the multiple unit injection system, except that it uses a different injection pump. In a wobble plate pump, all of the pump plungers are actuated by a single wobble plate instead of a camshaft with a separate cam for each pump plunger. The fuel metering is accomplished by a single axially located rotary valve, in contrast to the rotary movement of the individual plungers in the multiple unit injection pump.

Distributor-Type Injection Systems

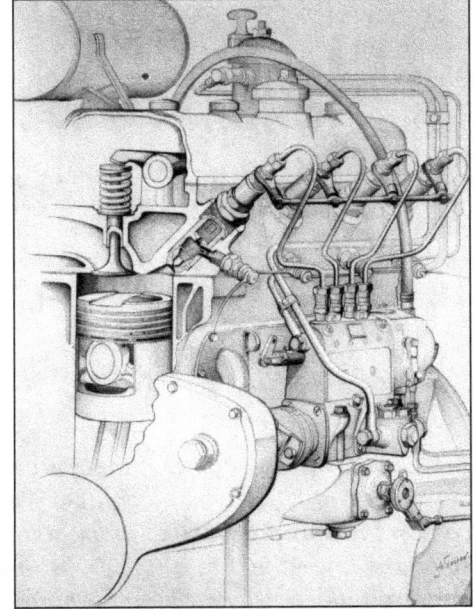

Before diesel fuel pumps could generate the pressure to successfully inject fuel directly into the chamber, indirect injection provided the means to atomize and ignite a diesel fuel/air charge. This Mercedes-Benz 260 D engine features an injection pump and diesel fuel lines. (Photo courtesy of DiamlerChrysler)

CHAPTER 1

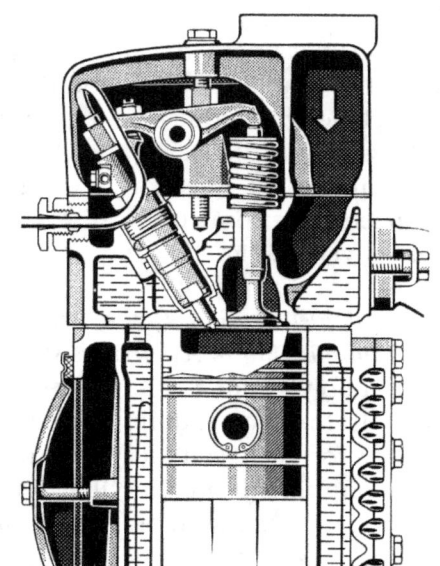

Direct diesel injection made its debut at Mercedes-Benz in 1964, in the OM 352 engine for commercial vehicles. Notice the piston bowl shape and intake port are quite different from modern high-swirl designs. (Photo courtesy of DiamlerChrysler)

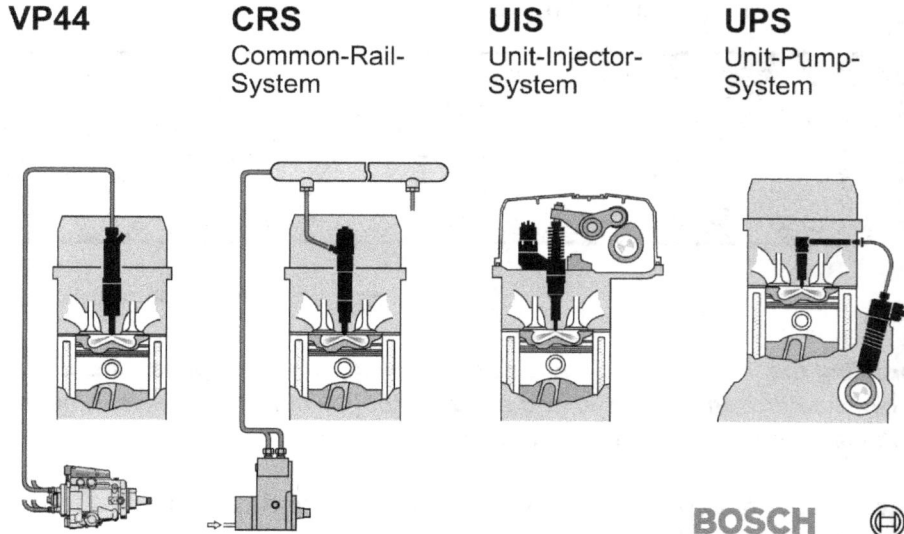

This diagram displays the four basic approaches to fuel delivery. From left to right: The VP44 is one of the more significant radial distribution pumps manufactured by Bosch. It was used on Dodge Cummins-powered Rams. The common rail is the current state-of-the-art system. Unit injection is still used for some commercial and specialty applications. Unit pump is an early design used on the first direct injection as well as early indirect injection diesel engines. (Photo courtesy of Bosch)

are characterized by the fact that pumping, metering, and distribution operations take place at low pressure. The high pressure required for injection is built up by the injector at each cylinder. A lift pump lifts fuel from the tank and delivers it to the float chamber, then a second low-pressure pump delivers the fuel to the distributor. Fuel passes through the distributor to the metering pump, where it is divided into measured charges. The fuel charges are then delivered back to the distributor, where they are sent to the injectors in the proper sequence. The measured charges are then sprayed into the cylinders at the proper time and under high pressure by the fuel injectors.

Unit Injection systems operate in the same manner as the multiple unit injection system. The difference is that rather than using a centrally located unit to house the high-pres-

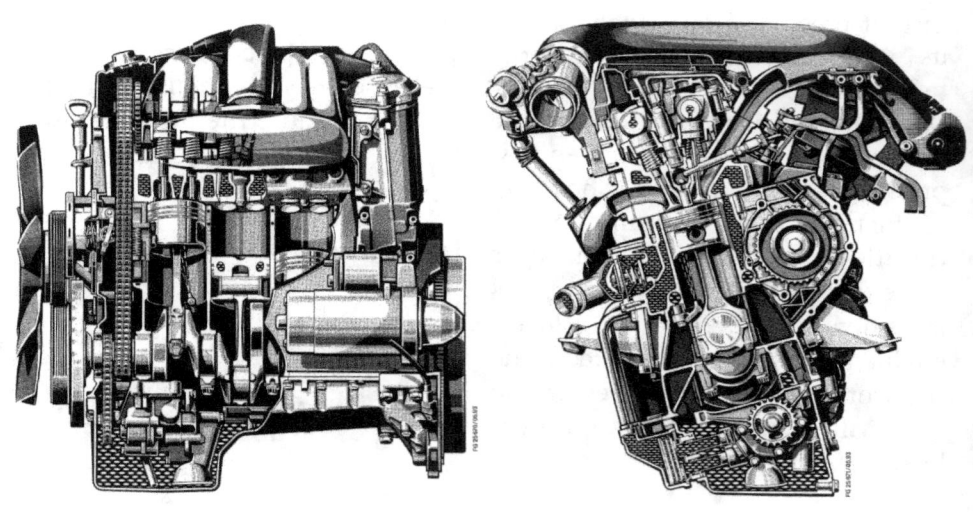

The OM 604 D 22 engine of the Mercedes-Benz 220 Diesel (W 202 series), introduced in 1993, was a compact yet powerful diesel using an overhead cam, with center positioned indirect injection arrangements. It's only been since the late-1990s to early-2000s that common rail has become the preferred fuel delivery system. (Photo courtesy of DiamlerChrysler)

sure pumps, control racks, pressure regulators, and delivery valves, they are all incorporated into each injector. This eliminates the need for high-pressure lines or any other apparatus besides the fuel supply pump.

Common Rail Injection

The common rail direct injection system, primarily developed by Bosch, is perhaps the most significant technology to arise in the long history of the diesel engine. The Bosch high-pressure injection system, with its distributor-pump, unit injector, and common rail have transformed the ponderous, smoke-belching diesel engines of yesterday into the sporty, fuel-efficient, clean, and powerful machines of today. Common rail injection, with its ability to shape the fuel curve of each power stroke by dividing each injection into several pulses (pre-, main, and post-injections), allows optimum control of fuel and load for maximum performance.

Here's a quick overview of how it works: In the common rail system, injection pressure is generated separately. A high-pressure pump generates up to 1,600 bar of pressure in an accumulator (the rail), as determined by the injection pressure setting in the engine control unit. The pressure is built up independently of the engine speed and the quantity of fuel injected. The fuel is fed through rigid pipes to the injectors, which inject the correct amount of fuel in a fine spray into the combustion chambers. The Electronic Diesel Control (EDC) system has extremely precise control over all the injection parameters such as the pressure in the rail, the timing, and duration of injection, as well as performing other engine functions.

This technology is being rapidly and radically improved. Bosch is currently working on the fourth generation of the common rail system. In the first and second generation, the injection process is controlled by a magnetic solenoid on the injectors. The hydraulic force used to open and close the injectors is transmitted to the jet needle by a piston rod. In the third-generation system, the injector actuators consist of several hundred thin piezo crystal wafers. Piezo crystals have the special characteristic of expanding rapidly when an electric field is applied to them. In a piezo inline injector, the actuator is built into the injector body very close to the jet needle. The movement of the piezo packet is transmitted friction-free, using no mechanical parts, to the rapidly switching jet needles. The advantages over the earlier magnetic and current conventional piezo

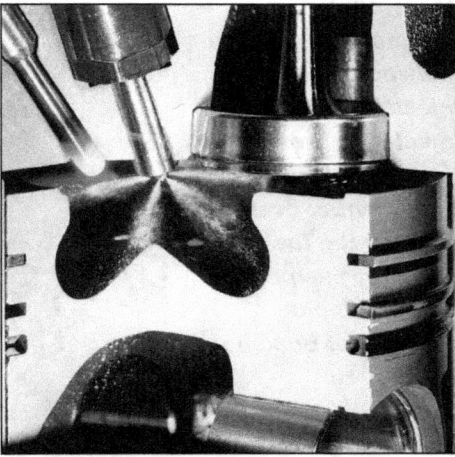

Modern direct injection uses high-pressure injection to atomize the fuel, which is sprayed into a turbulent air charge. The combustion cup in the piston shapes the air charge so the fuel will be injected into an oxygen-rich environment. (Photo courtesy of Bosch)

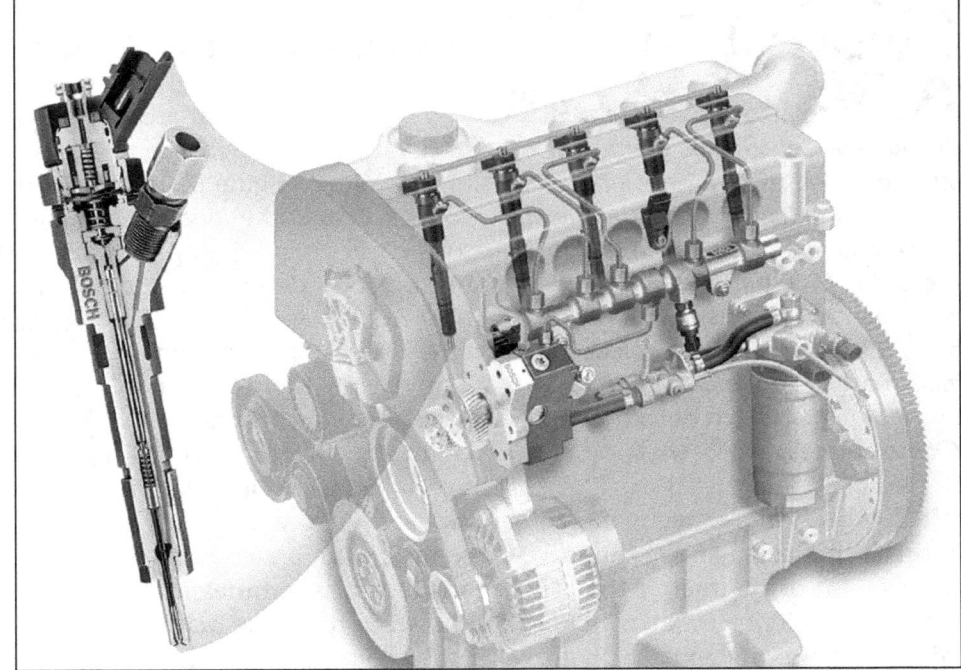

The common-rail system uses a high-pressure pump that pressurizes a main rail (sometimes referred to as the accumulator), which provides a reservoir of high-pressure diesel fuel. When the engine management computer activates the injectors, they deliver precise quantities of fuel with exact timing. This system is the primary reason today's diesel engines are so efficient. (Photo courtesy of Bosch)

CHAPTER 1

The evolution of common-rail injection is using piezo injectors. These injectors cycle so fast that they allow much more control over shaping the fuel curve for each power stroke. (Photo courtesy of Bosch)

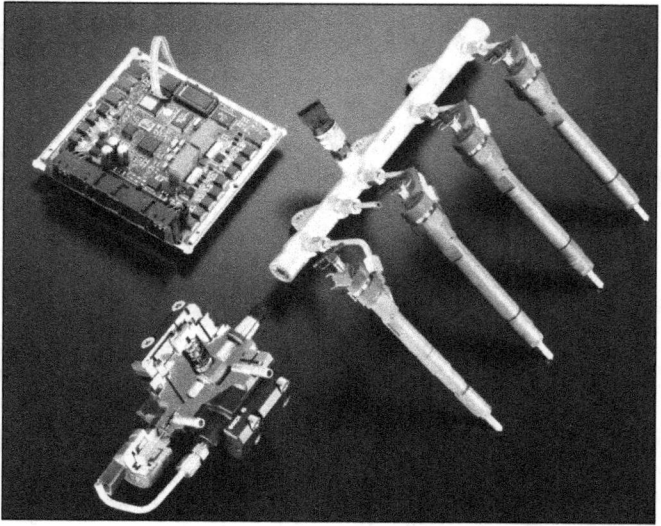

Because diesel engines operate at such low RPM there is very little turbulence to fully atomize the fuel in the combustion chamber. The high pressure (1600 bar and above) of common-rail systems and the spray pattern that promotes turbulence and mixing are key to releasing more of the heat in the fuel to optimum work. (Photo courtesy of Bosch)

injectors are a more precise metering of the fuel injected and an improved atomization of the fuel in the cylinders. The rapid speed at which the injectors can switch makes it possible to reduce the intervals between injections and split the quantity of fuel delivered into a large number of separate injections for each combustion stroke. Diesel engines become even quieter, more fuel efficient, cleaner, and more powerful.

For its fourth generation of common rail system, Bosch is currently exploring designs using even higher injection pressures of more than 2,000 bar, as well as injectors with variable injection geometry.

Engine and Exhaust Brakes

There is one final area we need to cover before moving on to exploring the diesel engine performance in greater detail: the need for some sort of engine braking mechanism. Since diesels have no throttle, they don't offer much engine braking when you release the accelerator pedal. To work around this, engineers have devised two main technologies to provide engine braking: a compression brake and an exhaust brake. The compression brake is known as the "Jake Brake," in honor of the company that makes it, Jacobs Vehicle Systems, Inc.

Jacobs says its Jacobs Engine Brake is a compression release device that mounts on, or within, the engine's overhead valvetrain. It changes the timing of the engine exhaust valves, turning the engine into a giant air compressor. The resulting stopping power is proportional to engine RPM, but you have to use the brakes to stay within the RPM limits of the engine. This type of engine brake is typically used on heavy-duty commercial vehicles (semi trucks and buses), enabling safer vehicle speed control in several driving conditions, from flatlands to steep downhill descents.

Exhaust brakes, on the other hand, mount in the vehicle's exhaust system and restrict exhaust flow when activated. This supplementary braking system helps to slow your vehicle by restricting the flow of exhaust gases and increasing backpressure inside the engine. The increased backpressure creates resistance against the pistons, slowing the crankshaft's rotation, and thus your vehicle, so long as it's in gear. Exhaust brakes are more commonly found in light-heavy duty diesel trucks on the road today. We'll explore all of this in more detail in subsequent chapters.

This aftermarket exhaust brake from BD Diesel Performance uses a double-action spring air cylinder to restrict exhaust flow and give you some engine braking power. The 3.75-inch inner diameter flows a lot of air when it's open, so it doesn't hurt your performance when it's not in use. (Photo courtesy of BD Diesel Performance)

CHAPTER 2

INTRODUCTION TO DIESEL PERFORMANCE

In the first chapter, we took a short course in the thermodynamics of the internal combustion engine. There we learned a little about heat engines and how they make power. Even taken abstractly, this knowledge gives you an advantage in choosing products and techniques to improve the performance of your diesel engine. In this chapter, we begin the practical application of that knowledge.

The most effective way to increase the power output of an internal combustion heat engine is to increase the average force of the power stroke and minimize friction within the engine. You can also free up power by reducing the rotational inertia of the reciprocating and rotating components such as the rods, pistons, crankshaft, and flywheel (if equipped with a manual trans), as well as by reducing parasitic power lost to driving external accessories. Reducing the weight of the rotating assemblies is time consuming and expensive. These heavy-duty (and consequently heavy weight) parts are designed for high cylinder pressure, high heat, and high torque loads sustained inside a diesel engine. Chasing down efficiency in driving the water pump, fuel pump, alternator, air conditioning, etc., is difficult and not practical or cost effective unless you're building a purpose-built racing vehicle where all other considerations are second to finding power.

In this book we concentrate on the easiest and cost effective (not to mention most fun) way of increasing the power output of the engine: increasing the average force exerted on the piston during the power stroke. I'll also show you some of the research and development Gale Banks Engineering is working on.

The Diesel Power Stroke

The power stroke of a four-stroke engine can be thought of as the theoretical average pressure generated by the heat that combustion exerts on the piston top while it travels the distance of the stoke. This theoretical average is called the mean effective pressure (MEP).

The equation that describes MEP is:

MEP = 150.8 x Torque/Displacement

(Note the capacity units are in cubic inches. To use this equation, you need to convert metric units (cc's and liters) into inches. To convert cc's into cubic inches, multiply the number of cc's by 0.0610237. Multiply the number of liters by 61.023744 to convert it to cubic inches.)

What this formula tells us is that the two factors that influence the power output of an engine are the size of the engine (displacement) and the cylinder pressure. This knowledge is fairly well known by performance enthusiasts (remember the muscle car era?). In other words, the larger the surface area on which a given combustion pressure acts, the more force is produced. Or, with a given surface area, higher pressure produces more force.

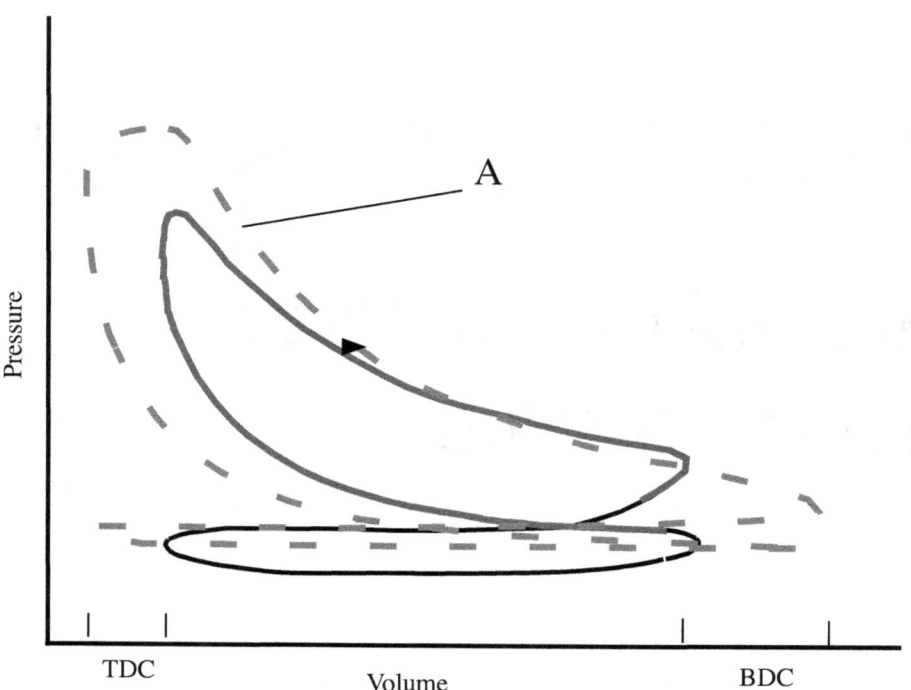

The dotted trace compares the pressure and volume curves of an imaginary gas engine and diesel engine. The diesel (dotted) has higher peak pressure that remains higher as the volume of the chamber expands. This area under the curve (A) is part of the reason diesels are more forceful and efficient than gasoline engines (solid line).

What isn't so obvious in this equation is the time and distance in crankshaft rotation degrees that the force acts. The equation uses a constant of 150.8, which is multiplied by a known torque value, then divided by the cubic inches of displacement (CID). The displacement of a Cylinder is determined by:

(Bore/2)² x 3.14 x Stroke

The displacement is basically the distance over which the force of the MEP acts (distance and force being the two dimensions that define work). As we stated at the beginning, the power stroke is the force acting over a distance within the engine, and the average force acting over that distance is the MEP.

In order to increase the power output of an engine, we need to increase the MEP. To do that, we have three options: (1) increase the displacement, (2) increase the peak cylinder pressure on the power stroke, and/or (3) increase the *duration* of the pressure acting on the piston.

Either option 2 or 3 above will increase the average pressure working on the piston top as it travels in the bore. However, a diesel engine is particularly designed to increase the duration of the pressure acting on the piston. The duration of the fuel injection pulse is key to this process. As you inject fuel you create heat and pressure—a longer injection creates more heat and pressure over a longer period of time. That is really one of the more unique qualities of diesel engine design that makes it both powerful and efficient.

Since this book is about enhancing the power output of diesel engines, we should have a reasonable grasp of the units of measure of power of a rotating heat engine. The MEP equation above is derived from the equations that describe horsepower and torque. For more info, see the Horsepower and Torque sidebar on page 22.

Applying the MEP formula to the '06 6.6-liter Duramax LBZ engine's stock torque rating of 650 ft-lbs at 1,600 rpm we find that the MEP acting on the piston top is 243 psi (150.8 x 650/(6.6 x 61.023744) = 243). The performance challenge then is how to increase that figure without causing driveability and reliability issues that outweigh the performance benefit.

Using the MEP equation, or at least knowing what the cylinder pressure is at various engine outputs, helps you with tuning choices. Here's why: As with all things in life, there are limitations. To make more power without increasing the displacement, you have to increase the cylinder pressure during the power stroke. How much pressure you can add is limited by the stress limits of the pistons, rods, rings, cylinder walls, and the hardware that holds it all together. Keep in mind also that the engine has to handle the peak cylinder pressure, which is much higher than the average.

With diesel engines, the most common way to make more power is to increase the air density in the cylinder. Beyond the bolt-on intake and exhaust parts, you can re-tune the engine to modify its electronic controls. You can increase the boost of the stock turbo or install one that flows more mass air. You'll also need to add fuel to increase the heat and therefore pressure in the cylinder.

INTRODUCTION TO DIESEL PERFORMANCE

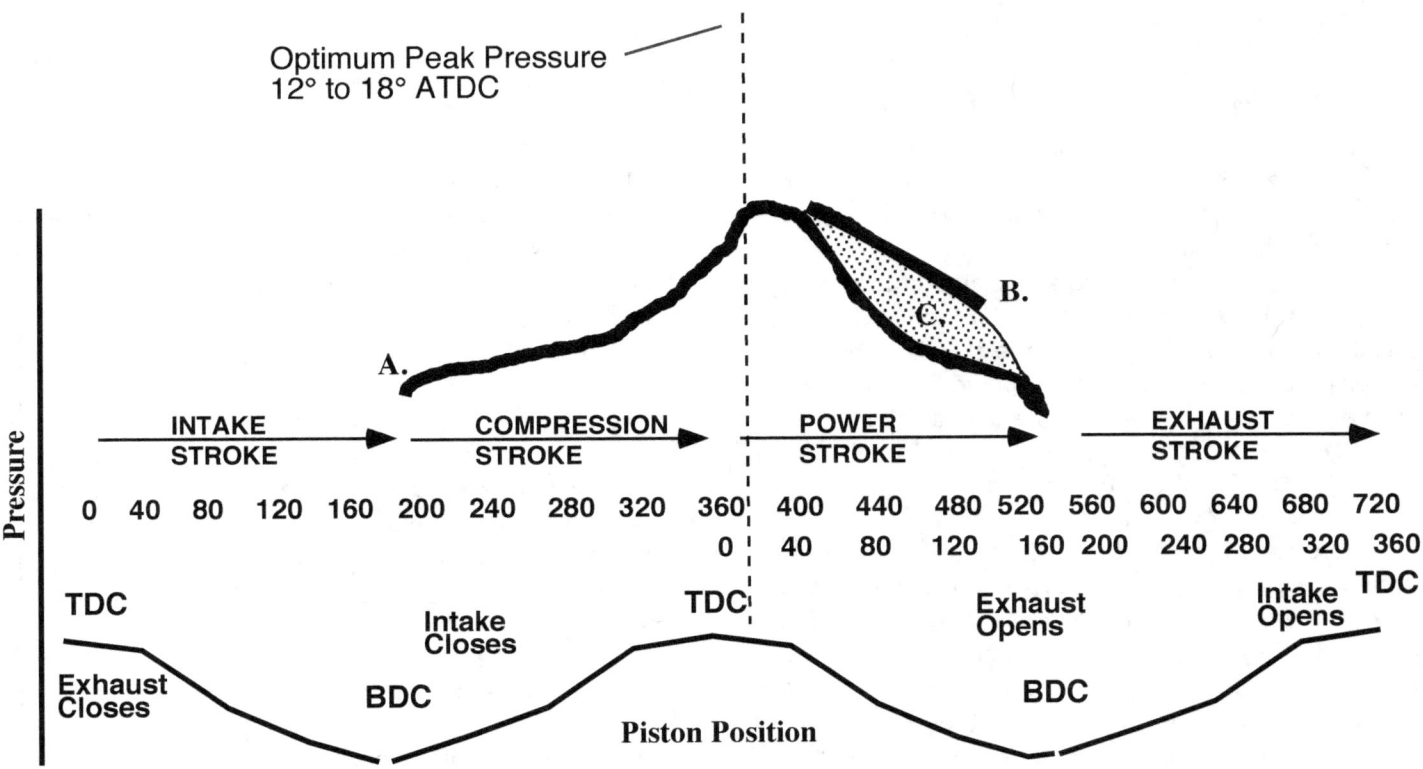

This theoretical pressure trace (A) of a diesel engine shows the relationship of pressure to piston position and crank angle degrees. The piston position indicates the volume change of the chamber. When tuning when and how much fuel to inject, you have the option to change the pressure curve (B), allowing you to go after the area (C) to make more power and improve efficiency.

Simply increase the air density in the chamber and add fuel. That's essentially the goal of diesel performance in a nutshell. Of course, it's not as simple in practice. For example, add too much fuel at the wrong time in the combustion cycle and you get high exhaust gas temperatures (EGT) and smoke. Run that way for long and you'll be in danger of hurting your engine.

Successfully blending theory with the real world requires engineering smarts and experience. Not everyone has the time to learn all this stuff on his or her own, so if you're really interested, pay particular attention to the rest of this chapter, as I've asked Gale Banks to share his vast experience in enhancing the power of diesel engines.

Gale Banks on Diesel Performance Strategy: It's all About Mass Flow

This section on diesel performance is the result of some great interviews I had with Gale Banks:

When you're talking about naturally aspirated motors, meaning motors without a supercharger or a turbocharger, most people use airflow to talk about power enhancements. But when I talk about supercharged or turbocharged engines I prefer to talk about density.

To understand why that's significant let's start with the basics: engines are air pumps. A four-stroke engine pumps its own volume every two revolutions. So if you have a 427-ci engine, it pumps 427 cubic inches of air every two revolutions, not counting volumetric variables. The question is how much does that air weigh? What is its density?

Air Density

Let's look at air in nature. Air weighs about 0.07 pounds per cubic foot (seven hundredths of a pound per cubic foot). That would be near sea level under standard conditions, say 70 degrees. Of course, the air's density varies as its pressure and temperature change. For example, at a higher altitude, air with the same temperature weighs less. There is less pressure because there is less air mass pushing down on it at the higher altitude. Then again, if the air gets colder, a cubic foot of air weighs more than when it's warmer. This is

CHAPTER 2

Horsepower and Torque

Horsepower and torque are the basic measurements of engine performance. Torque is a measurement of how much force the engine generates, while horsepower is the rate of work an engine is able to do.

Horsepower and torque are related in that force is required to do work. If you look under the hood of these equations you'll have a greater understanding and appreciation of your engine. Since horsepower is dependent on torque, let's look at torque first. The equation for torque is:

Torque = Force x Length

Torque is a twisting (or rotational) force exerted from a center point of rotation. Therefore, the only way to measure torque is using a distance from the pivot. In other words, you measure the twisting force's magnitude through a lever arm. If you have a 1-ft lever arm and you push or pull it with 50 lbs of force, you'll make 50 ft-lbs of torque. To express this in inch-lbs, simply multiply the ft-lbs by 12, which in our example is 50 x 12 = 600 inch-lbs.

Horsepower is the rate of work the engine performs Work is defined as the distance a force moves an object. For example in the British system a unit for work is the foot-pound. It denotes the force (pound) and the distance of one foot. So one foot-pound of work equals the force required to move one pound, one foot. Note that torque is sometimes expressed as pounds-feet, while work is expressed as foot-pounds. They are related but they are also different quantities.

Power is defined as work divided by time or:

P = Work/Time

One horsepower can be expressed as the power required to move one pound 550 feet in one second. (1 hp = 550 ft-lbs/1 second = 33,000 ft-lbs/minute)

The equation for deriving horsepower from engine torque is:

HP = RPM x Torque/5252

In this equation, 5252 is the distance in feet that the end of the one-foot lever travels per second.

When you divide the product of engine speed in RPM and the twisting force in pounds-feet by the displacement in feet per second, you get the rate of work, or power, in the quantity we call horsepower.

The basic principles of diesel performance are the same no matter what truck you're starting with. There are also a variety of companies making quality parts for your diesel. (Photo courtesy of BD Diesel Performance)

so because as hot air expands, the molecules move farther apart and therefore there is less mass (less molecules) in a cubic foot of air, which means there is less oxygen.

Oxygen is the key thing when you're talking about engine performance—it's the active ingredient in the atmosphere that reacts with the fuel. More oxygen means more potential power. In other words: If you don't have more oxygen, putting in more fuel won't help.

Fuel Ratio

In a gasoline engine you have a narrow range of air/fuel ratios that will work. It's like 15:1 to about 12:1. 14.7:1 is the chemically perfect stoi-

INTRODUCTION TO DIESEL PERFORMANCE

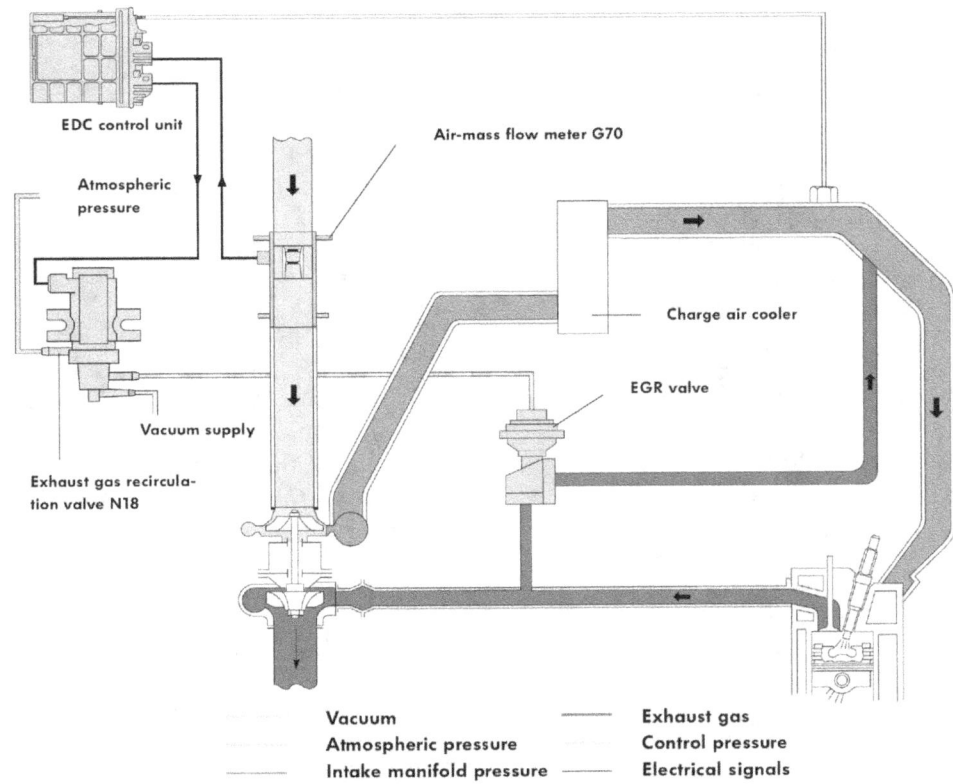

Here's the layout of the airflow path of a turbo diesel. The key to making reliable, low-emissions power is to increase the air density in the cylinder by increasing boost pressure and charge-air cooling (intercooling) efficiency. Then you need to add fuel and improve the exhaust flow. (Photo courtesy of Bosch)

chiometric air/fuel ratio that theoretically will burn all the fuel. So if you have 14.7 parts air and one part fuel (by weight), you'll have enough oxygen to burn all the fuel, but no more. (Again, this is true only in standardized conditions.)

As you go richer you get into the power mixtures. For example, mixing 12 parts air to one part fuel, a 12:1 ratio, is another way of saying you've got more fuel per unit of oxygen. Of course this leads to the question: Why can't you make full power with a chemically perfect 14.7:1 ratio? Well, the excess fuel provides more cooling and so prevents detonation up to a point. It allows the engine to use a higher compression ratio.

Ultimately, the power that a gas engine will make is a function of the octane of the fuel. The higher the octane, the more power you can make because you can have higher compression and not have detonation. Strictly speaking, detonation is not caused by compression; it's

When you increase the boost pressure with a turbo you're doing work on the air and therefore heating it up. Heated air has more pressure when confined to a given volume, but this does not increase density. To keep the density of your boosted air up, you'll need an intercooler. An intercooler, like the air-to-air intercooler shown here, is basically a heat exchanger that transfers heat from the heated and boosted intake charge back to the atmosphere (like a radiator does with the hot engine coolant).

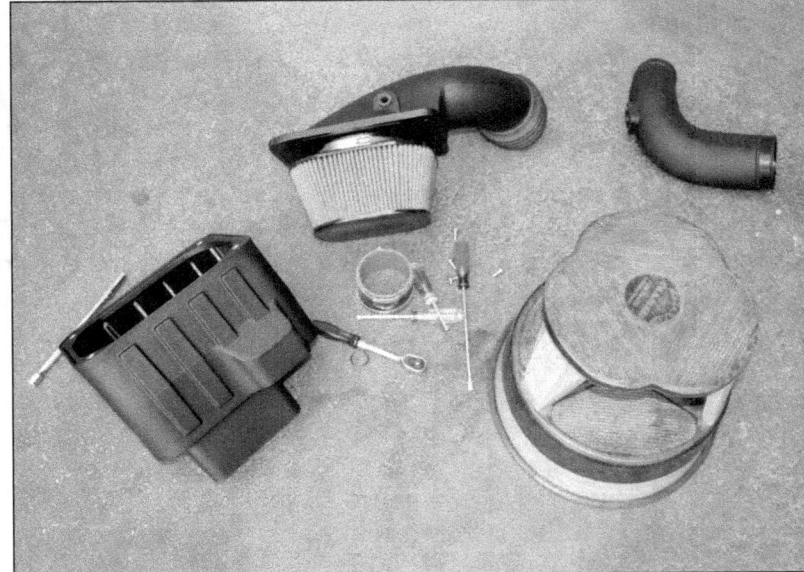

Installing a free-flowing intake system is step one. Look at the generous filter area and pipe diameter of this Banks intake. Step two is a free-flowing exhaust, and step three is electronic tuning to deliver more fuel and air density to the cylinders.

CHAPTER 2

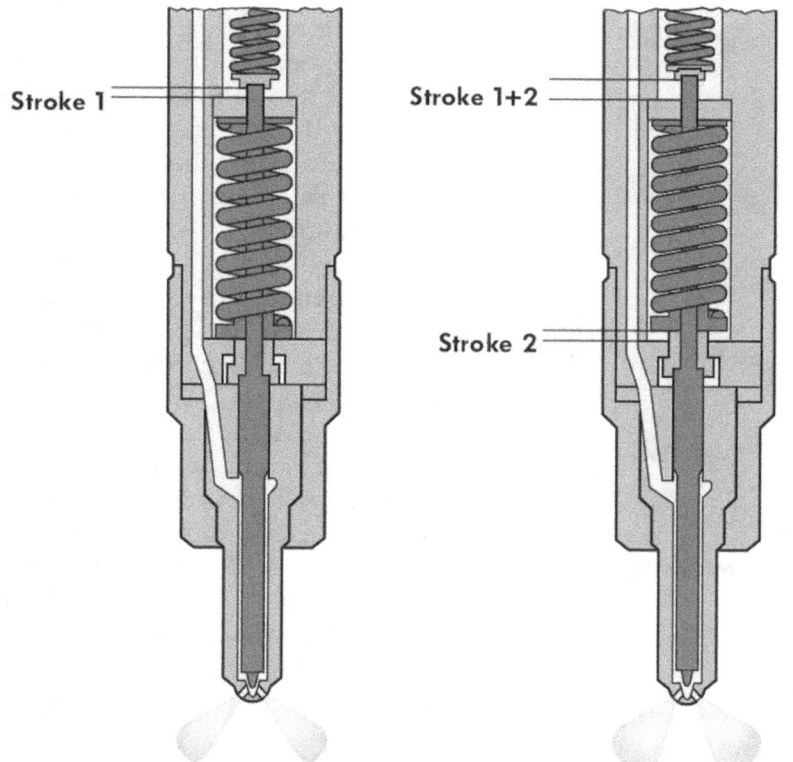

On some systems, fuel delivery is electronically controlled at the fuel pump. The injector responds to the fuel pulse mechanically. A low-pressure fuel pulse causes a small gap to allow a pilot injection. As the injection pump delivers more fuel than can actually flow through the small gap, the pressure in the injector rises. The force of the second spring is overcome, and the injector needle is lifted further. The main injection cycle now follows at a higher injection pressure. (Photo courtesy of Volkswagen)

Direct injection diesel engines require much more of the injectors than port fuel injection. The smaller injector is the gasoline injector.

caused by the high temperature of the charge as it's being compressed. Higher compression ratios generally lead to higher temperatures in the chamber, but the physical compression ratio, i.e., piston travel and combustion chamber size, is just one factor in determining the temperature rise in the chamber. The intake air temp is also a factor, since a set amount of compression will raise the temperature a specific amount. Cam timing is another factor since the piston can't compress air until the intake and exhaust valves are closed.

Detonation Defined

Detonation in a gasoline engine is the uncontrolled ignition of the air/fuel mixture in the cylinder after the spark plug has fired. The spark plug fires and the temperature rises at such a rate that the fuel ignites somewhere else in the combustion chamber on its own. It might auto ignite in many other places or it might be in just one. Then what happens (as a result of having all the fuel burning real quick) is the peak pressure in the cylinder occurs before the piston gets to TDC on the compression stroke, rather than after you reach TDC on the power stroke. When the pressure occurs too early, it tries to force the piston back down the hole, which is why you hear that telltale knock. Detonation is not good for power, economy, or longevity. It puts a lot of heat into the piston and usually destroys it.

Diesel Engines are Different

Gasoline engines like to run between roughly a 12:1 and 15:1 air/fuel ratio, which is pretty narrow. Diesel engines are different.

Varying the density of the air flowing into the cylinder controls the output of a gasoline engine. The density is varied using a butterfly valve (often in the throttle body) or some other mechanism controlling the airflow stream into the intake manifold. The diesel has an efficiency advantage because there is no throttle blade. The new Valvetronic BMW system takes this lesson from diesel engines, controlling airflow solely by varying the valve lift rather than with a throttle butterfly, which gives you better fuel economy and the potential for better power.

Diesels without a turbocharger have no throttle in the intake tract. So how do you change the speed of the diesel engine? You don't vary the air density—you vary the fuel ratio. Diesels will run from 50:1 to 22:1 air/fuel ratio. When you're idling, it doesn't take a lot of fuel because it doesn't need to suck air past a butterfly, so there's not a lot of intake

INTRODUCTION TO DIESEL PERFORMANCE

pumping losses. Consequently, you don't need to burn very much fuel. This shows up in very cool exhaust temps at idle. If you measure the exhaust temperature of an idling diesel, it's only a couple hundred degrees. Starting on cold morning, a diesel will take forever to warm up, unless you put it under load and feed it a lot of fuel.

When you want more power out of a diesel, you just richen it up. You might idle at 50:1, but when you start adding fuel, it will make more power all the way up to the point where there is insufficient oxygen for the fuel delivered. When you get to say 20:1, the diesel is probably starting to smoke. When you see smoke from a diesel exhaust, it's because it doesn't have enough air to completely burn all the fuel. If it doesn't have enough air, you have to figure out a way to get more air to it. Excessive smoking is power that you can see but not use. That is not smart in my book. Any guy who thinks smoking diesel engines are cool doesn't know what he is talking about. The question now is: How do you get more air into a diesel?

[Editor's Note: Diesel fuel burns in several stages, each of which releases a different amount of energy. Complete combustion results in the formation of carbon dioxide and water, plus products containing sulfur and other elements present in the raw fuel. More heat (power) is produced in the earlier stages of combustion, which form carbonaceous materials (soot). Less heat is produced from the final stages of combustion, which are necessary to lower emissions of environmentally targeted compounds such as soot. Complete combustion requires more carefully controlled combustion conditions and a lot more air than partial combustion. That is why under maximum power, such as racing conditions, a diesel engine may smoke. More fuel is being injected than can be fully burned to carbon dioxide and water, given the best power-with-efficiency range of the engine. However, the extra fuel is being burned partially and is releasing additional energy to make greater horsepower at the expense of smoke/soot formation.]

The Turbocharger was Invented for Diesel

Around 1903, a Swiss gentleman named Dr. Alfred J. Buchi invented the turbocharger. He invented the turbocharger for a diesel in a locomotive that needed to operate at higher altitude. The engine was really lying down at high altitude, and it was determined that it didn't have enough air to make the power it could make at sea level.

Buchi came up with an exhaust-pressure-driven compressor that forced air into the engine, improving the density of the intake charge. Remember that a naturally aspirated engine will only pump its own volume every two revolutions. That amount is fixed, so forced induction is all you can do to get more power beyond what the engine will pump naturally. Forced induction increases the air density.

But there's a drawback. When you increase the pressure of the air, you increase its temperature. You're doing work to the air with the impeller in the turbocharger and you're making the air hotter. So while you're getting higher pressure, you're not getting as much density as you could get if, when you increase the pressure, or boost, you cooled the air afterwards. If you do after cool, or intercool, the charge air, you'll have greater power

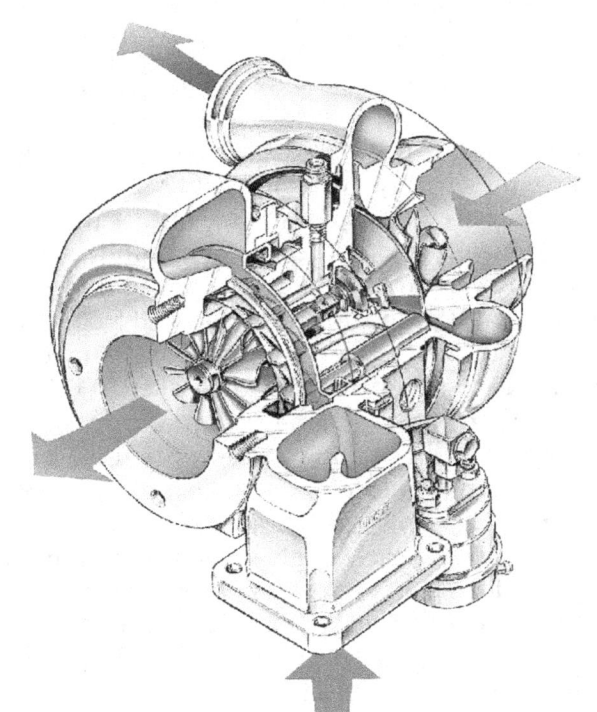

The turbocharger uses exhaust energy to drive a compressor that forces more air into the engine than would occur at normal atmospheric pressure. Forced induction increases the density of the air inside the engine. (Photo courtesy of Garrett)

potential at the same boost than if you don't cool the air.

The increased boost raises the density of the air going in and a turbocharger does it almost for free. Turbochargers work by the expansion of hot gases. This simple statement contains a lot of information. First, you need enough airflow from engine displacement and/or RPM to get the turbine wheel moving fast enough to make boost, or compressed air. Secondly, the wheel won't move enough until there is also heat applied, with the gases expanding as they move through the wheel into the exhaust system. Try it out in your turbo diesel. You can cruise at 2,000 rpm and have no boost, but under heavy fuel loads, you will make substantial boost—20 to 50 psi or more. The difference came not from airflow, which was based on RPM, but on the expansion of hotter gases resulting from burning more fuel.

In this way, a turbocharger varies its production of boost with engine requirements based on fueling and power production. It's pretty much an ideal piece of equipment to work with a diesel engine. This is because diesel exhaust gas temperatures so accurately reflect the air requirements of the engine based on desired power production. If the turbocharger is producing around 30 psi, that means it is putting about three atmospheres of air into the engine (atmospheric pressure is about 14.7 psi). Zero boost equals one atmosphere (relying on atmospheric pressure to fill the cylinder, aka naturally aspirated), but you added two more with boost pressure. Now you can add fuel to match. In effect, your engine thinks and acts like it were three times as big in displacement.

An aftermarket turbo, like this Super B single turbo from BD Diesel Performance, can make more boost and flow more air and still stay in its efficiency range. This keeps the intake air temperature down and density up. BD recommends this turbo for up to 425 hp. (Photo courtesy of BD Diesel Performance)

Turbocharging vs. Supercharging

There are two ways to run a supercharger: drive it mechanically off the engine, or using exhaust backpressure (which is commonly referred to as turbocharging). A supercharger requires power from the crankshaft to drive it. In some cases, it costs 50 hp, and on higher-output race engines, it could cost 500 hp. In other words, if you have an engine that makes 500 hp using a supercharger that takes 50 hp to run, the engine is actually making 550 hp, but you can only use 500. That means more load on the bearings, higher cylinder pressure, etc., to reach a given horsepower number. You're putting in more fuel, enough to make that extra 50 hp, but you're not getting it back out. Superchargers are also driven off the front of the crank, which gives you a load on both ends of the crank. This puts a hell of a load on the engine. You won't find many diesel engines with superchargers.

Backpressure Compared to Cylinder Pressure

Of course, supercharger advocates point out that a turbocharger increases the exhaust backpressure. But if you look at it, this drawback is minute compared to the peak cylinder pressure. Peak cylinder pressure in a modern diesel is 2,200 to 2,500 psi. Compare that to exhaust backpressure of around 30 psi. The turbo does its job almost for free. I'm not saying you can ignore backpressure, but compared to other available means of powering a compressor, the turbo is the most efficient tool we have today.

With the turbocharger, you're also not putting any excessive stress on the engine. The extra stress on

This is the Duramax piston in the cylinder bore. The recess in the piston is called the combustion cup. The flat edges of the piston squish the air into the combustion cup at top dead center (TDC). This combustion chamber arrangement is typical of a direct injection diesel.

the bearings and pistons is nominal. The engine lasts longer and makes more power because the parasitic losses are lower, which also means better fuel economy. Turbochargers are also easier to regulate. With a supercharger, you can't change the boost relative to the engine speed like you can with a turbo. This is because the supercharger is driven directly off the crankshaft, meaning boost pressure is permanently tied to engine RPM. This gives you fewer options for controlling boost, and it also means the supercharger is costing you power at all RPM and loads, whether you want boost or not.

A supercharger not only costs parasitic horsepower at all times, it also provides additional air through compression (increased pressure) only in relation to engine RPM. Engine load or fueling does not have an effect. Thus, the system is best used where engine load is predictable versus RPM and does not change. In practice, an engine cruised under light load at the same RPM where heavy power could be needed is another driving situation.

On the other hand, you can almost turn off a turbocharger simply by bypassing it using a wastegate. You can also use a computer to regulate or change the peak boost (or the density output). Turbochargers used today on diesel engines are the most sophisticated turbos on earth, using variable geometry, or pairs of turbos run in series, where one raises density before a second raises the density even farther.

The bottom line is that more boost gives you more density in a properly engineered, intercooled turbo system. In a way, a well-designed turbo setup is like having a higher compression ratio, without the drawback of the smaller combustion chamber. With the turbo diesel, you get more density per cubic inch of air using the same physical compression ratio.

Defining the Limits

Cylinder pressure makes power, but it also pushes the insides of your diesel engine apart. To get high torque and good power out of a low-speed diesel, you need a lot of cylinder pressure. On the other hand, if you can get a diesel to turn 5,000 rpm, you don't need as much cylinder pressure because you're firing it more times per minute and therefore getting more power strokes per minute. The individual power pulses might not be as powerful, but if you spin it fast enough, you can make more horsepower on the average.

The power limits of a diesel engine are determined by its physical strength, thermal strength, and emissions control. Unfortunately, the formation of nitrogen oxides (NOx) is countered with after-treatment, included treating the exhaust catalytically and chemically to remove NOx. This causes backpressure after the turbine and hurts performance.

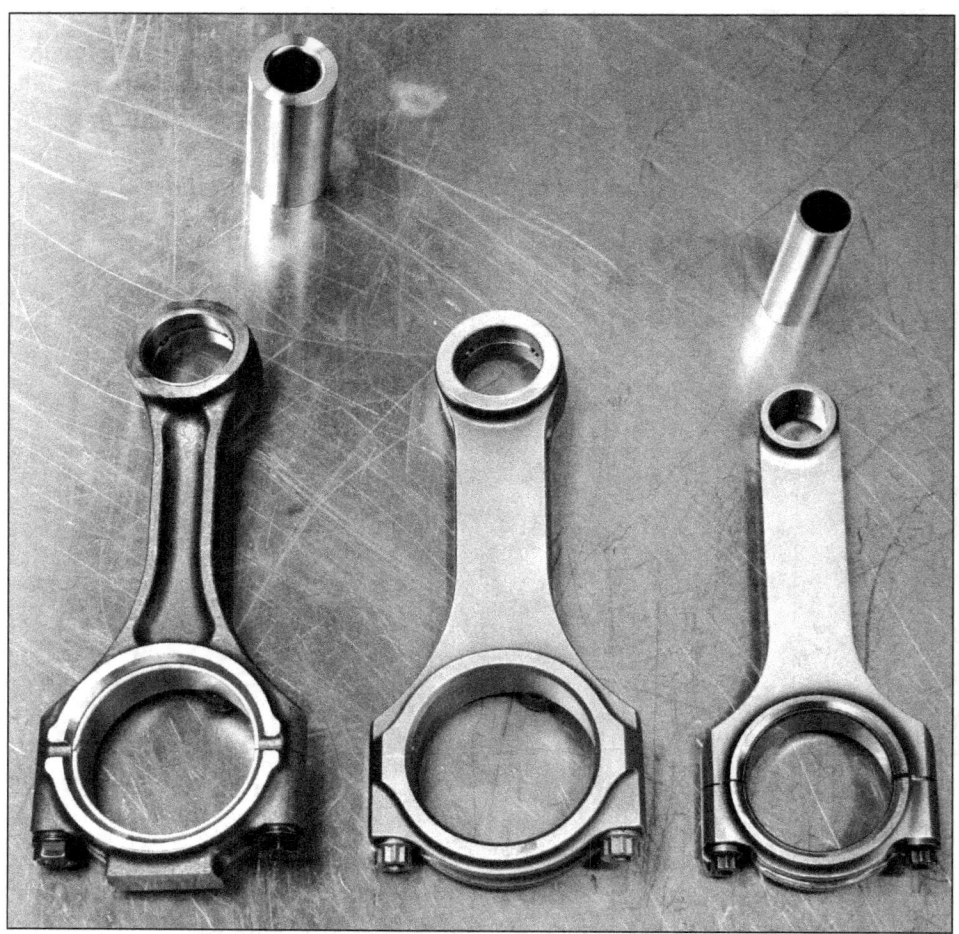

Comparing the stock Duramax connecting rod (left) with a custom Banks forged rod (center) and a Chevy small-block forged rod (right) gives an idea of the reciprocating masses involved. Compare the wristpins as well. Diesel components have to be built to withstand high cylinder pressures and long service lives.

Once you get the highest pressure, coolest air you can get, you want to add fuel to get the most potential power from the oxygen content of the intake charge. Different engines have different points where the air/fuel ratio becomes an issue in terms of smoke. It depends on the swirl in the combustion chamber, the shape of the injector nozzle, the shape of the piston's combustion cup, etc. "You might have an engine that smokes at 22:1, while some can run as rich as 18:1 and won't smoke. It just depends. We spend a lot of time working on cylinder heads to change the characteristic known as the swirl, which allows us to add more fuel and not have the engine smoke. My whole deal is that performance diesel engines should not smoke," says Gale Banks.

"So fuel flow does give you more power up to a point. That point is defined by two limits for a street-driven diesel: the smoke threshold and the engine reliability at a given cylinder pressure. Once you get up to a given cylinder pressure, in other words, the more fuel you put in the engine, the more energy you release. You've got to keep the crank from hitting the ground and the heads from going through the hood. If either happens, then you've got too much cylinder pressure. You've got to contain this energy. The engine has to live through it."

This is the cylinder head face of a B-series Cummins engine. It is flat and called the fire deck, as opposed to a combustion chamber on a gasoline fueled spark-ignition engine. The head must be held tightly to the block, particularly in modified engines with increased boost and cylinder pressures.

INTRODUCTION TO DIESEL PERFORMANCE

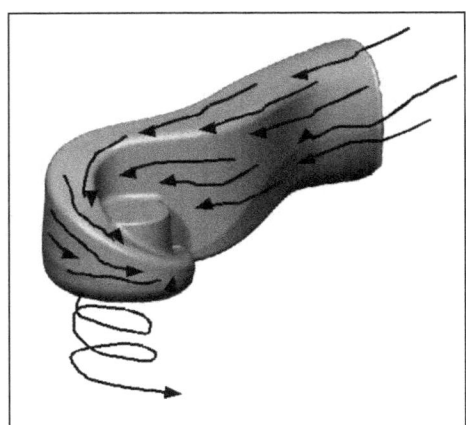

In the direct injection engine, diesel fuel is injected directly into the main combustion chamber, resulting in more efficient combustion and lower fuel consumption. The intake port is shaped in such a way that it induces a swirling movement of the intake air and, as a result, produces greater turbulence in the combustion chamber and piston recess. This is critical to helping the fuel atomize so it can react with the oxygen in the combustion chamber to create heat and pressure.

Combustion Basics

Older diesels were forced to burn fuel particles that were comparatively large and slow moving. Due to their mass, these particles had sufficient momentum to keep moving through the air up to the point most of their mass reacted with the oxygen in the cylinder. However, the velocity was not sufficient to completely vaporize the fuel. At some point the fuel stopped moving, stopped burning, and formed soot.

To understand this process, think about each fuel particle being like an onion, and you are burning off the layers of skin. It doesn't just explode. You're actually burning layers of fuel molecules off of this droplet. If it stops moving it stops vaporizing. Then it consumes all the oxygen around it and goes out, and that's incomplete combustion. This is how the soot that gets everywhere is formed. In many older diesel engines, this soot would get past the rings into the oil and turn it black very quickly. Otherwise, it comes out the tail pipe as smoke.

The fuel velocity/combustion problem in these older diesels was caused by their lower injection pressures, which were around 1,500 psi. In comparison, the injection pressures of today's diesel engines are almost 20 times that.

These older diesels smoked, but they really smoked when you tried to make a lot of power with them or tried to accelerate. When you punched the throttle down, you put in a lot more fuel, which made the power come up, but there's not enough air coming in until the engine sped up. This is because the early diesels were either naturally aspirated or used turbochargers with serious lag.

With modern turbochargers and high injection pressure, we have a situation where the fuel particles are very small and move at very high speed. This is the result of extremely high pressure forcing the fuel through smaller holes in the injectors. This vaporizes the fuel much better, so it's better able to burn. The particles still have very high momentum and they keep moving through the air even though they are very light. There is not a lot of mass to them so they burn faster and more completely, so there's much less smoke. A number of other factors keep the smoke down, including high compression ratios to heat the air upon compression by the piston, specialized camshaft timing and valve events, and improved piston bowls.

Velocity is incredibly important in understanding how to tune a diesel. Gasoline vaporizes quickly; diesel vaporizes slowly. It's far less volatile. The rate of vaporization is far less at any given temperature

Peak Cylinder Pressure and Crank Angle

The ideal time for peak cylinder pressure is when the piston is somewhere after TDC. Expressed in crank angle (crankshaft degrees), the best time is between 12 and 18 degrees after TDC. The optimum point varies with the stroke, the bore, the rod length, and the piston speed (RPM). In other words, the alignment of the thrust from the piston, the wrist pin, the rod, and crank (among other factors) dictates when the best time will be. The mechanical advantage changes as the crank rotates. When the piston is at TDC there is no mechanical advantage whatsoever. If you put peak cylinder pressure right then, who knows which direction the crankshaft will want to rotate. Put the peak pressure just after TDC, when the piston is moving back down the bore, but before the volume in the cylinder/combustion chamber is too great. This gives you the most power.

CHAPTER 2

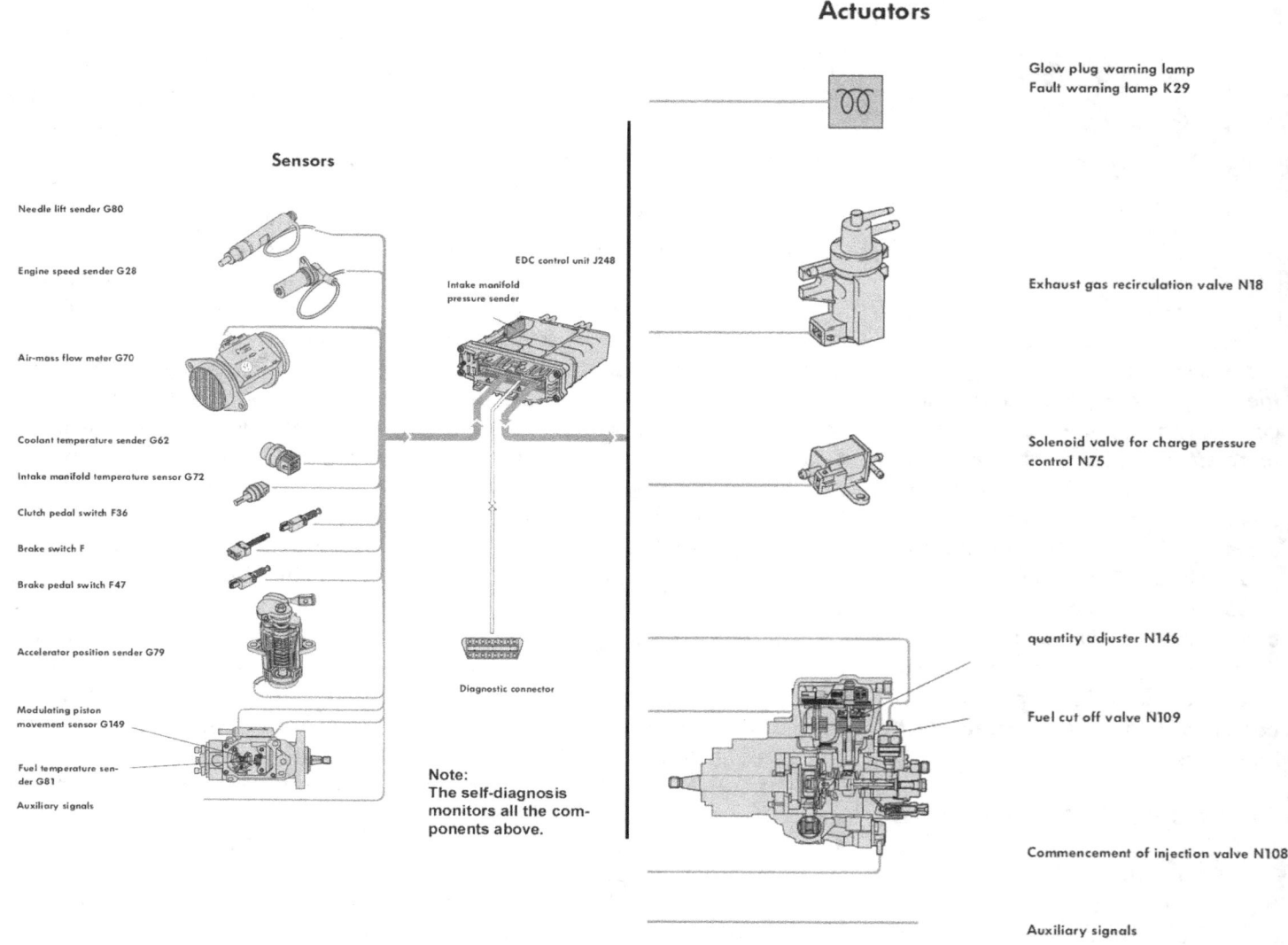

Modern computer controlled diesel engines use an extensive suite of sensors, not unlike electronically controlled gasoline engines. Diesels use intake temperature, mass airflow (MAF), manifold absolute pressure (MAP), crank angle, coolant temperature, ambient air pressure, and other sensors to produce clean, quiet power. (Photo courtesy of Bosch)

than gasoline. You can still vaporize diesel fuel, don't get me wrong, but it takes a lot of heat, which is why the combustion process is much different than gas.

Electronic Engine Contols

Modern diesel engines use direct injection and computer controls to deliver incredible power, efficiency, and driveability. The engine design and control method also provides the opportunity to enhance the power output and custom tune your engine to your requirements using an aftermarket tuner or interface. But to tune successfully without hurting your engine requires that you know something about the system of computers, sensors, and actuators that make it all happen.

When discussing the sensor suite and electronic controls, it's useful to break the subject into: sensors on the intake side before the compressor, intake after the compressor, exhaust before and after the compressor, coolant and lubricant temps, and the rest of the various actuators controlling engine functions.

The sensors on the intake side before the compressor are temp

INTRODUCTION TO DIESEL PERFORMANCE

sensors, mass airflow sensors, and barometric sensors. The barometric sensor measures ambient pressure, which can vary with altitude. Using the air temp sensor and the pressure sensor to check against the MAF, the computer can calculate air density at an acceptable resolution. You could calculate it even more accurately if you had a humidity sensor, too.

Messing with these sensors, or trying to trick them, takes away the computers ability to have an accurate calibration of the air entering the engine, which can cause it to inject too much fuel and start smoking or set trouble codes. If you trick the engine crudely, that's the kind of performance you'll get. More often than not the tricks lose power.

After the turbo compressor come the sensors that measure intake manifold pressure, and in some cases, intake temperature. The sensors, their locations, and the information they read varies from engine to engine and make to make.

In some cases, an air mass sensor serves as a back check to verify the air mass at specific RPM checkpoints. If the values from the sensors don't match, you'll usually get a trouble code. Maybe there's a boost leak. Or, given X-amount of air mass at certain boost level, the computer wants a certain amount of exhaust gas recirculation (EGR).

EGR absorbs temperature from the combustion process. It's a method of regulating peak temperature to reduce NOx formation while still producing adequate average cylinder pressure to make power goals. The problem with EGR is that it occupies space, so to get more oxygen in the cylinder, you've got to have more boost and more intercooling. According to Gale Banks, earlier engines have 5 to 7 percent EGR, but future engines will probably have 18 to 25 percent EGR.

On the exhaust side, manufacturers don't use oxygen sensors on diesels because they don't last in a diesel combustion gas stream. Banks uses oxygen sensors on the dyno, but they deteriorate very rapidly due to the contamination from the diesel fuel, soot, etc.

Working together, the sensors and actuators are designed to determine the most advantageous time to create peak cylinder pressure given the load demands on the engine. This is dependent on the temperature of the charge after being compressed by the piston and the amount of oxygen that's available to react with the fuel. By comparing the mass airflow with the boost level at RPM data points, the computer determines the health of the turbo system to determine if it's within parameters.

There are essentially two ways to compute how much air is flowing through the motor: speed density and mass airflow. If you're clever at it, which most manufacturers are, you're doing both, though a given setup might depend on one more than the other. "I prefer to depend on mass airflow measurements and calculations. If for some reason the sensor output doesn't compare with a calculated speed density map of fuel and timing, then the computer can make a logical assumption that the mass flow sensor is not operating correctly. Then it defaults to the speed density map and forces a trouble code, but the engine is still running. I like mass airflow, because you know just so much more and you can tune to the real conditions influencing combustion and system health. Most of the automakers are moving this way," says Banks.

The task of the MAF meter is to measure the fresh air mass supplied to the engine. This fresh air mass is used to calculate the exhaust gas recirculation (EGR) rate and the permissible injection quantity. This particular sensor uses a hot film that is regulated to a constant temperature. The intake air cools the hot film as it flows past. The amount of electrical current necessary to keep the temperature of the hot film constant is used to calculate the intake air mass. If the MAF fails, the engine control unit (ECU) defaults to a fixed air mass value. (Photo courtesy of Bosch)

Other sensors include crank angle, engine speed, and manifold temperature. GM has a vane position sensor on its variable geometry turbo (Ford doesn't, though it uses the same brand of variable vane turbo as GM). Ford is the only manufacturer to use exhaust backpressure in its calculations. Of course, trucks use trans temp and vehicle speed sensors, but nobody is using factory EGT sensors yet, though many performance enthusiasts add them.

According to Banks, the next big thing for tuning is pressure-sensing

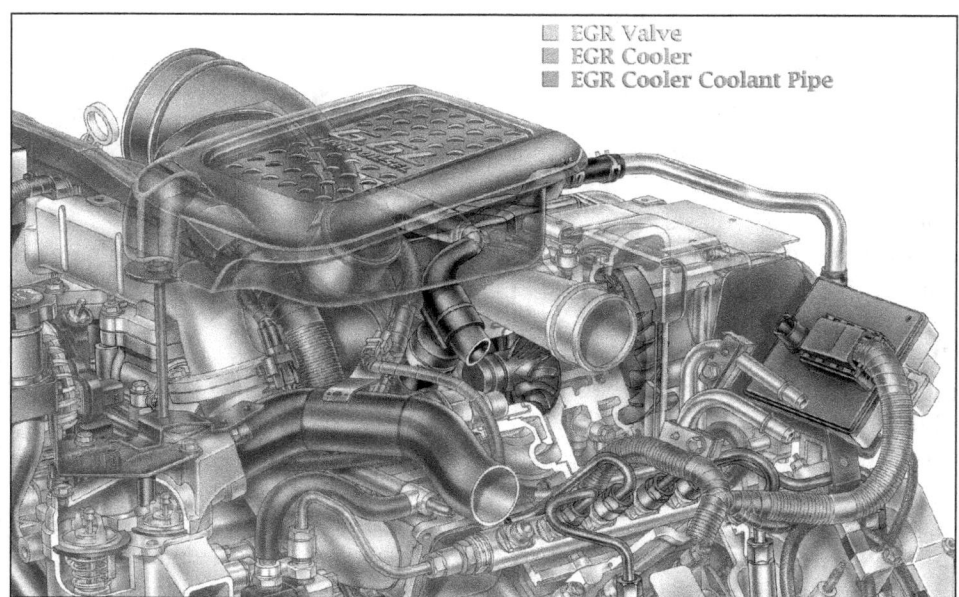
The EGR system recirculates cooling exhaust gases, greatly reducing NOx emissions. The EGR absorbs heat energy to fine tune cylinder pressure to reduce NOx formation while retaining sufficient cylinder temperature and pressure to make adequate power. (Photo courtesy of General Motors)

Here you can see the total diesel performance package coming together. Add increased airflow (upgraded turbos), improved air density (massive intercooler), and the proper fuel and tuning to match (upgraded injectors, fuel pump, and tuning). Now you just have to worry about the drivetrain holding up! (Photo courtesy of BD Diesel Performance)

glow plugs. A German company called Bayru is already making one. "That will allow us to monitor the cylinder pressure of each cylinder, and then adjust each accordingly to get proper power balance through the widest range of operating conditions. We'll also be able to detect problems with the fuel injector. As the fuel injector ages, it doesn't give you the same fuel flow for a given pulse. They change over time and not at the same rate. So to get your emissions to be constant over 100,000 miles (or whatever is required for the 2010 levels) isn't possible today because of the variability of the injectors. With this new sensor you can trim your fuel injectors by the cylinder, which should improve fuel efficiency and keep the power balance stable. Pretty cool."

Engine coolant temperature is big for diesels. In fact, the '07 Duramax uses two coolant temp sensors. Coolant temp has to do with derating the engine. While most performance enthusiasts are trying to up the amount of power their engine makes, in some cases the manufacturers are trying to reign that power in.

Factory Derating Tactics

Some diesels use slip detectors to detect slip in the transmission. According to Banks, the technology is most developed in the Allison transmission. These systems monitor the engine speed, trans input shaft speed, and transmission output shaft speed. By comparing input and output speeds, the computer can look at the torque converter, torque converter clutch, and transmission clutch-pack slip. Once it sees a predetermined amount of slip, the computer pulls fuel out of the engine to lower output and prevent you from killing the transmission.

INTRODUCTION TO DIESEL PERFORMANCE

Common Causes of Overheating

Many diesel owners experience overheating problems. It seems the Duramax gets a lot of negative attention in this regard. We asked Banks to comment on the issue.

His explanation is that the radiator can only dissipate X amount of BTUs and that amount varies under different conditions. "It's a function of the ambient air temperature, the velocity of the truck, and the power output of the engine under those conditions," says Banks. "If you're towing a heavy trailer at high altitude up a steep grade, that's about the worst conditions to tow. Because of the low air density, the cooling system transfers less heat. At sea level you can reject more heat because you have more air mass to absorb the heat.

"At full load, I like to see the temperature rise across the engine and drop across the radiator to be somewhere between 8 and 12 degrees Fahrenheit. So with the water coming out of the engine at 240 degrees F, I expect to see water temperatures of 228 to 230 degrees F at the radiator exit. If the difference gets below 8 degrees F, you might have your water moving too fast. You need some residence time for the heat to transfer."

Banks says he hopes to bring some big radiators to market. He says the guys at Valeo make really great radiators, but some people end up wanting smaller ones. From the OEM's perspective, it's all about building a commercial product that works for most people, and if it doesn't work for some (i.e., performance enthusiasts)... too bad. This attitude is driven by economics, of course, not the temperament of the design engineers.

Ford also uses this technology in its new TorqShift transmission, but not the E-4OD, which uses only engine RPM and output shaft speed, so it cannot isolate slip in specific gears.

DaimlerChrysler also uses a derating strategy for the Cummins with automatic transmissions to lower engine output slightly during shifts. Of course, this derating prolongs transmission life. The Cummins engine also has a derate built into the engine computer that pulls back power if the boost pressure gets too high. Some factory computers also derate the engine based on coolant temp. If the coolant is too cold or too hot, the computer dials back the power to keep the engine from overheating and save on wear and tear.

Summary

We pick up with Gale Banks in later chapters. To sum up this chapter, we'll end with a few generalities on the performance potential of diesels and a recommended order of operations for enhanced performance.

The three most common turbo diesel engine configurations are: (1) mechanical injection pump without intercooler, (2) intercooled with mechanical injection pump, (3) intercooled with electronically controlled injection pump. We don't discuss naturally aspirated diesels in the book because all diesels worth using for performance are turbocharged. In regards to the potential of each type of turbo diesel, the non-intercooled turbo diesel with mechanical injection offers the least potential, with room for perhaps a 15 to 20 percent increase in torque. The intercooled mechanical injection diesel can generally see torque increases of 25 to 30 percent. Diesels with electronically controlled injection offer the most potential, especially common rail diesels. You can expect at least 60 percent more torque with proper tuning from engines of this design.

Order of operations for external diesel performance upgrades:

1. Improve airflow before and afterturbo:
   Install an aftermarket intake system to increase the density of charge. Go for an exhaust system to reduce backpressure behind turbine and improve turbo spool up.

2. Improve air density:
   Increase boost; if necessary, install larger, more efficient turbos; increase charge air cooling efficiency with a larger, more efficient intercooler; consider nitrous.

3. Add fuel to meet air mass flow requirement:
   Tune engine management computer and consider increasing rail pressure.

4. Upgrade driveline.

CHAPTER 3

INDUCTION AND COMBUSTION

Tuning the Airflow Path

Diesel engines respond extremely well to increases in the density of the intake charge, so when you increase the mass flow through the engine, you increase power. The airflow components of your diesel engine include the intake ducting and manifold, the compressor of the turbocharger, the cylinder head, and the exhaust system, including the turbine of the turbocharger. The design of these components determine the upper limits of the mass flow through the engine, which is another way of saying they limit the horsepower and torque potential of your engine combo.

Diesel engines also have a couple unique design challenges to consider. The airflow through the whole engine is limited by the restriction imposed by the intake port's duty to swirl the intake charge. This swirl helps the engine make power despite the tight piston-to-valve clearance dictated by the 18:1 (or so)

Improving the efficiency of the airflow path, from the intake through the tailpipe, is a key aspect to improving diesel performance. You need to get air into and out of the engine to make power; then you just need to worry about getting enough fuel. (Photo courtesy of BD Diesel Performance)

compression ratio. With the intake port holding you back in a way, intercooling and efficient turbo design are critical to modern turbo diesel performance.

Though the gross mass flow through the engine's airflow path determines the amount of power it is capable of producing, the trick for most diesel enthusiasts is getting the most airflow from what you've got. This is where volumetric efficiency (VE) comes into play. Roughly speaking, your engine's VE is its ability to fill the cylinders with a fresh intake charge. The more air is piled in, the higher the VE. Improving your engine's VE is the goal of most of the bolt-on performance components.

Volumetric Efficiency

To be precise, VE is a measure of how much air the engine actually flows compared to its displacement. For example, the cylinder volume of a 6.0-liter, six-cylinder engine is one liter or 61 cubic inches. If the engine has 100 percent VE, each intake stroke fills the cylinder completely with air. If it fills only partially, say 80 percent of its potential, then it is only 80 percent volumetrically efficient.

VE is influenced by the design of the airflow path components and the camshaft. The more efficiently air flows through the intake, into and out of the combustion chamber, through to the exhaust system, the higher the potential VE. Typically, the torque peak occurs at the point of the engine's highest VE. Naturally aspirated performance engines fight tooth and nail to get their VE as high as possible, which increases the specific output for a different displacement. Of course, the diesel engines we're talking about get a little help from their turbochargers. With a turbocharger, more often than not, the additional density of the pressurized intake charge will echo the engine combo's naturally aspirated VE.

From the standpoint of a performance diesel enthusiast, increasing VE contributes to increased power output because there is more mass in the cylinder (increased density) and it takes less energy to fill it (the system is more efficient). What's the best way to increase the VE of your engine? To get a better understanding of this process, we need to get down to the molecular level.

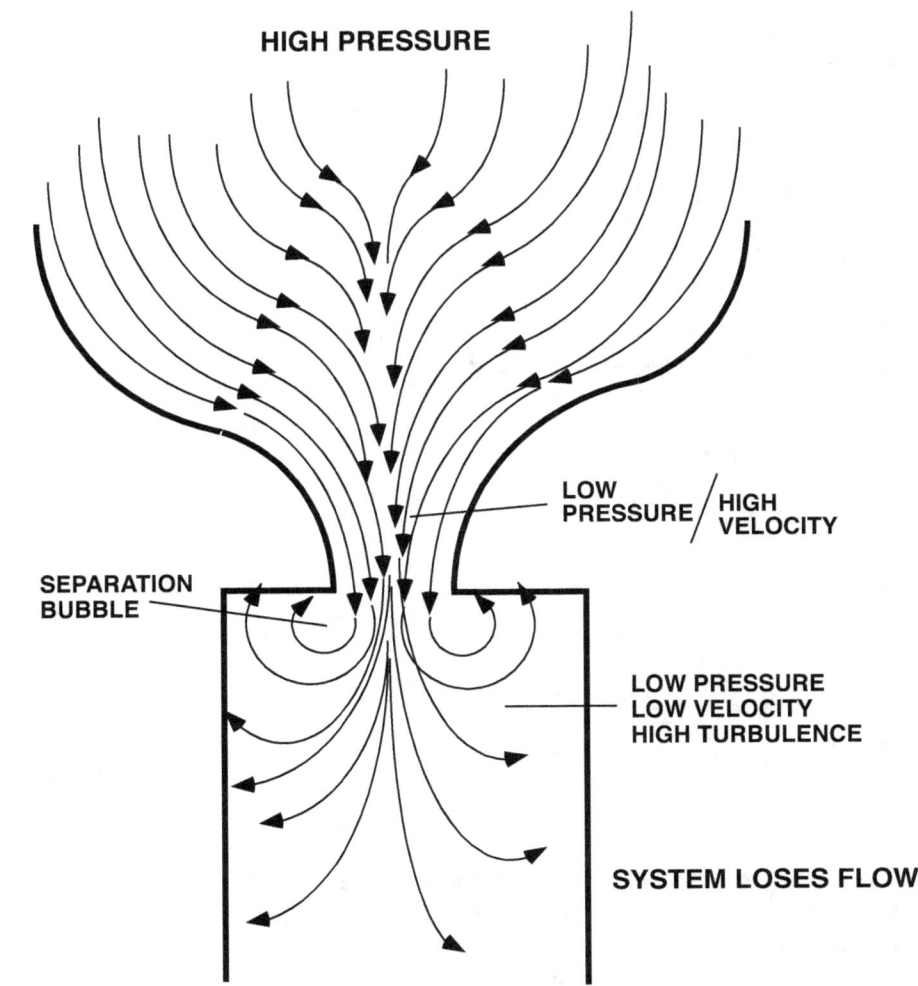

Improving airflow is fundamental to improving the performance of your diesel. This drawing illustrates what happens to airflow when the (intake or exhaust) runner wall terminates suddenly. The pressure is released and the flow detaches from the wall, causing turbulence and lost flow. This is the main reason you should match the ports of your intake and exhaust manifolds to the head ports.

The air we breathe is just over two-thirds nitrogen and less than one-third oxygen. These same oxygen molecules react rapidly with the fuel molecules to create heat and raise the pressure in the combustion chamber to make power. Nitrogen doesn't burn, but it sure takes up a lot of space in the intake manifold and combustion chambers. Don't forget that humidity, i.e., water vapor suspended in the intake air. So there's a lot more flowing through your engine than just the oxygen you want to burn. When you're thinking about airflow, it's useful to think of air as a liquid even though its density can change very easily. This attribute gives air a spring-like quality. Fortunately for performance enthusiasts, air's behavior is well known and quite predictable, which allows us to tune the engine combo—shape intake and exhaust passages, swap turbos, etc.—to improve flow, increase VE, and build more power.

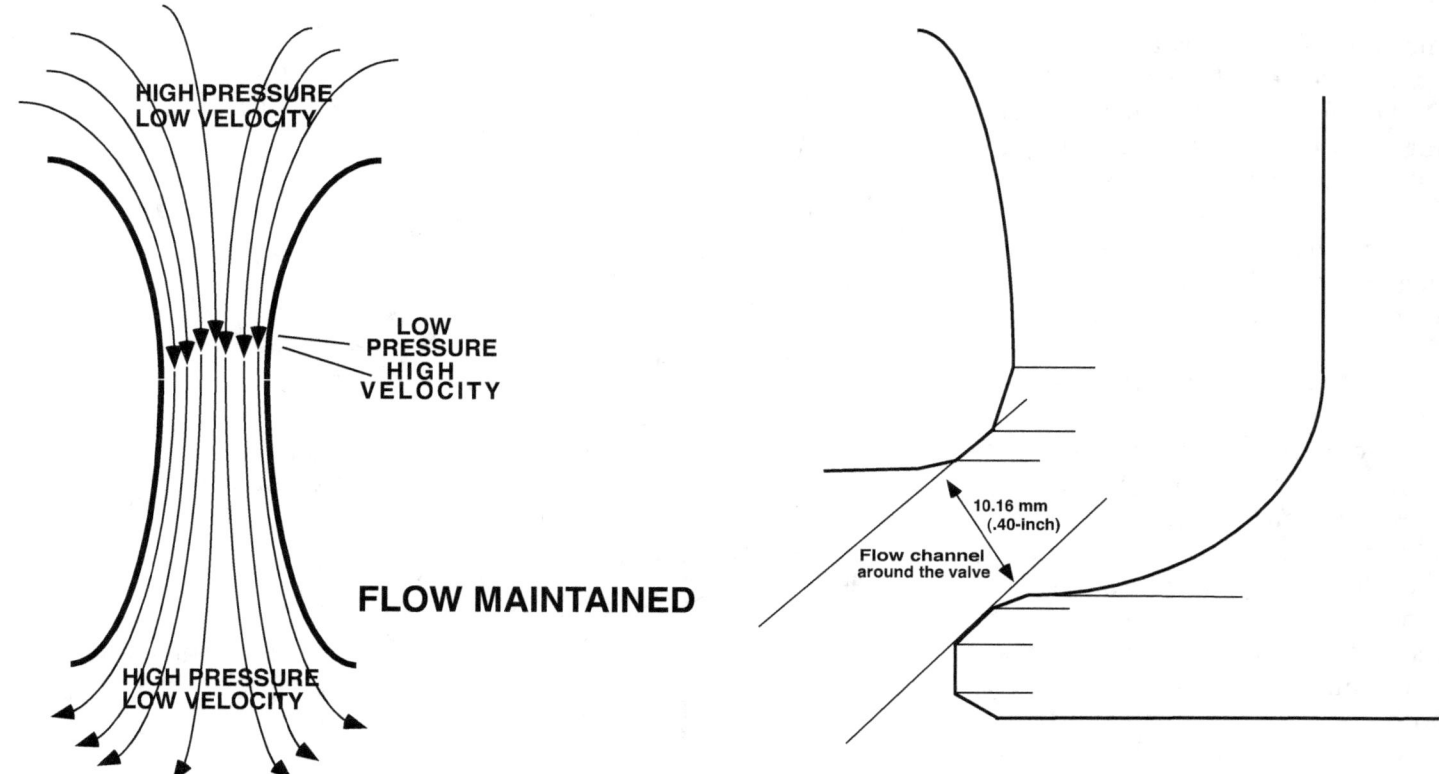

Here, the runner wall gradually slopes away, keeping the flow organized to maintain a high flow rate. This, more than anything, should clue you in to seeing that the shape and the entire flow channel impacts airflow—up and downstream, i.e., intake manifold, head ports, and exhaust system.

Valve face and seat angles have the most influence on low-lift flow. Getting good low-lift flow numbers makes an engine come alive. Sharp angles seem to work best, while blended angles seem to increase the boundary layer and reduce the effective airflow channel size.

Laminar Airflow

Air behaves like water except that it expands when its temperature rises. At certain speeds, it acts as a fluid, which is why aerodynamic studies use fluid dynamic equations and oil-filled "wind tunnels." What engine builders have found is that a fluid, even a gaseous fluid, flows smoothly over the walls and shape of a tube until it has to make a turn greater than about 9 or 10 degrees.

Smooth airflow is called laminar flow. Laminar flow is when the gas or fluid "seems well organized," as Joseph Katz put it in *Race Car Aerodynamics*. Laminar flow tends to (but not always) produce the highest flow volume with the least amount of drag. Turbulent flow is when the air starts to tumble. It becomes disorganized, generates friction, and slows down the flow. When you force a fluid to turn more than 10 degrees, it wants to separate from the shape that it's flowing over, which is when it starts to tumble and slow down.

Since we're discussing what happens inside a tube, such as an intake manifold runner or intake port, we have to consider the walls, or sides, of the tube. To simplify our discussion, let's first look at flow in two dimensions. The long-side radius (outside of a bend) and the short-side radius (inside of a bend) have the greatest impact on fluid flow because gases and fluids have mass, and therefore, inertia. The gas and fluid flow on the long-side radius picks up speed, forcing a pressure drop in that area. Meanwhile, the fluid flow on a short-side radius slows down because the flow separates and tumbles, increasing pressure in this area.

Daniel Bernoulli, a Dutch-born mathematician who lived from 1700 to 1782, first described this effect with his equations, so it became known as the Bernoulli effect. In essence, Bernoulli's equations state that if air speed varies as it flows around an object, the pressure of the air will vary inversely to the square of the air speed. So as air speed increases, pressure drops. As air speed decreases, pressure rises. In a tube with bends in it, such as an intake runner, the consequence is that you get less average mass flow through this area and the bend becomes a restriction.

Now, let's add the third dimension and consider the shape through which gas or fluid flows best. Obviously, a straight tube offers the least resistance to flow. But the realities of packaging an engine to fit under the hood of a passenger vehicle almost always remove that option. If we must turn the fluid, what shape generates the least turbulence while allowing maximum flow?

In general, we only have a few shapes that are practical: square, rectangular, round, oblong, and hybrids of these, such as a D-shaped port. So which one is best? It depends on what you need the air to do.

Each shape influences flow depending on how it is positioned relative to the changing direction of the airflow. For example, it's easy to see that a circle with less area than a square will not flow as much mass as a square shape. Now, bend the air and use a round shape on the long-side radius. What happens? The gases respond as Bernoulli's equations state. The air on the long-side radius, since it has to travel farther, wants to speed up and drop pressure. The round shape has less area than a square port so the airflow slows down and keeps its pressure more consistent with the short side. This minimizes tumbling, keeping the air more organized, thus allowing the port to flow more mass. For enhanced flow performance, that's a good thing.

Sometimes the engine architecture, head bolts, water passages, etc., won't allow you to use the optimum shape. The engineers have to figure out the next best choice and apply it. The bottom line is that by precisely controlling the shape and volume of the intake runner (including the intake port), you can direct equal airflow mass to the intake valves with sufficient velocity and swirl to make power within a predetermined power band.

We've been concentrating on the flow dynamics that occur in a tube because it is analogous to the behavior of air as it flows in and out of the engine's intake and exhaust tracts. But in order to simplify the presentation of the concepts we've been speaking of the flow as if it were at a constant rate. In reality, the engine is a pulse-flow device, with the pulses originating in the four strokes of the process.

The fact that your diesel engine is a pulse-flow device introduces the complication of pressure waves bouncing around in both the intake and exhaust systems. Of course, these pressure waves influence VE. If a pressure wave arrives at the intake port when the valve is open, it could help fill the cylinder and improve VE. If a pressure wave arrives at the exhaust port while the piston is working to push the exhaust gases out it will decrease exhaust flow, increasing pumping loss, and decreasing VE.

The difficulty lies in designing components that at least neutralize the negative effects of these pressure waves, or better still, use the energy to increase VE. On the intake side, this influences the design of the plenum. On the exhaust side, pressure waves are managed with the exhaust manifold design, including the tube diameter, collector shape, and even anti-reversion chambers.

The intake plenum is the large reservoir of air from which each intake runner pulls air. The air in the plenum vibrates in response to the pulse signal from each cylinder on the intake stroke. If you have straight walls on the plenum, the "wave forms" stay organized as they reflect. Because they're organized, they tend to have more energy and have more opportunity to combine constructively, randomly varying the pressure and speed of the intake charge coming down the runner. However, you want consistent pressure in order to tune the engine precisely, so this is not desirable. The solution, to avoid these resonance issues, is to use a rounded shape for the plenum. If you have to use straight walls, as is the case when fabricating a sheet metal manifold, you should make asymmetrical surfaces to inhibit the organization of these waves.

Cylinder Head Tuning: Swirl and Flow

The four-valves-per-cylinder advantage has by now become an accepted part of the performance diesel design. Essentially, the four-valve arrangement, two intake and two exhaust valves, increases the area of whereby intake and exhaust gases may flow into and out of the head over a two-valve arrangement. The benefit of this is much improved VE. In addition, the smaller individual valves have less inertial force, so they require less valvespring pressure to control. Therefore, a four-valve head can rev higher than a two-valve head with a given spring pressure, all else being equal.

Once you get the air to the valve, you have to make a sacrifice, because the air has to turn. Since the air can't flow through the metal of the valve, it has to go around it, and the port walls are shaped to get the air to turn and start the swirl. Diesels need a significant amount of intake

CHAPTER 3

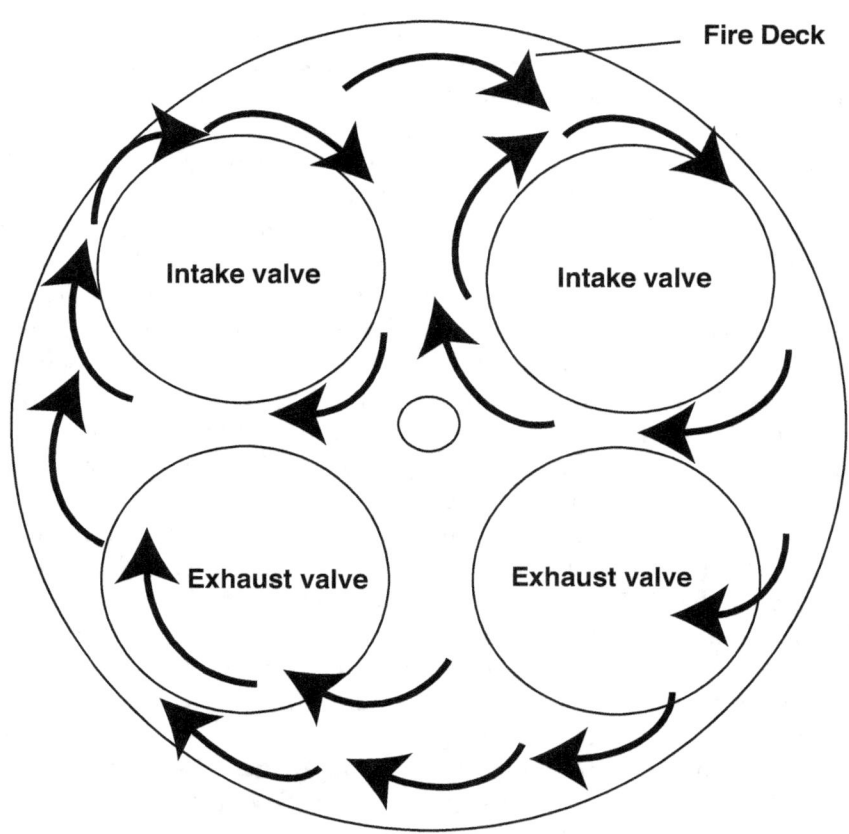

The new four-valve heads have more area through which to flow air. The design also facilitates a stratified swirl in the chamber. Tumbling turbulence doesn't work well for diesels; the air needs to swirl.

As you can see here, Gale Banks takes the engineering of his air intake systems seriously. The intake setup needs to work with the rest of the system to keep flow and density up. This particular setup probably won't work with the stock hood.

charge swirl because of the shape of the combustion area and the top of the pistons. Unfortunately, this means turbulence and lost mass flow. As enthusiasts, the only thing we can do is to minimize the flow loss while maintaining a sufficient amount of swirl.

Swirl is critical to atomizing diesel fuel in the chamber, so the strategy for minimizing flow loss around the valve is tricky. The swirl energy and flow rate is very sensitive to the port's floor height. Properly designed port walls should turn the air so it approaches the valve in a direct a manner as possible to set up a cone-shaped flow of air around the full circumference of the valve. We're talking intake side here, but essentially, you try to get the cone-shaped flow pattern around the exhaust valve as well, you just don't have to worry about the swirl.

Airflow between valve and valve seat is critically dependent on the angles you use on the seat and the shape within the combustion chamber, particularly on the shrouded side next to the cylinder wall. In general, you get better flow with a series of sharp edges on the cuts than by blending the cuts together. Since you're limited to rather modest valve lift in a diesel, you have to work hard on the low-lift flow rates, with special attention to swirl at the higher lift area for intake.

So far we've discussed the air entering the cylinder. The exhaust side is just as important since the spent gases have to be removed from the cylinder to make room for a fresh intake charge. Essentially, the exhaust side shares the same concepts as intake air except that the exhaust gas is much hotter and in addition to the mass of gas exiting through the valve, we've got pressure waves bouncing around in the exhaust system. The

INDUCTION AND COMBUSTION

Porting the intake ports on a direct-injection high-performance engine has got to be one of the most delicate operations in the performance world. While you can't see the angles inside the port, Banks says you can't hog it out and go for high flow numbers and still make non-smoking power. Don't remove too much material and ruin the swirl characteristics.

The exhaust port doesn't need to generate swirl, it just needs to flow lots of mass. Typical performance porting works on this side.

fluid dynamics are similar and the valve seat area functions in much the same way, even though the gases face the flat side of the valve at the entry to the exhaust port. For an in-depth look at the exhaust system, check out Chapter 4 on turbos, where we discuss in detail the exhaust system from the exhaust valve to the turbine.

Gale Banks on Airflow and Combustion

I've had Chevy, Ford, and Dodge Banks Power Ram-Air systems on the market for a while now. They work well because when driving through the air, you build up pressure on the front of the vehicle. If you can inhale some of that air, two things happen: First, you effectively reduce the frontal area of the vehicle because you've just inhaled some of the air mass that causes the drag. Second, it gives you a way to generate pressurized air through the filter and duct work right to the inlet of the turbo compressor. The higher the pressure and the cooler the temperature of air you can get to the inlet, the more power you can make.

The compressor is going to add pressure and temperature to the air, if I'm able to do part of that with ram air off the nose of the vehicle and get cold air, then the compressor has to do less work to get the air density I want in the intake manifold. If I can relieve the amount of work the compressor has to do and produce the power I'm looking for, then it takes less backpressure and less turbine horsepower to put that density in the engine.

Aside from careful attention to balancing flow numbers with swirl energy, the bowls and seats of this Banks ported head show familiar performance porting. The bowls are smoothed, the valve seat precise, and the area leading into the seat is blended.

HIGH-PERFORMANCE DIESEL BUILDER'S GUIDE

CHAPTER 3

As you can see, the length of the intake port from the manifold face to the valve on this Duramax head makes porting a challenge. It's tough to reach all the way through.

Driving the turbine is the thing most guys ignore. I want to take advantage of the work the engine and vehicle nose is doing compressing the air, instead of paying for it twice with increased backpressure from spinning the turbo to make higher boost. When you've got to make more turbine horsepower to overcome a screw up in the intake system, the extra backpressure makes it harder for the pistons to push the exhaust out of the valves. In other words, boost is not a free ride. To make boost, you make backpressure, which takes power out of the crankshaft.

The power used to overcome friction in the intake and exhaust is not available at the crankshaft. Reduce the friction in these areas, and with no other changes, the engine will have more output at the crankshaft. If you can diminish that loss with a better intake design (intercooler, intake manifold, ducting) and exhaust system after the turbine, you can improve power output and efficiency. That's what good engineering is all about (not to mention most aftermarket performance parts).

The OEMs have for years designed diesel engines with poor manifolding like the Cummins. The Cummins inline six has the worst intake manifold that I've ever seen. But consider that the intake manifold design dates back to that Case tractor 30 or 40 years ago, where it was only supposed to make 120 horsepower. When you're trying to make 300 horsepower through that torturous air route—you just can't. All you can do is turn up the boost. How do you get more boost? You make more exhaust backpressure. That's not efficient.

With any open-intake design, particularly a ram-air system, think about rain entering the system. Ideally,

The intakes of the Banks Type R road racing Duramax pull from the high-pressure area on the nose of the truck. Pulling air from here reduces the mass the vehicle has to push through and also delivers higher pressure and density to the inlet of the compressor. Street intakes are less extreme, but follow the same principle.

The airflow path on the Type R makes all the right moves. It makes the air turn as little as possible and guides it gently. A setup like this isn't practical for the average street truck, but consider the flow path when you're choosing your intake, intercooler plumbing, and exhaust systems.

INDUCTION AND COMBUSTION

This Banks Cummins exhaust manifold design includes stainless steel tubing and a 3/4-inch thick steel flange. Four stainless steel expansion bellows are welded into the manifold to allow for the different expansion rates of the flange and the tubing. The Holset HY55 turbocharger builds plenty of boost.

Here's the Cummins head fresh off the block. You can see the ancient intake very clearly here. Unfortunately for performance enthusiasts, part of the intake is cast as part of the head, which makes it much harder to port for extra airflow.

you want a ducting that removes the water because you're going to drive in the rain. You want ram air off the nose of the vehicle if you can route the air that way. On the ford it's very difficult, but on the Chevy and Dodge it's possible, so we're building an opening that faces forward.

If it's raining, hopefully you won't be driving as fast, so you're not ramming the rainwater into the intake. We also design the intake so the rain would have to climb a significant vertical distance (nearly 2 feet) in the intake system. That keeps a lot of the water out of the air box. Plus we cut slots in the back side of the duct that exhausts the water. That results in cool, higher-pressure air getting to the air filter.

The next consideration is the shape of the housing and the air filter, which should complement each other to achieve maximum flow. If it's designed right, the air should load all the surface area of the filter. You don't want one section of the filter to have dirt on it after 10,000 miles, and the other part of it to be clean. That would show it isn't flowing correctly. So within the limits of the vehicle body, we shape the filter, then the box, to achieve maximum flow to the face of the filter.

Next we look at the pleats in the filter. We look at the number of pleats, the depth of the pleats, then number of the pleats per inch to get more surface area. If the pleats are too close together, and the air is just flowing through the top of the pleat, which reduces the efficiency. The goal is to get the air in the housing to have equal pressure all the way around the filter and to get the air into the filter so we're using all the surface area is used efficiently.

Most air filter material is oiled cotton gauze; some are five layered, six layered, seven layered, eight lay-

The best intake designs draw air from a high pressure area on the body, use a housing that shapes the air to promote flow through the air filter, and will feature a filter element that cleans the air with minimal airflow restriction. The design should also prevent liquid water from entering the engine. (Photo courtesy of Gale Banks Engineering)

ered, and so on. Most of the filters I use have eight layers. The more plies, the better it filters; but of course, this reduces its maximum flow rate. So you have to decide the purpose of the filter. I'm providing two styles, one that filters more for the work truck product, and one that filters less but has more flow for the sport and racing line. All the ducting is the same, but the high-flow filter is five ply. Now the K&N is a four-ply filter, so we still go for a little better filtering than pure flow in both our applications. The work truck guys are driving on dirt roads, fields, and in groves. The eight-ply still flows enough to provide enough horsepower without too much restriction.

I design intake ducts to have the smoothest widest radius I can within the limits of the vehicle body. But I also use the factory-style bellows joints to join the ductwork mounted to the engine and the body. This is to compensate for the engine rock under load. Without the bellows, the system will separate and allow unfiltered air into the intake. I understand why some other aftermarket manufacturers don't do it—it's expensive. But in the long run, the system performs better and lasts longer.

Placing sensors properly is critical for optimum performance and accurate engine calibration. When you choose an aftermarket intake system, you have to be aware that the map sensor needs a proper signal to work correctly. If you put a sensor in a bigger duct, it will read a lower airflow level than what is actually happening. That might be good for horsepower, or it might be bad for horsepower. It might set trouble codes because the computer sees conflicting information, and sometimes that code will derate the engine, which nobody wants.

This brings in the concept of matching your whole system. If the intake system is designed to increase airflow and allows sensors to accurately report the airflow to the computer, you'll be able to tune your engine far more accurately and produce more power safely with fewer emissions. This makes a good argument for the idea of buying matching components from the same manufacturer. If you're trying to tune your engine and the sensors aren't sending correct information, it won't perform as well as it should.

Airflow After the Compressor

Improving the airflow after the turbocharger compressor essentially involves improving airflow through the intercooler (its efficiency) as well as through the intake manifold and the intake ports in the cylinder head.

Efficient intercooling means low restriction to reduce intake charge pressure drop across the intercooler, and effective transfer of heat from the intake charge to the ambient environment. Due to their size, some intercoolers take up more frontal area than others so you need to take that into consideration. If you block air that would otherwise flow into the radiator, you might be more likely to overheat your engine.

All intercoolers are not created equal. Banks tries to work with the best, "We work with Valeo and we're looking to work with Visteon. Valeo currently supplies the factory intercoolers for the Duramax and the Cummins. I don't know who has the Ford business. Valeo has a great product, but they're frustrated because the factories won't pay for the higher performing units, so we teamed up and brought the technology to the customer. We paid for the tooling on the bigger cores, which is what Valeo's engineers wanted to do all along and then we developed the designs with them." (For more info on intercoolers, see Chapter 4.)

A good intercooler is highly efficient, pulling temperature from the air without forcing too much of a pressure drop across the intercooler. You also need to allow plenty of airflow to the engine's radiator.

INDUCTION AND COMBUSTION

The Stock Dodge Cummins Intake

Some intake designs are better than others. And while the 5.9-liter Dodge Cummins makes the most torque and has the most brawny bottom end, its intake system could use some help. Check out the system and see for yourself.

The stock Cummins air intake leading to the compressor forces the air to make sharp turns that restrict airflow. As we learned, intake air, like any fluid, flows best through gentler bends.

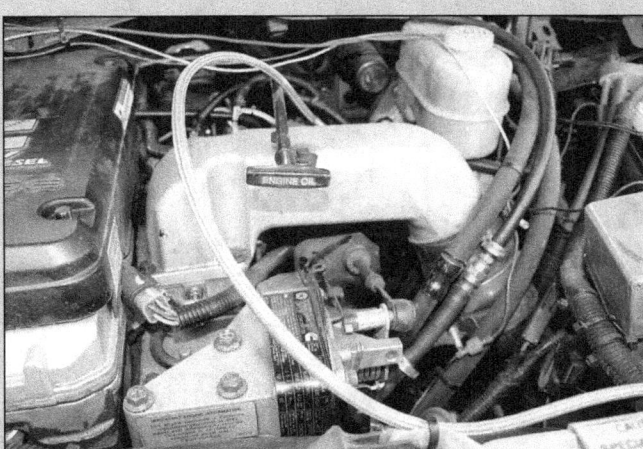

The air has to run through this chicane between the compressor and the cylinder head intake port.

The entry to the intercooler is also cramped and restricts flow. Obviously, the engineers had other things to worry about than absolute power potential.

The Cummins head design shrouds the intake ports with the partial intake manifold that's cast as part of the head. This causes uneven airflow and therefore uneven power output from cylinder to cylinder.

The exhaust system isn't a model of mass flow either, but compared to the intake manifold and the head, the exhaust is relatively modern. Of course, aftermarket companies have much better performing parts available.

HIGH-PERFORMANCE DIESEL BUILDER'S GUIDE

CHAPTER 3

The stock port match on the Duramax is terrible. Check out the arrows. If you have to rebuild your engine, this is an area that'd offer significant airflow improvement, especially if you're upgrading your turbo. (Photo courtesy of General Motors)

Cummins and Duramax Intake Manifolds

Once you get to the intake manifold, the airflow path gets nightmarish. The Cummins intake manifold that is partly cast into the head and the poor Duramax port-matching come to mind.

Each Duramax head has eight intake ports (two per cylinder), so the mismatch is a significant source of restriction. Ideally, you want the intake manifold to match perfectly to the cylinder head ports so there's no flow or velocity lost between the manifold and the head. The Duramax has no port match whatsoever, and the intake manifold is just a clamshell. The port has square corners and the flow going into the port has to go around a 90-degree angle. It's a terrible, absolutely crude assembly.

So there's room for improvement on the intake manifolds of both the Duramax and Dodge. Ford probably has the best manifold and it certainly has the best port match.

You'll never get the ports to line up on the Cummins, because the ports don't come up to a surface where you could seal a gasket around each port. So with the Cummins we're flowing the shape of the manifold into the outer perimeter of the port, the top, the bottom, and the end ports, and then it's just a common chamber. With this design, the front and rear cylinders are starved for air because the manifold chokes them off. Having equal distribution to all cylinders is crucial for precise tuning and high performance.

Air Distribution and Power Balancing

Why is it important for the air distribution to be equal between the cylinders? You're injecting the same fuel amounts into each cylinder (the injector nozzles are matched precisely), so if you put in different amounts of air, then the air/fuel ratio will be different. This produces different cylinder temperatures and different power outputs per cylinder.

When most people talk about balancing an engine, they're talking

To work around Cummins' torturous intake, Banks designed this Big Hoss intake manifold to evenly distribute the air between cylinders.

INDUCTION AND COMBUSTION

This early plastic prototype model of the Big Hoss Duramax intake manifold shows the mating surface. The runner length and volume, and plenum volume and shape, are designed to work with a twin-turbo system.

about balancing the reciprocating parts, which can include adding counterweights to the crankshaft to physically balance the engine. However, power balance is just as critical. The engine's life is compromised if the power balance is off. This is also true for everything that's driven off the front of the crank.

The crankshaft does not turn a constant RPM. If you watched the instantaneous speed of the crankshaft as it rotates through 360 degrees, it speeds up as each cylinder fires, accelerating momentarily and then decelerating because there's load on the end. If the power stroke is equal every time, then the power balance is correct. If the air/fuel ratio is not the same in each cylinder, the power balance is toast. This puts different amounts of energy into the crank throws as the cylinders are firing, which in turn gets the crank twisting erratically and ultimately breaks it. If you want to build a durable, high-RPM, high-output engine, you need power balance. Power balance isn't talked about as much as it should be, but anybody building endurance engines talks about power balance. That's how you make the engine survive.

Banks watches the cylinder temperature at each port as a direct measure of the amount of energy consumed in that cylinder and a direct measure of the air/fuel ratio. "We try to get the exhaust temps to within 25 to 50 degrees of each other across the engine. I've seen stock engines with a 200-degree difference between cylinders. Cold cylinders have a lot of air; hot cylinders are starved for air.

"My Duramax Big Hoss manifold has good plenum volume feeding each of the intake ports and it has a balance tube that balances pressure from bank to bank. The reason for the balance tubes versus a common chamber for all eight cylinders is that I'm using two turbos.

"The reason I'm bringing this up is that the intake manifold is part of the port design. The intake port is continuous from the intake manifold plenum through the gasket surface through the valve into the cylinder. So port design tuned length is what we're talking about. The Cummins design prevents us from doing a tuned intake port.

"The Duramax and the Powerstroke have individual intake ports right to a gasket surface. Strictly speaking, they're all four-valve designs with two intake ports per

Gale Banks is designing components and devising the techniques to allow direct injection diesels to make power at high RPM. This intake runner design, running nearly straight from the plenum to the valve, is part of the puzzle. A low-restriction, torque-producing balance tube manages the pressure waves in the plenum.

CHAPTER 3

If you're thinking about some ported heads, remember that swirl energy and flow need to be balanced. Banks engineers devote an incredible amount of time to the flow bench with a swirl meter. This tool is really indispensable in producing port work that increases flow and maintains the swirl energy.

ting more air into the engine, but they're degrading the combustion process, so the brake specific fuel consumption goes way up. You need to be more scientific, measure the swirl, and increase the flow to do it right.

"We measure the valve lift 1-mm to 20-mm, or 0.050-inch to 0.700-inch. Essentially you're trying to get more flow at every lift point, from right off the seat to maximum lift, without killing the swirl. This is hard.

"When we dyno the engines with ported heads, we measure the smoke. Every test we do on the engine dynamometer, in most of the developmental testing on the chassis dyno, and even on the street. We have an instrument that measures the smoke by shooting light through it and reading how much light is absorbed by the smoke.

"Swirl is important on the cylinder. Some are designed with one port generating most of the swirl. In other words, one port is restricted right behind the valve head, because it is designed to turn and accelerate the air to generate swirl, which slows the flow. That was an early tactic, most now use both ports to generate swirl because swirl is so critical to making the diesel combustion process work."

Porting for Flow and Swirl

Unfortunately for diesel enthusiasts, you can't just port the heads out to get big flow numbers and still get good combustion. Do that and the engine will just go to smoke. "It's just astonishing," says Banks, "it's really easy to mess up a diesel head with porting unless you just don't care about the combustion process and smoke. I'm not saying they don't gain power, they're get-

Valve lift versus flow versus swirl versus piston-to-valve clearance makes porting a direct-injection diesel about the most challenging operation in the automotive performance industry. Monitoring flow at all valve lifts is key for diesel engines since their camshaft profiles are dictated by the tight piston-to-valve clearance.

intake port, but the exhaust port just needs to flow. It has no impact on smoke, no impact on combustion. All you're trying to do is get the remaining energy out of the cylinder. You just need the highest flow at all lift points."

Camshafts and Valvetrain

Most diesel engines have very restrictive ports and don't really support high valve lifts. After the valve lifts 10 or 12 millimeters, the flow just quits increasing. So lifting the valves extremely high doesn't usually help a lot. One of the tests Banks does is to take the valve out of the port, plug the stem hole, and check the flow without the valve. This gives them an idea of the max possible flow. They'll then run the head with the valve on the flow bench and keep increasing lift until it stops picking up flow. This tells them how much lift to spec in the cam.

"Moreover, you don't need and can't use increased duration that sometimes justifies more lift because diesels are more duration limited than gas motors," says Banks. "You're overlap-limited with a turbo gas motor because you'll blow the boost right through to the exhaust. But with diesel, it's hard to get overlap because you're running the piston and valve clearance so close. There aren't valve reliefs in the stock pistons of most diesels. We've added reliefs on the Cummins and now on the Duramax, but the minute you cut valve reliefs in the pistons you kill the swirl. It's like teeth—they grab the swirling air and just stop it. So we're experimenting with how to make valve reliefs without slowing the swirl and forcing it to smoke early. That's key to be able to use camshafts with much higher lift, otherwise there'd

Comparing the stock cam (left) with an experimental performance cam for the Banks Type R Duramax engine, it's easy to see the additional duration on the cam lobe grind. Turbo diesels, like turbocharged gas motors, don't produce good power with too much overlap and thus the lobe separation angle remains close to stock specs.

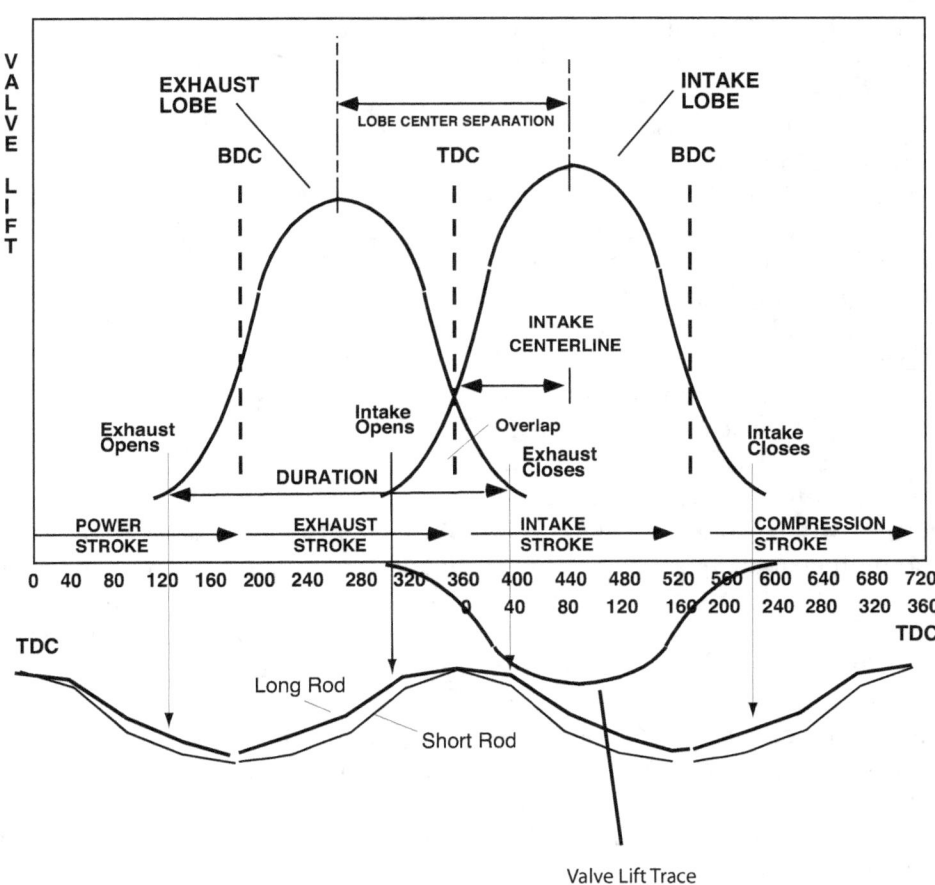

This illustration shows a hypothetical cam profile in relation to crankshaft degrees and the position of the piston in the bore given a long rod and a short rod dimension. It also shows the relationship of valve lift and timing in relation to piston position. It's interesting to see how all these events must happen in concert to make good power.

be no point."

Diesels are, in addition to the reasons we addressed above, naturally limited in the amount of duration they can handle. To explain, lets look at the cam timing events beginning with the opening of the intake valve. You can open it at a pretty traditional spot, but closing the intake valve is critical. On the intake stroke, the piston drops down the bore and the intake valve opens a few crankshaft degrees before TDC on the exhaust stroke. However, on the compression stroke, if you don't close the intake valve early, you won't have any compression and you won't have enough heat to ignite the fuel. On a gas engine, you don't close the intake valve until well after BDC because even though the piston is rising you're still running air into the cylinder. But with diesel, you need the extra compression so you have to close the intake valve early. That's the main reason you're duration limited. Other than that, the valve tuning points are pretty much the same as with a gasoline engine. Overall, the valve timing is a tough obstacle for a diesel engine because it limits how much air you can pack into that cylinder. The solution to this, of course, is high boost and high charge density.

Heavy Valves

The valve gear in most diesel engines is incredibly heavy. That's not a problem if you're only spinning the engine to 3,000 rpm, but when you're going for higher engine speeds you need a lightweight valvetrain. Banks is working on lightweight lifters. "Some cam designs are flat tappet, some guys convert them to roller tappets and make special cams for them, which is good if you want to spin the engine fast. And as far as the Duramax is concerned

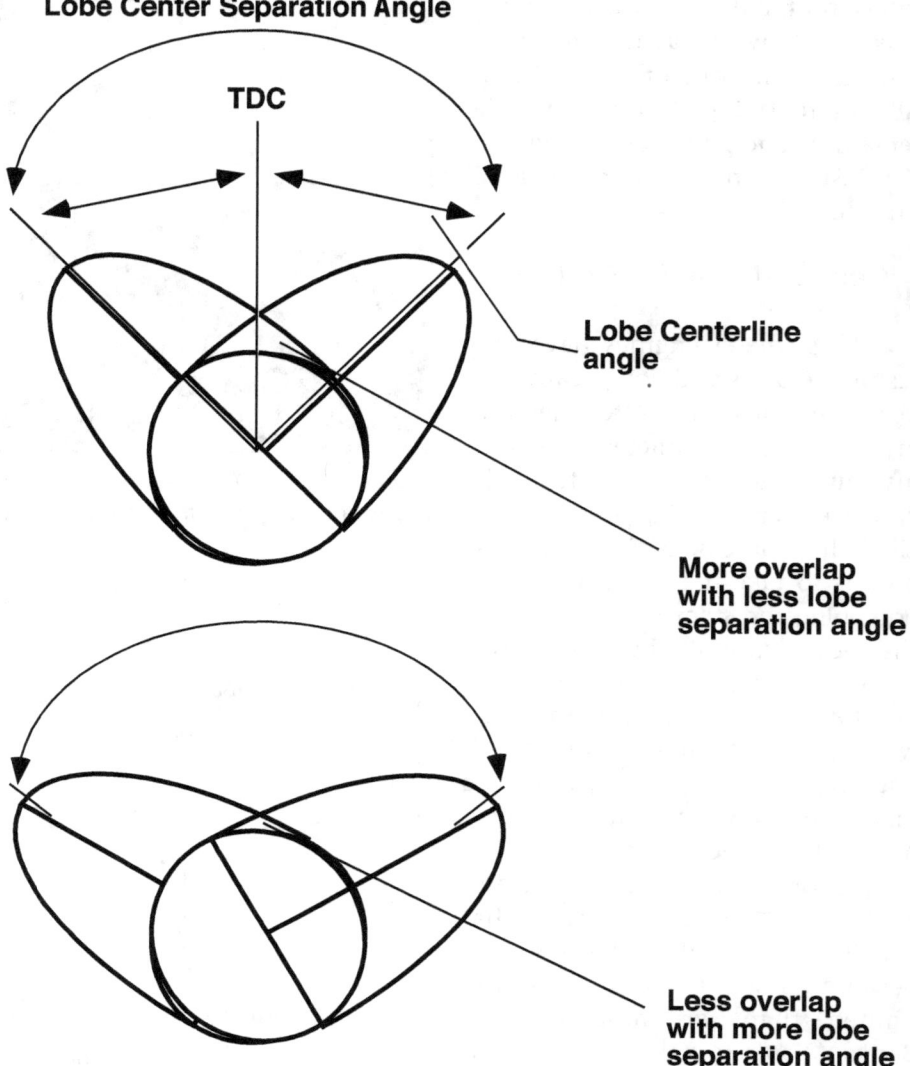

A camshaft's lobe separation determines the overlap (the time when both the intake and exhaust valves are open) allowing the incoming charge to help evacuate the cylinder of spent gases. Turbocharged engines need less overlap since the pressurized intake and exhaust work differently than a naturally aspirated engine.

we're doing a much lighter-weight roller tappet and bushing down the lifter bores. We're also remachining the block to provide oil passages so we can pressurize the oil for the lifters. In stock trim, they're splash oiled or oiled down from the rockers. That's fine for the stock RPM and for an engine that's not going to see severe duty in a road race truck or even in an off-road or off-shore racing application.

"As far as the valves are concerned, I think most high-performance diesel guys are looking for better material in the exhaust valve," says Banks.

The stock exhaust valves in many diesel engines are superior to the materials used in gasoline engines, but in some cases you can still improve.

"713 Inconel exhaust valves are

INDUCTION AND COMBUSTION

usually better than what comes in most diesels and are recommended if you're running a combo that sees high EGT over a long duration. The Inco valves are heavy though. They're high nickel and really dense. So you have to match the valvesprings to go with them for the RPM you want to run."

Pushrods

Banks is also working on various types of tubular push rods of various diameter that would be lighter and stiffer than stock. The best valvetrains are stiff and light, and sometimes it's hard to get both. If the pushrods are not stable it causes valve control problems, so you're sometimes better off having a stiff pushrod that's heavier than a light one that flexes.

In wrapping up the chapter, I should point out that much of the discussion on high-end valvetrain parts is to get you up to speed on the inner workings of your diesel engine, not to suggest that you need these upgrades for your street truck. Remember, and I need to stress this, it is very early in the development cycle for diesel performance products, and aftermarket manufacturers are learning as they go. Most of the valvetrain mods discussed are expensive and typically would be found on racing engines. With that said, they can be applied to a street driven diesel with much success, provided one is willing to accept the expense. Of course special tuning and an extended RPM range is required to take advantage of such mods.

Piston-to-valve clearance is a delicate issue in building a performance diesel. Fly cutting the piston top to provide clearance works, but it tends to kill the swirl, which is necessary to make good power without excessive smoke.

Banks' strategy to increase the potential engine speed of the Type-R Duramax engine included reducing the mass of the valves by shimming the guides and using high-flowing aftermarket valves and seats. This is cool stuff, but it's a little overkill for a street engine at this point.

HIGH-PERFORMANCE DIESEL BUILDER'S GUIDE

CHAPTER 4

THE TURBOCHARGER

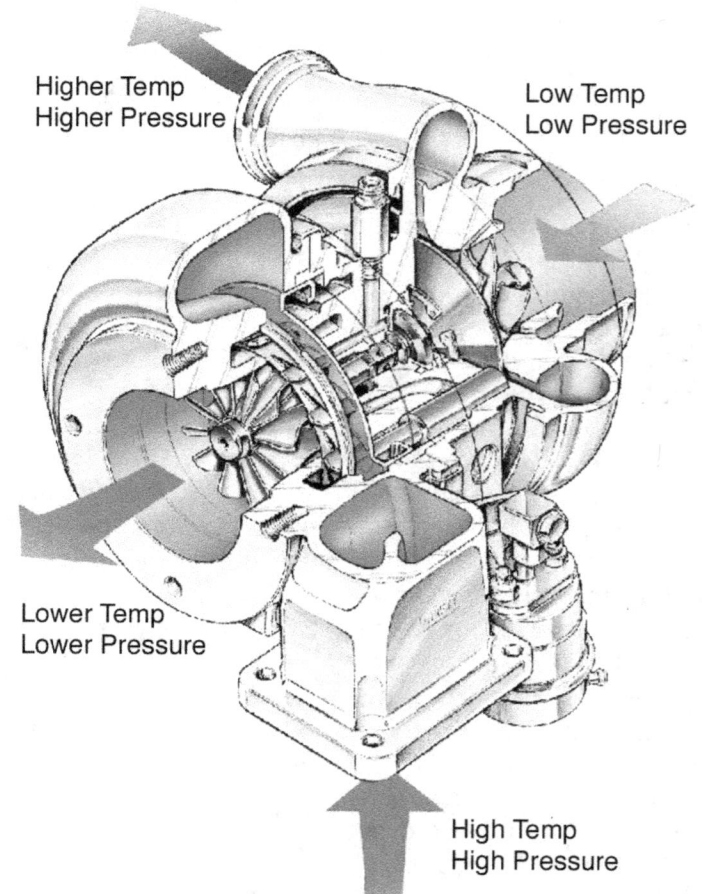

The turbocharger flows heat and pressure in specific directions. On the compressor side the turbo takes in cooler, lower-pressure air and does work on it and adds heats. The compressor compresses the air, which also raises its pressure and temperature. On the turbine side, high temperature and pressure exhaust gas does work to drive the compressor wheel. The heat energy and exhaust pressure spins the turbine wheel, and cooler, lower-temperature exhaust gas is released to the atmosphere. (Photo courtesy of Garrett)

Turbochargers are a popular automotive power adder for both gasoline and diesel engines. Most of the information readily available on turbos is written from a gasoline-engine perspective. In terms of the mass flow of the compressor, it doesn't matter what the fuel is or the means of ignition, so most of the current information applies to diesels as well. However, because of the differences in the mass flow requirements for diesel versus gasoline you need to adjust some of the tuning and component choices to get the best combination for your diesel application.

In this chapter I give a general explanation of turbocharger theory and then apply that theory to diesel engines. This gives you the "mental map" of how it all comes together to make a powerful diesel combination. You should also know what information you need to work with a turbocharger supplier to get the best turbo for your needs.

In the most general sense, a turbocharger is an exhaust-driven supercharger. The turbo basically consists of a turbine and a compressor. The turbine is the side driven by the exhaust gas (turbine wheel and housing), which in turn drives the compressor (compressor wheel, housing). The turbine and compressor are connected by a center section, which includes a bearing system to help the wheels spin freely.

When upgrading your turbo combination, realize that it's all about finding the best compromise. Matching a turbocharger system with your engine is the art of balancing the following:

- Coordinate the air/fuel ratio and airflow demands of the engine under different loads and engine speeds with that of the turbocharger compressor map.
- Match the turbine to the engine mass flow and load to match the compressor map with engine mass flow demands.
- Build the system to respond quickly to changing load and engine speed demands and to get great fuel mileage with great service life and reliability.

As you can see, it's a challenge to get it right. That's why you shouldn't go into this neighborhood alone. You really need to educate yourself or work with an experienced diesel tuner to select the right parts. Let's get started.

The Basics

Many people think a turbo increases the volume or the pressure of the air in the engine's intake system. However, the real purpose of the turbocharger is to increase the density of that air.

Density is determined by dividing the weight or mass of a substance

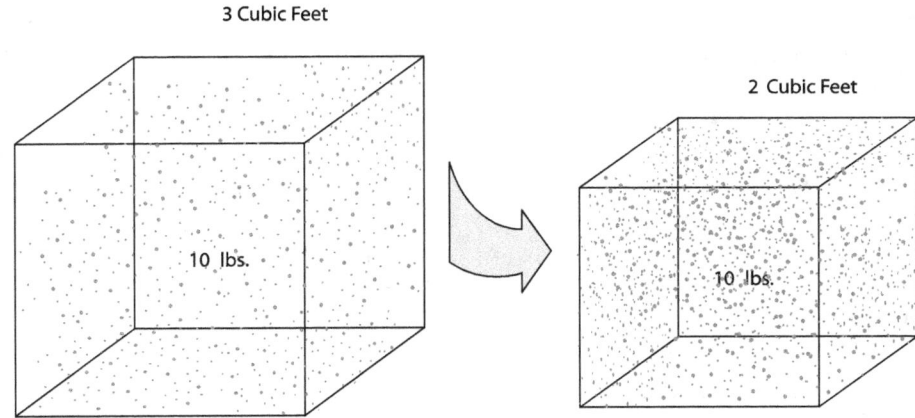

Density is defined as mass divided by volume. In other words, more matter in less area equals higher density. Density is related to the old problem of putting 10 lbs of crap into a 5-lb sac, which is more or less what your turbocharger is doing to your intake.

by its cubic area or volume. So the density of a cubic inch of lead is higher than a cubic inch of air. Because gases such as air can be compressed, we can put more air mass within a cubic inch, thus raising its density. That's what a turbocharger does.

However, as the turbo compresses the air, it is doing work to it, and thus heats it up. This tends to reduce its density. Let's take a look at the gas law to help us understand how a turbocharger system manages these conflicting processes.

The Gas Law

The basic law that describes the relationship between the pressure, volume, weight, and temperature of a gas is called the Ideal Gas Equation,

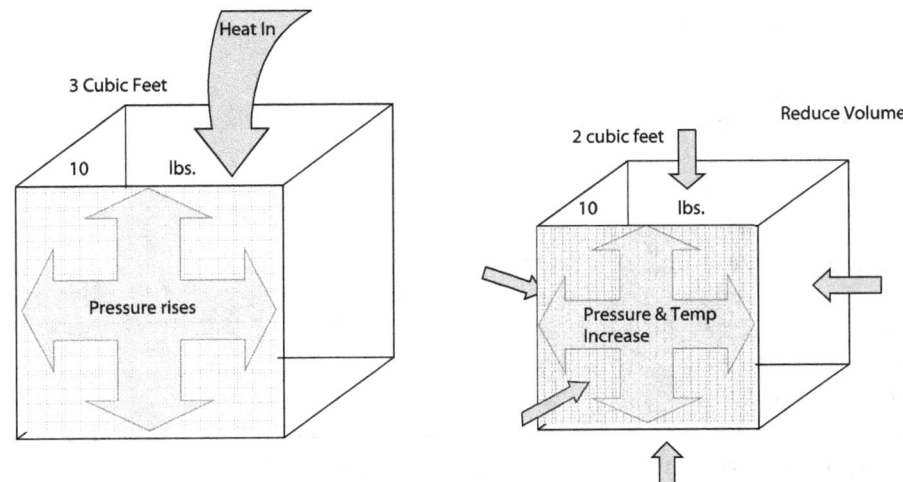

The Gas Law describes how an ideal gas behaves when its volume, pressure, and temperature are changed. When a gas is heated and the volume of its container kept constant, the pressure rises with no change in density (right). If the volume is allowed to expand, temperature will rise but pressure remains constant, while its density will be reduced. If the volume is reduced, the temperature and pressure rise proportionally (left).

or just the Gas Law. It is usually stated by the equation:

$$PV = nRT$$

Where: P is pressure, V is volume, n is the weight of the gas in moles (molecules), R is a constant (called the Molar Gas Constant, which has different values depending on the units used for the other quantities), and T is the temperature.

Let's rearrange the equation to: P = nRT/V. Now we can see that if more boost pressure is measured, it could be because more molecules of air are present (n) for a given volume (that is, the constant capacity of the engine and boost air system). Or, more pressure (P) could be measured simply because the air is at a higher temperature (T). Now we see that measuring boost pressure is not so straightforward.

If you change the turbocharger and see more boost, or if one engine has more boost than another, is the horsepower more, less, or the same? The answer is "maybe," depending on temperature. You can get the same or even lower horsepower if you change a component of the turbocharger to increase boost at the expense of hotter air. Two major causes for this problem are (1) turbochargers are efficient at producing boost only over a certain range of pressure, temperature, and airflow; and (2) the engine still needs to "breathe" out the exhaust side to make power (that is, minimize pumping losses).

Furthermore, this formula tells us that for a given amount (mass or weight) of gas, increasing the pressure and keeping the volume the same will increase the temperature proportionally. Increasing the temperature and keeping the volume the same will increase the pressure proportionally. And finally, increasing the volume while keeping the pressure the same means the temperature must increase, and so on.

Of particular importance to the subject of turbocharging is that a temperature rise at a given pressure increases the volume, meaning a decrease in density. You can increase both the pressure and the temperature without increasing the density. This is what makes an intercooler necessary for optimum power output.

Heat and Adiabatic Efficiency

The tricky aspect of turbocharging an engine is making sure it increases the density of the charge air, *not just (boost) pressure*. As the gas law shows, the pressure of a gas can be raised without increasing its density.

Adiabatic efficiency is a measure of compressing a gas without adding or losing heat to or from sources outside the thermodynamic system. If we could compress a gas by some physical means without adding any more heat to it besides the heat generated by the act of compression, and we did not let any of that heat escape, we would have perfect adiabatic compression, or 100 percent adiabatic efficiency.

Because compressing air heats it up, and because its volume is not held constant throughout the intake ducting between the turbo and the cylinder, its density varies at different points in the system. You can use the air/density ratio equation to determine the effectiveness of your compressor and intercooler at increasing the density of the intake charge. It also shows how temperature and pressure interact to change the density of the intake charge.

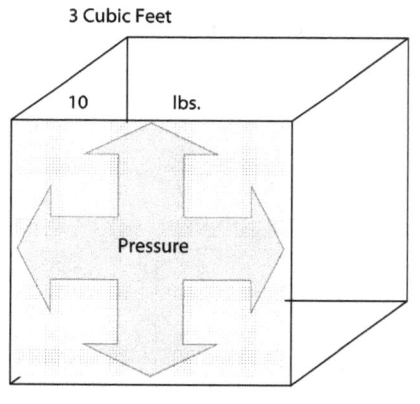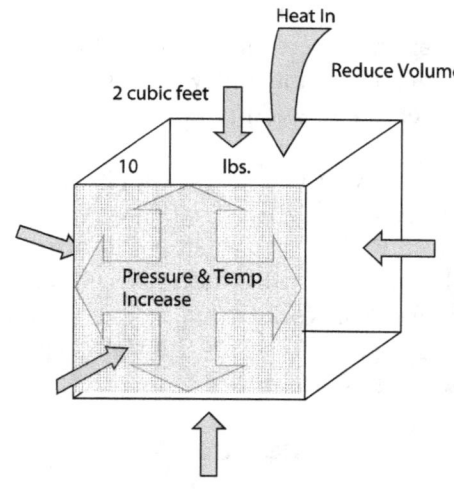

An adiabatic process is one where no heat is lost or gained. For example, a 100-percent efficient adiabatic compression of a quantity of air does not add heat to it, even though the temperature and pressure rises in the process. The temperature rises because the heat energy of the air in volume A is now contained in a smaller volume B. Consequently, a 90-percent efficient process raises the temperature and pressure proportionally higher. A turbo's compressor does adiabatic work at less than 100-percent efficiency, so the work done by the turbo adds heat.

THE TURBOCHARGER

A more efficient turbocharger builds boost without introducing as much heat into the intake charge. This helps keep your intake change dense and the power up. This BD Diesel Performance Super B Special turbo is rated to make 525 hp. (Photo courtesy of BD Diesel Performance)

Density Ratio = Inlet Temp/Outlet Temp x Outlet Pressure Absolute/Inlet Pressure Absolute

$$DR = (68 + 460)/(131 + 460) \times (7.4 + 14.7)/14.7$$
$$DR = 528/591 \times 22.1/14.7$$
$$DR = 0.8934 \times 1.5034$$
$$\text{Density Ratio} = 1.34:1$$

The air density ratio measured across the turbocharger and intercooler for this example is 1.34:1, or a 34-percent density increase over atmospheric. The beauty of this equation is that it takes into consideration most of the real factors operating on the intake charge, such as the cooling effect of the intercooler. That's why the factories use intake temperature and pressure sensors along with mass flow and ambient air-pressure sensors. If the engine management computer knows the pressure and temperature of the air, it can calculate density and mass flow. Once it calculates those it can calculate the proper amount of fuel to inject.

The Air Density Ratio

The demands for fuel efficiency tend to favor using a smaller engine with more boost. This, of course, means using higher pressure ratios. Increasing the pressure ratio means either operating the turbocharger at much higher shaft speeds or splitting the pressure increase by using dual-stage compression systems (staged turbos).

Now onto the formula for calculating the air density ratio. Measure inlet temp in degrees F and inlet pressure in psi. The formula adds 460 to convert Fahrenheit to the Rankin scale and also adds standard sea level pressure of 14.7 psi to get absolute pressure. If you're really hardcore, use measured ambient atmospheric pressure (which will vary) instead of 14.7 for a more accurate figure. Let's use the example of a turbocharged engine operating at an ambient temperature of 68 degrees F and standard atmospheric pressure (14.7 psi absolute). Imagine it making 7.4 psi of boost in the manifold and recording a temperature in the manifold of 131 degrees F. We can plug in these figures and find the density ratio:

BD Performance's stock and performance Ford 6.0-liter replacement turbocharger is engineered to flow air for 550 hp. It offers quick response, low exhaust temperatures, and better fuel economy than stock. (Photo courtesy of BD Diesel Performance)

Choosing a Turbo

An efficient, effective turbocharger setup is one where the

CHAPTER 4

Which of these is right for your turbo diesel combo? That depends on your particular application, including your mass airflow requirement, RPM, displacement, and power goals. (Photos courtesy of Travis Thompson)

turbo is allowed to operate in the heart of its efficiency range. How do you choose the right turbo? Well, that depends on what else you've done to your engine.

When designing a turbo system, you have to look at the application. Is your driving mainly high-performance street? Do you use your diesel truck mostly for work? Is it mostly a drag racer with some street driving, or mostly a streeter with an occasional full-boost blast down the quarter-mile? The type of driving you do most makes a big difference when choosing your turbo.

Keep in mind that diesel engines require different turbine and compressor characteristics than gasoline engines. This is because diesels need to move far more air compared to gasoline engines, and because the exhaust temps are cooler, so the turbine responds differently to load and fueling. With that said, we look at the compressor side first, and we move on the turbine side later in the chapter. This is partially because turbo manufacturers and distributors are much more open with compressor maps and info than turbine maps. Starting with the right compressor gets you going on the right foot.

Let me apologize in advance for all the dry number crunching tech to come. But when you're looking to make huge power gains, you need to do some planning. This involves determining the mass flow of air at the power level you desire, then using the equations to determine what manifold pressure and temperature is going to flow the mass needed to achieve the power level. You do this at two points: the power peak and the torque peak. Once you have the mass flow rates at peak power and peak torque you overlay them on a compressor map to judge the match of the compressor to your engine combination and power level.

The first equations are general and designed for a quick estimation and a first step in the planning process. The later, more-detailed equations take into consideration and adjust for the temperature and pressure of the charge air to determine the mass flow under operating conditions. One determines the manifold absolute pressure needed to flow a certain mass rate for a selected power level, while the second solves for the mass flow under operation conditions. In addition, a few compensation values are added to the results to guide you. The more variables are taken into consideration, the more accurate your estimations will be, and the closer you'll get to your ideal turbo.

The best way to size a turbo is to work backward from your horsepower goal. It pays to be realistic here—so please try to stay within the principles of physics. The Power and Mass Flow chart uses your horsepower goal and your air/fuel ratio to help you estimate your fuel and mass airflow requirements. This can help you choose the best compressor for your application, as most turbo manufacturers recommend their turbos based on lbs/min, lbs/hr, or CFM or mass airflow.

Garrett offers turbo upgrades for 1998 to 2006 Dodge Ram 2500 and 3500 trucks with Cummins 5.9L engines. The kits start with the GT37R dual ball-bearing turbo and are available in stages that can support up to 550 hp and 1,100 ft-lbs of torque. (Photo courtesy of Garrett)

THE TURBOCHARGER

The Engine Size, Boost, & Air Mass Flow Rates chart uses your cubic inch displacement, redline RPM, and your prospective boost level to help you calculate what kind of mass airflow to look for in a turbo.

Power and Mass Flow

The information in the Power and Mass Flow chart was calculated assuming a brake specific fuel consumption (BSFC) of 0.4 pounds of fuel per horsepower per hour and an air/fuel ratio of 20:1. While BSFC varies with load and RPM, a good average number for a diesel is 0.4. By multiplying horsepower by 0.4 we get the pounds of fuel used to make the power (hp x 0.4 = lbs/hour/hp).

To help you choose a turbo or fuel system, simply reference the planned horsepower level and move across to the right to find the mass flow in the measurement unit used by your turbo manufacturer of choice.

Engine Size, Boost & Air Mass Flow Rates

Choosing your turbocharger is directly associated with mass flow. The Engine Size, Boost & Air Mass Flow (page 56) charts are based on standard cubic feet per minute (SCFM) of air. SCFM is a measure of airflow with atmospheric conditions at a barometric pressure of 29.92 inches of mercury, 60 degrees F, and no water in the air (dry vapor pressure).

The SCFM ratings in the chart were calculated using 100-percent VE and 14.7 psi of ambient pressure (0 psi boost). To scale for a different volumetric efficiency, insert the term that reflects those conditions into the formula. For example, to calculate CFM at 85-percent VE, use the formula CFM = RPM x CID/3456 x 0.85. To calculate flow under boosted conditions (as in the center and right columns), add a multiplier representative of the boost increase. For a boost pressure at the gauge of 10 psi, use the formula CFM = RPM x CID/3456 x ((10 + 14.7)/14.7). Just swap in any boost level for the "10" in the formula (we used 14.7 and 29.4 psi in the chart).

To find a fuel or mass air requirement in lbs/hr, just multiply the number in lbs/min by 60.

Please note that I'm using a trick with VE term of the equation to build these charts that while not the most accurate, is common in the industry and is considered a good estimating technique in modeling airflow.

Compressor Maps

Using the information in these charts and the specs of your particular application, you should be able to get a good idea of how much mass flow you're looking for in a turbo. Take that number to your favorite

Power and Mass Flow

HP	Fuel lbs/hr	Fuel lbs/min	Airflow lbs/hr	Airflow lbs/min	Airflow CFM
700	280	4.67	5,600	93.33	1,225
680	272	4.53	5,440	90.67	1,190
660	264	4.40	5,280	88.00	1,155
640	256	4.27	5,120	85.33	1,120
620	248	4.13	4,960	82.67	1,085
600	240	4.00	4,800	80.00	1,050
580	232	3.87	4,640	77.33	1,015
560	224	3.73	4,480	74.67	980
540	216	3.60	4,320	72.00	945
520	208	3.47	4,160	69.33	910
500	200	3.33	4,000	66.67	875
480	192	3.20	3,840	64.00	840
460	184	3.07	3,680	61.33	805
440	176	2.93	3,520	58.67	770
420	168	2.80	3,360	56.00	735
400	160	2.67	3,200	53.33	700
380	152	2.53	3,040	50.67	665
360	144	2.40	2,880	48.00	630
340	136	2.27	2,720	45.33	595
320	128	2.13	2,560	42.67	560
300	120	2.00	2,400	40.00	525
280	112	1.87	2,240	37.33	490
260	104	1.73	2,080	34.67	455
240	96	1.60	1,920	32.00	420
220	88	1.47	1,760	29.33	385
200	80	1.33	1,600	26.67	350
180	72	1.20	1,440	24.00	315
160	64	1.07	1,280	21.33	280
140	56	0.93	1,120	18.67	245
120	48	0.80	960	16.00	210
100	40	0.67	800	13.33	175

Engine Size, Boost & Air Mass Flow

5.9 liter, 360 ci

RPM	Naturally Aspirated		14.7 psi Boost		29.4 psi Boost	
	SCFM	lbs/min	CFM	lbs/min	CFM	lbs/min
5,500	573	44	1,146	87	1,719	131
5,000	521	40	1,042	79	1,563	119
4,500	469	36	938	71	1,406	107
4,000	417	32	833	64	1,250	95
3,500	365	28	729	56	1,094	83
3,000	313	24	625	48	938	71
2,500	260	20	521	40	781	60
2,000	208	16	417	32	625	48
1,500	156	12	313	24	469	36
1,000	104	8	208	16	313	24
500	52	4	104	8	156	12

6.0 liter, 366 ci

RPM	Naturally Aspirated		14.7 psi Boost		29.4 psi Boost	
	SCFM	lbs/min	CFM	lbs/min	CFM	lbs/min
5,500	582	44	1,165	89	1,747	133
5,000	530	40	1,059	81	1,589	121
4,500	477	36	953	73	1,430	109
4,000	424	32	847	65	1,271	97
3,500	371	28	741	56	1,112	85
3,000	318	24	635	48	953	73
2,500	265	20	530	40	794	61
2,000	212	16	424	32	635	48
1,500	159	12	318	24	477	36
1,000	106	8	212	16	318	24
500	53	4	106	8	159	12

6.6 liter, 403 ci

RPM	Naturally Aspirated		14.7 psi Boost		29.4 psi Boost	
	SCFM	lbs/min	CFM	lbs/min	CFM	lbs/min
5,500	641	49	1,283	98	1,924	147
5,000	583	44	1,166	89	1,749	133
4,500	525	40	1,049	80	1,574	120
4,000	466	36	933	71	1,399	107
3,500	408	31	816	62	1,224	93
3,000	350	27	700	53	1,049	80
2,500	292	22	583	44	875	67
2,000	233	18	466	36	700	53
1,500	175	13	350	27	525	40
1,000	117	9	233	18	350	27
500	58	4	117	9	175	13

turbo manufacturer's website or catalog (I got these from Turbonetics) and see which turbos will give you the flow you need. Of course, many turbos flow a given amount of air, so you want to look for one that flows the right amount of air at the highest level of efficiency, which keeps your intake charge temps down.

For example, say you want to double the power output of your stock '04 Duramax LB7, which comes from GM making 300 hp at 3,100 rpm and 520 ft-lbs at 1,800 rpm. You're not going to spin it faster; you just want to double the horsepower. Check the Power and Mass Flow chart and you'll find it takes 80 lbs/min of air with a 20:1 air/fuel ratio to make 600 hp. Referencing the Engine Size, Boost, & Air Mass Flow chart we find that to achieve that mass flow rate (80 lbs/min) at that RPM (just over 3,000 rpm), it takes 29.4 psi on the boost gauge (44.1 psi absolute). We use the charts as guides, but you need to use the formulas and plug in the specific data for your application.

So we need to look for a compressor that flows 80 lbs/min within the most efficient area of the map. This keeps charge temps down, plus ensures the turbo can still match the flow requirements of the engine at other RPM and loads. Most compressors run in the range of 55- to 80-percent efficient, which means the compressor will heat the air more than it would if it was 100-percent efficient.

To fine-tune our search we need to compensate for the heat gain during the compression process. We want to get the most boost at the lowest temperature, which means choosing a compressor to provide the mass flow we need at the highest efficiency to avoid heating the air and lowering the density. This is not

THE TURBOCHARGER

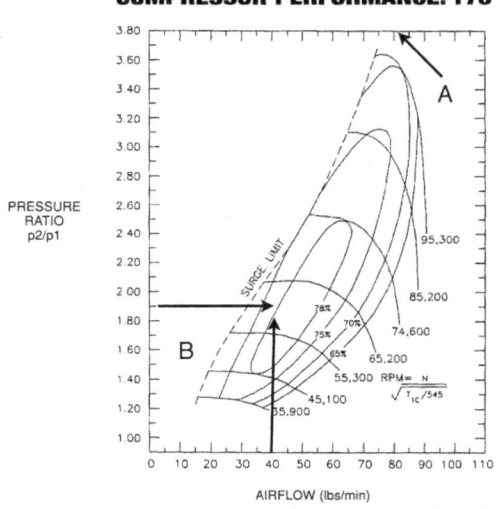

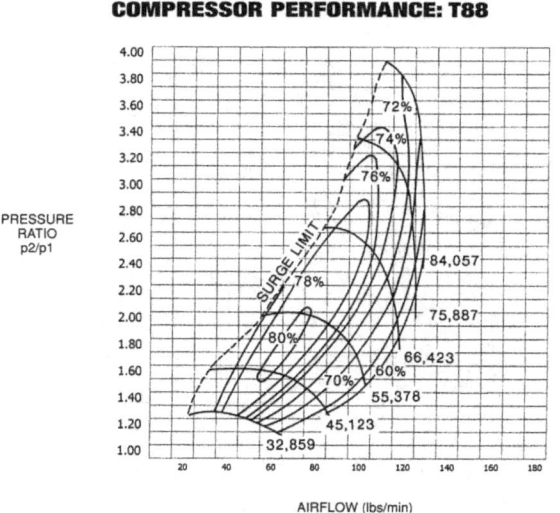

Above Left: This compressor does not support our mass flow goal (A) of 80 lbs/min at a 3.8 pressure ratio. Though the compressor flows more than the required mass, it just doesn't do it in a range that matches the engine demand. Using two of these in a twin-turbo setup would be closer since each compressor would do half (B) of the work. This compressor is even too small to use a pair though because at torque peak flow rates it'd be on the wrong side of the surge line. (Photo courtesy of Turbonetics)

Above Right: This compressor is way to big for our purposes. The pressure ratio/mass flow points are beyond the surge line. (Photo courtesy of Turbonetics)

always possible at high boost and power levels, which is why intercoolers are an integral part of a turbo system.

Manifold Pressure and Temperature

To be completely accurate when designing your turbo system, you'll also need an idea of the pressure and temperature you'll need at the valve, i.e., after the intercooler, to meet your power goals. Use this formula courtesy of Honeywell/Garrett to find your manifold absolute pressure (MAP), or gauge pressure plus actual ambient pressure, required to meet your goal. This formula helps you estimate the psia needed once you account for the temperature change caused by the inefficiency of the turbo and the pressure loss from the intercooler.

$$MAP = \frac{Wa \times R \times (460 + Tm)}{VE \times N/2 \times Vd}$$

Where:

MAP = units of psia, or psi absolute
Wa = actual airflow (lbs/min)
R = gas constant (639.6)
Tm = intake manifold temp in degrees F
VE = volumetric efficiency
N = engine speed (RPM)
Vd = engine size (ci)

To use this formula, you need to know the intake manifold temperature. You can get this with a scanner tool from your truck's OBD system, use an infrared thermometer, or you can estimate. Air temps after the intercooler typically range between 100 and 130 degrees F according to Garrett. Before the intercooler (after the turbo) you'll see temps in the 170 to 300 degree F range.

Using the values in our hypothetical Duramax scenario and 100-percent VE we find we'll need 49.9 psia with an intake temperature of 130 degrees F to reach our goal. If we reduce the intake charge temp by 30 degrees F (with a better intercooler or lower ambient temp) it only takes 47.5 psia to make 600 hp at 3,000 rpm. This is a more accurate estimate than the ones given with the earlier formulas because it takes more vari-

Part No. 30647

Specifications	
Trim Size	T-91
Inducer Diameter	3.580
Exducer Diameter	5.000
Flow Rate	130 lbs/min

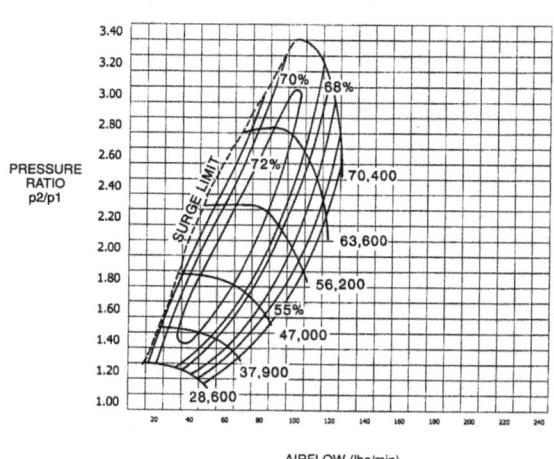

This map shows a compressor able to flow way more than we need, but it still won't do it at the pressure ratio we need. (Photo courtesy of Turbonetics)

Part No. 30648

Specifications	
Trim Size	T-100
Inducer Diameter	3.940
Exducer Diameter	5.000
Flow Rate	180 lbs/min

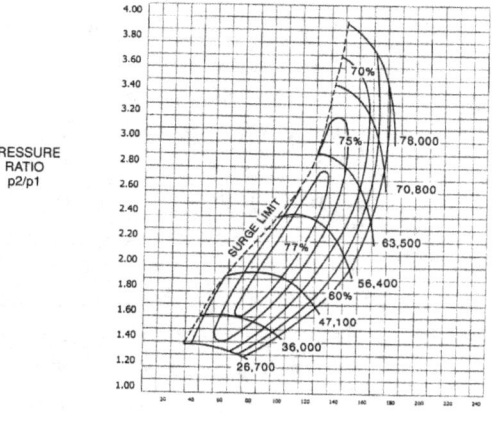

Okay, we're in trouble. There is a compressor out there that would build the boost we need to run 80 lbs/min of air through a 403-ci engine at 3,000 rpm but unfortunately, this T-100 it isn't readily available yet. (Photo courtesy of Turbonetics)

Part No. 30327

Specifications	
Trim Size	T-66
Inducer Diameter	2.580
Exducer Diameter	3.584
Flow Rate	68 lbs/min

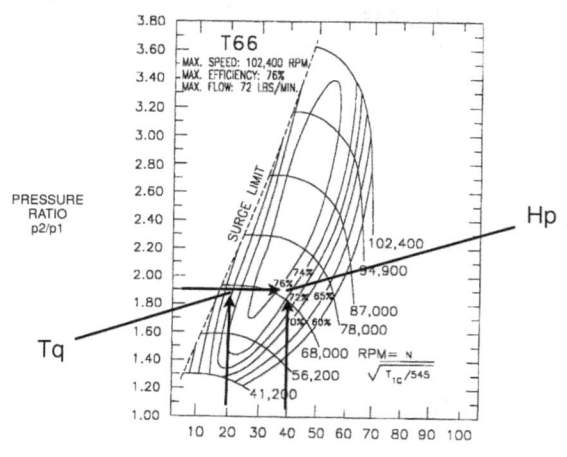

Going with a twin-turbo combination allows more options. This map is a pretty good match if it only has to flow half the mass at half the pressure ratio. Both horsepower and torque peaks are in efficient islands. The torque peak is kind of close to the surge line, but it's still a good match. (Photo courtesy of Turbonetics)

Some turbochargers have what is known as a ported shroud; a channel that allows over boost to be recirculated to the intake away from the compressor wheel. This technique moves the surge line to the left within a range of compressor RPM and pressure ratio. (Photo courtesy of General Motors)

THE TURBOCHARGER

Pressure Ratio Explained

Pressure ratio is one of those deceptively simple characteristics of the turbocharger. Pressure ratio is a ratio of the inlet air pressure and the outlet air pressure. Since inlet pressure varies, so does the outlet pressure, but the pressure ratio should be consistent all things being equal.

Pressure ratio is an indication of the amount of work the compressor is doing. Taking 13.7 psia and compressing it to 16.7 psia (a 1.22:1 pressure ratio) requires less work on the air than producing 27.4 psia (2:1 pressure ratio, or doubling the ambient intake pressure).

Matching a compressor to your engine demands you must calculate mass flow. It takes a certain amount of air and fuel to make a certain amount of power. The trick comes in matching the mass flow of the compressed air as it is squeezed through the cubic capacity of the engine. That's what the pressure ratio tells you when choosing the compressor. It's not just raw mass flow. The air volume has to be reduced a certain amount in order to fit through the restriction that is the engine.

That's why you have to calculate the manifold pressure and temperature required to flow the mass of air for your horsepower goal. Then you have to calculate the pressure drop through intake ducting from the compressor, through the intercooler, to the intake manifold before calculating the pressure ratio required to make your power goal.

[Editor's Note: Turbochargers work on the principle of pressure ratio. Popularly we think about the safe maximum boost pressure for a turbocharger, but the safe maximum boost, and the boost pressures achieved in practical usage, will vary with input pressure, or ambient air pressure. Expect and plan for less boost pressure in Denver than in Los Angeles, even though the safe maximum pressure ratio is the same.]

ables into account. Of course, you need to measure the actual temperatures to make it accurate. Keep reading; we're not done yet.

Plumbing Pressure Drop

Before making a compressor choice, you also need to adjust for the pressure drop across the plumbing from the turbo outlet to the intake valve. Diesels don't have the usual stuff in the way such as throttle bodies, but they do have an intercooler and bends and sensors and so on, all of which causes the pressure to drop and a reduction in the mass flow. How much? Ideally you should measure this. A probe that can capture the pressure at the intake manifold is preferred. For most enthusiasts, a good working number is a drop of 2 psia. Add that to your required MAP that we calculated. Thus our example is now at a rounded figure of about 52 psia. We're getting more accurate in our estimate with every variable we include.

Matching Pressure Ratio

At this point we know how much pressure and at what temperature the air will have to be at the intake manifold to provide the mass flow to make our power goal. So now you can choose your compressor, right? Not yet.

First we need to calculate the compressor's pressure ratio. This value, in concert with the mass flow in lbs/min we need, will get us a good match. To find the pressure ratio, we need to compensate for the pressure drop at the compressor intake from the air cleaner and the ducting.

This isn't as complicated as it sounds. If you can measure this value, great. If not, use 1.0 psia as the pressure drop from ambient to calculate the pressure ratio.
Continuing our example:

Pressure ratio = P1/P2

Where:

P1 = adjusted required MAP
(52 psia, from our example)
P2 = compressor inlet pressure
(ambient 14.7 psia - 1 psia = 13.7 psia)

52/13.7 = 3.8

So we're looking for a pressure ratio of 3.8, which is pretty high. That means we're going to want to choose a compressor that's very efficient at that boost ratio, at that pressure, near the torque peak, since that's where the engine would spend most of its time cruising or towing.

Estimate Mass Flow at Torque Peak

You need to find the mass flow at the torque peak to define the operating points of the combo. These

HIGH-PERFORMANCE DIESEL BUILDER'S GUIDE

points are located on a compressor map to model the operating range of a compressor and help you match it to your engine combo. You can use the charts to get you close, or you can use the formula below to solve for airflow in lbs/min:

Wa = MAP x VE x RPM/2 x Vd/R x (460 + Tm)

Where:

MAP = units of psia
Wa = actual airflow (lbs/min)
R = gas constant (639.6)
Tm = intake manifold temp in   degrees F
VE = volumetric efficiency
Vd = engine size (ci)

We can use the same figures from our example, including our latest required MAP:

Wa = 52 x 1 x 1,600/2 x 403/636.9 x (460 + 130) = 42.4 lbs/min

My Engine Size, Boost & Airflow equation used earlier predicts 42.6 lbs/min (the chart estimates 40 lbs/min at 1,500 rpm), so it's pretty close. Of course these values are without the adjustments for the pressure drop through the ductwork.

These values show us the highest demand made on the compressor, so using the compressor map, we can judge if the compressor is too small or large. Going too small puts the demand points near or past the choke line. If its too big it'll be too close or past the surge line.

If you've read our compressor map captions you can see we're running into difficulty finding a turbo that makes the boost we need to stuff 52 lbs/min through 403 cubic inches at 3,000 rpm. Even if we spun it up to 5,000 rpm, it wouldn't help us that much. We could go with a twin-turbo setup, which would essentially cut the work each turbo has to do in half. That would give us much better options for less expensive compressors.

Dual-stage turbocharging systems use two turbochargers stacked one behind another to achieve high overall system pressure ratios without the need to operate either compressor out of its efficiency range. By using a small, low-inertia turbo for one stage and a larger turbo for the other stage, dual-stage turbocharging systems work around the problem of finding one turbo with enough mass flow and pressure ratio capability to meet our lofty demands. Here's a "back of envelope calculation" for dividing the workload between two turbos:

52/2 = 26 psi per turbo
26/13.7 = 1.9 pressure ratio required for each turbo

With those pressure ratio and mass flow numbers, the combination is more attuned to what's available on the market today. So even though it'd be expensive to have the manifolds built and buy two turbochargers, you could in theory double the output as long as the engine could contain the pressure, you could deliver enough fuel, and get the fuel to react.

Blow-Off and Bypass Valves

Diesel engines don't generally use blow-off valves because they don't have a throttle blade too close the intake tract. But they do use other circuits to manage over boosting and causing the compressor to go into surge.

On gasoline engines, blow-off valves mount on the intake tubing between the turbo and the throttle blade. They are designed to vent excess pressure in the intact tract when the throttle body slams shut (when you let off the gas) to prevent compressor surge. The blow-off valve operates on the vacuum that develops

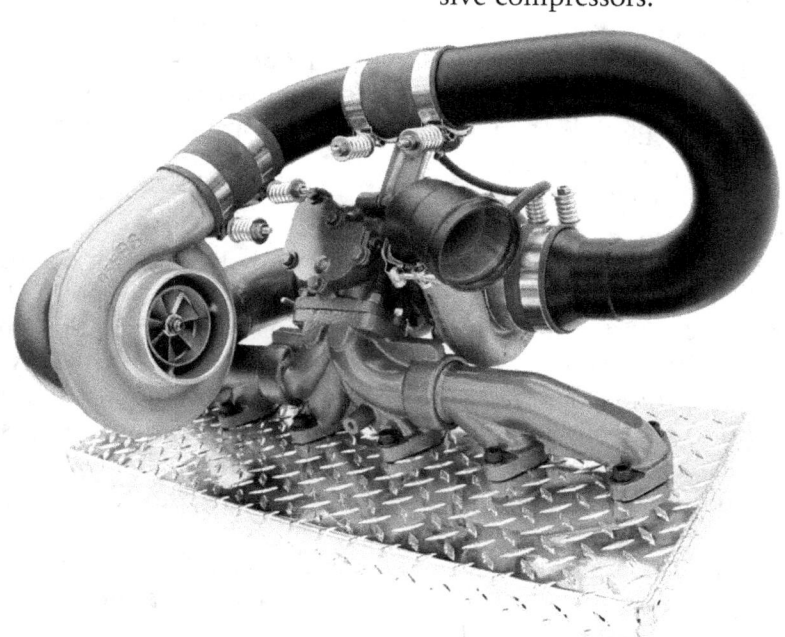

This BD Diesel Performance Super B twin-turbo can help you make an honest 575 hp. This one's designed for '94 to '06 Cummins engines. (Photo courtesy of BD Diesel Performance)

when the throttle valve closes. The vacuum is leveraged through the actuator to open the valve, venting boost pressure to the atmosphere. Bypass valves vent pressure to prevent compressor surge, but they divert the vented air back to the compressor inlet instead of to the atmosphere.

Intercooling Theory

Compressing air increases its temperature even with 100-percent adiabatic efficiency, which is impossible in the real world of turbocharging. Of course, the air is heated far more with the adiabatic efficiency of around 70 to 80 percent, which is the best-case scenario with current compressors. So we're heating air when we compress it and heated air is less dense for a given pressure (boost) than cooler air. Thus, the amount of air ingested by the engine is less, the efficiency is lower, and furthermore, the hotter air going in creates hotter exhaust gas temperatures, further limiting the amount of fuel that can be burned safety (i.e., without cracking or melting engine components). The object of turbocharging is to increase the density of the charge air (not just the pressure), so we need to cool it after compressing it—*while maintaining its pressure*. Of course, we've also got to flow the mass required to reach our power goal.

Thus the intercooler needs to:

1. Reject as much heat as possible
2. Flow a specified range of air mass
3. Perform the above with the least restriction to flow (pressure drop)

How does it do all this? The intercooler is a radiator (heat exchanger) that is usually made of aluminum, which is an efficient conductor of heat. The aluminum is shaped as a series of tubes with fins attached to the tubes. The intercooler transfers heat by conduction so the medium to which the heat is transferred must come in contact with the tubes and fins. Thus the fins and tubes are arranged to have as much surface area in contact with the cooler fluid (water or air) as possible.

We confine our discussion to air-to-air intercoolers, which are more common on diesel engines and more useful for a street-driven machine. Air-to-water intercoolers

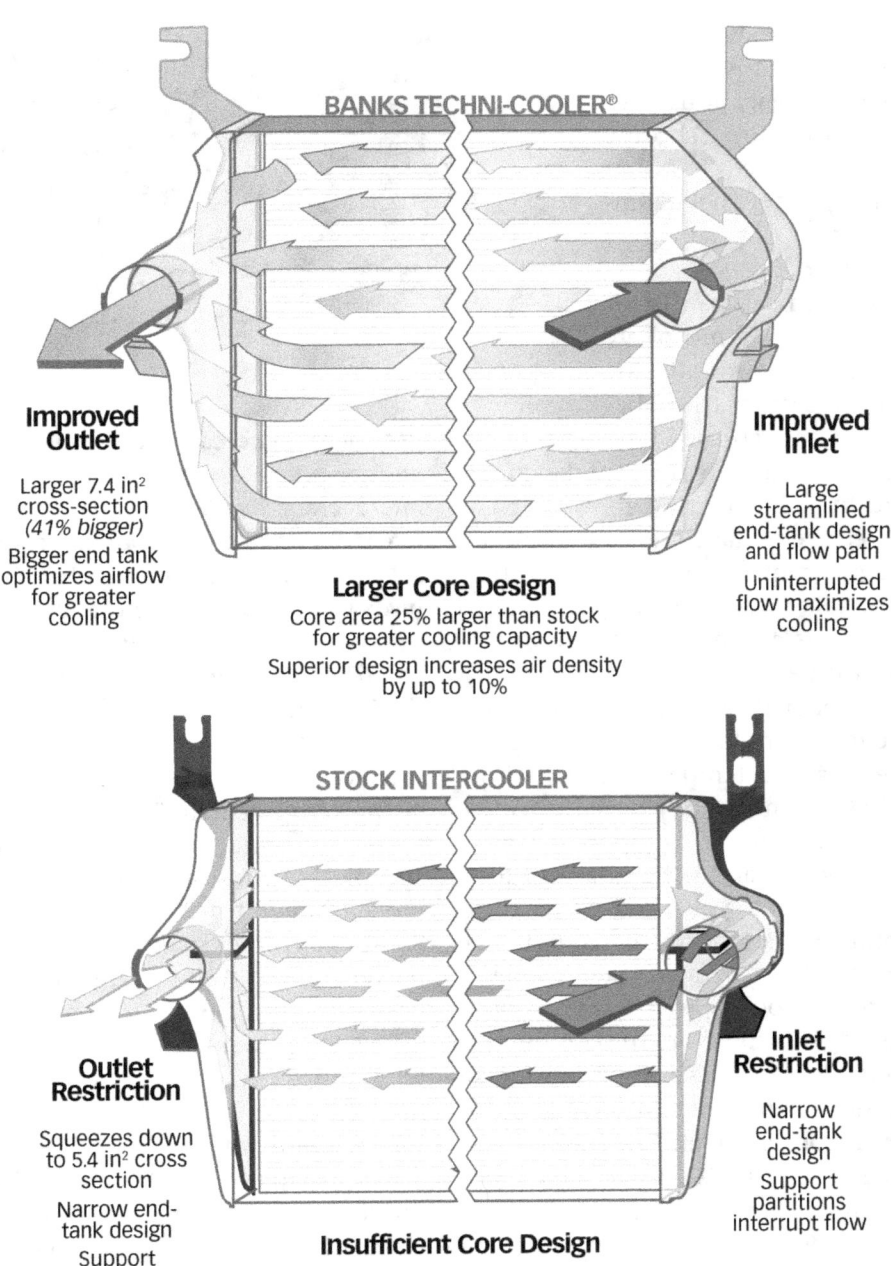

Check out this comparison of a Banks Techni-Cooler with a stock intercooler. The Banks intercooler is larger and flows far better internally. It reduces charge temperature more effectively for any given airflow compared to a stock unit. (Photo courtesy of Gale Banks Engineering)

are commonly used in racing applications, but because they become heat soaked rather quickly, they have limited use for a street diesel.

With an air-to-air intercooler, atmosphere flows over/around the surface area of the tubes and fins, absorbs the heat from the pressure intake charge within, and carries it away. The larger the surface area, the more air mass flowing over it, the more heat gets taken out of the pressurized intake air, the more effective or efficient it becomes.

For a given size of intercooler, the more air mass flowing through it, the less the temperature will drop. What this means is you have to size the intercooler to support air mass requirement and the amount of temperature drop you need to make to optimize the density of your intake charge. In general, bigger is better with intercoolers, so long as any pressure drop occurs from the cooling and increasing the density of the intake charge. If a pressure drop is caused by restriction of the airflow through the intercooler, that is a reduction of density and is not desirable.

When planning/shopping an intercooler upgrade, keep in mind the important performance variables: flow rating and efficiency. The industry doesn't have standard performance ratings for intercoolers because they are literally moving targets. The efficiency changes with the air mass flowing over the intercooler fins, i.e. the faster the vehicle moves the higher the mass flow rate over and through the intercooler. The air mass is what carries the heat away from the intercooler materials. That's why they give a range. Air-to-air

With over 50 percent more cooling surface area than most stock intercoolers, this BD Cool It intercooler has a core that measures 28 x 26 x 2.68-inches thick. This gives you a greater temperature drop with a pressure drop of less than 1 psi. (Photo courtesy of BD Diesel Performance)

intercoolers typically have a max efficiency range of 60 to 70 percent, with lower efficiency at lower vehicle speeds. Air-to-water intercoolers range from 75 to 90 percent efficient. Some intercooler makers offer horsepower ratings. These are typically based on the mass rate they'll flow calculated at maximum efficiency or temp drop. These are just recommendations, but they can give you a good staring point with your selection.

In summary, the function of the intercooler is to increase the density of the charge. Look back at the density ratio formula earlier in this chapter to see how important this is. A better, more-efficient intercooler drop the pressurized intake charge temp while keeping the density up—which is what making big power in a turbo diesel is all about.

Turbine Basics

Now that we've covered the compressor side of the turbo in detail, it's time to move on to the turbine side. While matching the compressor to a particular set of performance goals is moderately easy, the turbine match is technically challenging. With variable geometry turbines (VGT), the computer can control the exhaust restriction, and therefore the speed of the exhaust gas hitting the turbine blades, as well as the angle of attack. In other words, the computer can alter the amount of boost the turbo generates over an extremely large RPM and load range. This is way beyond choosing a turbine wheel and wastegate spring.

Even taking into consideration the wider operating range of a modern, computer-controlled VGT turbo, the rest of us will need to tap into some past experience to choose the right turbine side for our turbo application. Turbocharger manufacturers and retailers have turbine maps they don't distribute as freely as compressor maps. This means you have to rely on the advice of a trusted tuner or turbo manufacturer that can help you choose.

Matching Boost to Backpressure

A turbo is powered by exhaust mass flow spinning the turbine. When the exhaust valve opens there

A modern variable geometry turbine uses aerodynamically efficient foils to redirect the airflow. Most older turbo engines are stuck with choosing a single turbine size, which is where compromise inevitably comes into play.

THE TURBOCHARGER

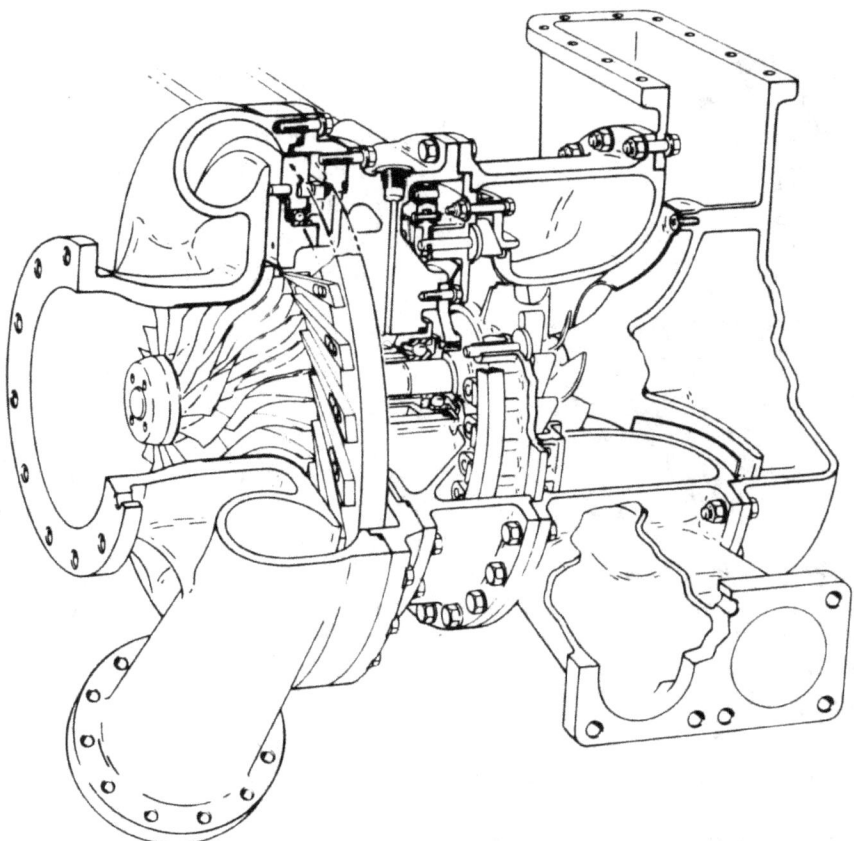

This is a drawing of an early variable geometry turbine. The airfoils within the turbine adjust the area/radius (A/R) ratio. In the most basic terms, this adjustment allows the turbine to act "smaller," for faster spool up, or "larger," for more mass flow and top-end power. (Photo courtesy of Gale Banks

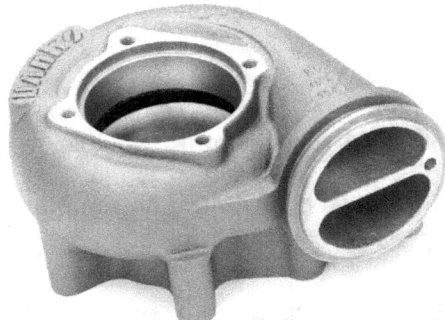

This is an example of a divided turbine housing from Banks. The divided housing helps your turbo spool quicker and helps make more power under the curve. (Photo courtesy of Gale Banks Engineering)

is still substantial pressure in the cylinder. The cam typically opens the valve at some point before BDC in order to use that pressure to allow the cylinder to blow down as the pressure is released. That pressure accelerates the exhaust gas out of the cylinder at a very high velocity. The energy of the high-speed exhaust mass spins the turbine, which spins the compressor to pressurize the intake.

Turbochargers raise the pressure in the exhaust system because they are an exhaust restriction. In general, adding a restriction to the exhaust costs you power. However, since the turbo captures energy that would otherwise be wasted, the turbo is able to move a sufficient quantity of air with less effort and fuel than a

Divided turbine housings tend to spool up quicker for a given mass flow than a non-divided housing. Divided housings keep mass velocity up following the Bernoulli principle. They work best when the exhaust manifolding is also divided to maintain mass flow velocity and isolate the low pressure pulses from other cylinders from reducing the average pulse energy driving the turbine. The compressor and wheel are in the foreground, and the wastegate is at the left. (Photo courtesy of General Motors)

belt driven supercharger. In other words, the turbo pressurizes the intake by pressurizing the exhaust. The trick is where and when in the RPM range these pressure differentials occur.

A properly matched turbocharger creates more boost pressure in the intake than exhaust pressure at low RPM and load. At a higher RPM and load, the pressures balance, i.e., intake pressure and exhaust backpressure is equal. As engine RPM and load is increased, at some point the exhaust pressure is greater than the intake pressure. This is known as the crossover point. It's one of those fine-tuning parameters you need to inquire about when selecting components. The most efficient and powerful combinations provide boost pressures greater than exhaust pressure near the torque peak. The crossover point should occur just before peak horsepower, which means there would be more exhaust pressure than intake pressure at peak horsepower RPM and load.

Unfortunately for enthusiast who are ready to tune for crossover, sizing and matching the turbine to the combination requires turbine maps, which most turbo manufacturers and dealers hold in confidence. This is one area where you must depend on a reputable dealer or manufacturer to help you choose the right turbo for your application. You have to buy the turbo from someone. That someone will, or should, have the turbine map and the experience to advise you.

Wastegates

When you're talking about exhaust backpressure caused by the turbine, it's critical to understand the function of the wastegate. For good responsiveness, a fairly small turbine

The Banks Big Head wastegate control unit is more precise so it doesn't start releasing backpressure until it needs to. Having more boost at lower RPM gives you more average power. Banks also offers a turbine housing with the upgraded wastegate control unit for several models. The combination produces more boost at low RPM, while also allowing more mass flow at higher RPM. (Photo courtesy of Gale Banks Engineering)

housing will spool up the turbocharger's boost quicker, so more fuel can be burned and the engine will make more power quicker. That same small housing is airflow limited when you want to make high power. Not only is its ability to flow the amount of exhaust gas limited, but when large amounts of hot exhaust gas are passed through it, the turbo will "overspeed," meaning it produces too much turbine wheel RPM (a destructive situation for the turbocharger) and overheat the boost air. Here is where a wastegate can save the day.

At a certain boost pressure, the wastegate opens to allow some of the exhaust gas to bypass the restrictive part of the turbine housing that feeds the wheel. These bypassed exhaust gases go directly to the down-stream exhaust pipe. This additional flow path moderates the total boost pressure produced and decreases backpressure, which reduces pumping loss. Thus, the RPM and load efficiency range for the whole turbocharged engine package has been extended.

The wastegate is controlled by means of a pressure actuator that receives a manifold pressure signal through a hose. Until the maximum boost level is reached, the wastegate is held shut by a spring inside the actuator canister. As the pressure limit is surpassed, the actuator opens the wastegate in proportion to the climbing boost pressure, allowing exhaust mass to bypass the turbine. By routing exhaust pressure around the turbine, the wastegate limits the turbo's ability to compress the charge air.

Wastegates have to be designed to resist releasing exhaust pressure too early or too late. A wastegate that opens too early will cost you power, but one that opens too late allows excess boost that may hurt the engine or drivetrain. According to the tech crew at Banks, most stock diesel turbocharger wastegate actuators do an okay job controlling stock boost lev-

This adjustable wastegate from BD Diesel Performance use a heavier spring keep the bypass valve closed, raising boost levels for increased performance. A locking jam-nut allows for precise boost pressure settings. (Photo courtesy of BD Diesel Performance)

els. But if the boost is increased, the stock wastegate actuator isn't usually up to the job and will bleed exhaust pressure too soon. This happens because turbine inlet pressure increases in response to the increased mass flow as engine manifold boost pressure rises.

Aftermarket companies design products to fix this situation. Banks offers its Big Head wastegate that uses a larger actuator with a higher rated spring and diaphragm to hold it closed until the system reaches the desired peak boost. When you control added boost pressure precisely you get more average power, or more power under the curve. In other words, peak boost comes quicker and is maintained throughout the engine's RPM range.

In addition to mechanical wastegate control there are aftermarket electronic boost controllers. These units monitor the boost in the system via fast acting sensors and control the pressure signal to the wastegate actuators with step motors or solenoids. By switching between ambient pressure and intake pressure, electronic boost controllers can shape the wastegate's pressure release profile. The advantage to these systems is that by controlling the pressure release more precisely, the wastegate won't bleed pressure off too quickly, again giving you more power in the area under the curve.

Housing Aspect Ratio

In practical terms, the housing aspect ratio is one way to estimate a turbo's most effective operating range. Quite literally, the A/R ratio (area/radius) is the ratio between the cross-sectional discharge area of the turbine scroll versus the radius of the circle between the turbine shaft and any point along the centerline of the

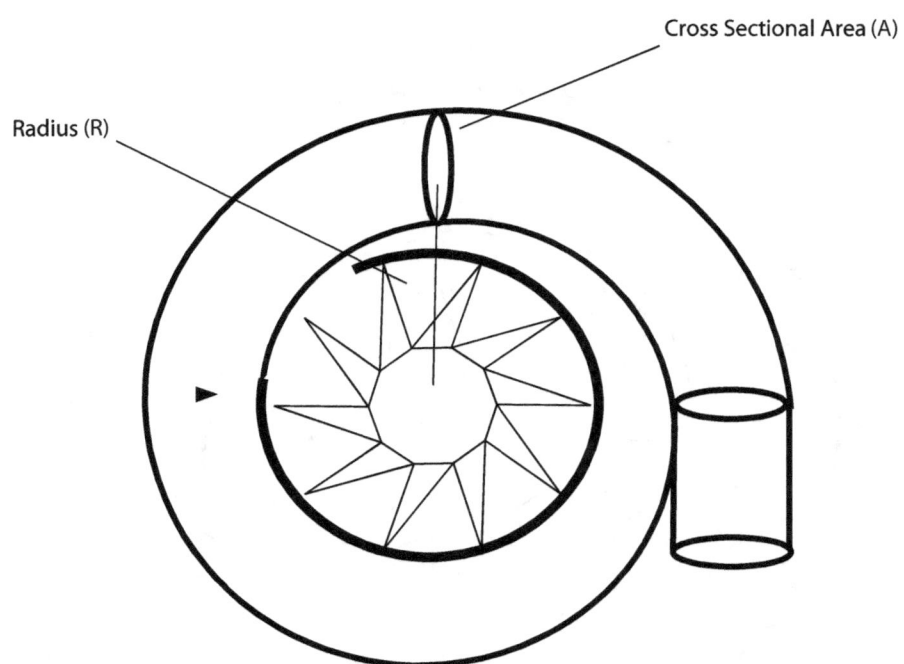

The shape and size of the turbocharger's two housings heavily influence its performance characteristics. One way of quantifying these qualities is by finding the A/R ratio of a housing, where A is the area of the compressor discharge area and R is the radius of the housing (between the center of the shaft and the centerline of the turbine scroll). In general, a smaller A/R increases velocity and low RPM spool time, but restricts mass flow. Increasing the A/R allows you to move more mass flow for extra top-end power.

turbine scroll. Assuming the radius is kept reasonable, the cross-sectional area measurement may be the easiest to compare among different brands of housings and turbochargers. For example, the turbos on Dodge Cummins engines have come with anywhere from 9 to 21 square centimeters in cross-sectional area, measured at the point where the turbine scroll opens up to the wheel.

In general terms, a turbo with a lower A/R builds boost more quickly than one with a higher A/R. The reason for this is that for a given R value, a lower A/R ratio means a smaller A, or cross-sectional discharge area. Since the gases must pass through the smaller area, they must speed up to maintain the mass flow, which accelerates the turbine wheel. Of course, the smaller area the gases must flow through the

more backpressure is created and the sooner the turbo (and thus the engine) "runs out of breath."

So, if you're trying to decide between two turbos, the one with the smaller A/R should theoretically give you better boost response and low-end boost, while a turbo with a larger A/R would give you better top-end power. As with the calculations for compressor size, there's no one-size-fits-best guess for picking an A/R ratio. Some combinations behave unexpectedly better or worse than predicted. Real world results are, of course, the best way to find out how well a particular turbo performs on your application.

Turbine Tech: How it Works

The exhaust pressure drives the turbine wheel in much the same way

CHAPTER 4

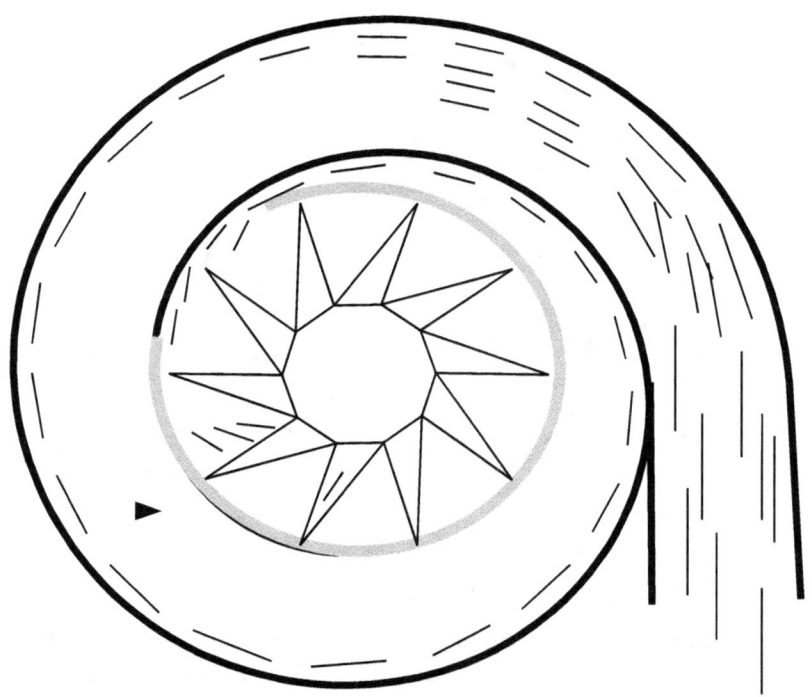

Hot, high-energy, high-pressure exhaust gas molecules enter the turbine and are turned to take a radial path and act on the turbine blades. A larger radius allows the air to make a gradual turn, decreasing resistance, and increasing the amount of mass able to flow through the system. A tighter radius increases the air's angle of attack relative to the blades. This tends to increase the velocity of the gas via the Bernoulli principle, which helps low-RPM spool up. But this restriction also reduces the mass flow rate and power at higher RPM.

that water drives a water wheel. However, instead of gravity and mass moving the wheel, the turbine wheel is moved by air pressure and mass. The air mass spins the turbine wheel, the turbine wheel spins the compressor, and the compressor is what gives us the boost we love so much.

This all takes place in the volute of what engineers call a centripetal turbine. The turbine converts exhaust gas pressure into kinetic energy by first directing the exhaust gases at the turbine wheel's circumference, then turning the gas with the shape of the blades at a constant velocity toward the center of the turbine wheel. It's during this process that kinetic energy is transferred into shaft power. The wheel's blades are designed to capture nearly all of the kinetic energy by the time the exhaust gas flows out the exducer. The size of the exducer more or less determines how much exhaust gas can flow through the turbine, so as with the discharge area, larger means more mass flow.

No Boost in Neutral?

One of the keys to understanding the turbine is to recall the relation of kinetic energy to velocity of the exhaust gas. Basically, when the velocity doubles, the kinetic energy is raised by a factor of four. Since velocity of the exhaust gas is related to pressure, and pressure is related to heat, the turbocharger doesn't really start making boost until the engine is loaded. When you rev your engine in neutral, it's only making enough power to overcome friction and the inertia of the engine. The engine isn't using much fuel to raise the cylinder temps and pressure, so there's no hot exhaust gas to spin the turbine and build boost. Under load, the engine burns more fuel to make power and it'll move more mass of exhaust gas. The exhaust gas molecules are hot and excited and making pressure. This high pressure wants to flow to the cold low pressure of the atmosphere and the only way to get out is through the turbine.

Going back to the Bernoulli principle, the exhaust gas pressure must speed up when squeezed down to the small opening of the turbine volute. In other words, the turbine's performance increases with the magnitude of the pressure differential between the inlet and outlet. The engine increases that pressure differential using higher engine speed and/or higher exhaust gas temperatures by burning more fuel.

As we discussed concerning the A/R ratio, how quickly the turbocharger spools up and how much boost it can make is determined by the specific cross-sectional area in the transition area of the inlet channel to the volute. A smaller cross-section produces a more pronounced restriction, causing backpressure to rise more quickly than with a larger cross-section. The result is that the turbo produces a higher pressure ratio. A smaller cross-section therefore results in higher boost pressures at lower mass flow rates (lower engine speeds).

Think of a water hose to illustrate how A/R is used to tune how the turbo responds to mass flow. The more of the opening you cover with your thumb, the higher the velocity of the stream, but the lower the flow.

THE TURBOCHARGER

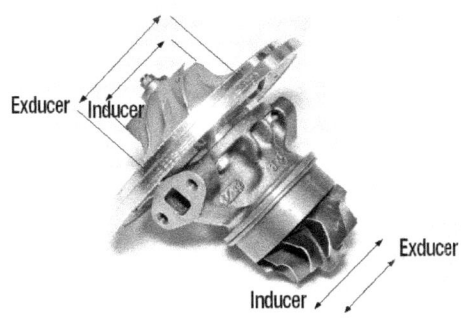

Inducer and exducer labels describe the function of two areas of the compressor and the turbine wheel. On the compressor side, the inducer is the center area of the wheel that inducts the air; the exducer is the perimeter of the wheel that releases the air into the "ram's horn" of the compressor. On the turbine side, the inducer is the perimeter and the exducer is the center area. (Photo courtesy of General Motors)

In the turbo, the higher velocity exhaust gas mass has the potential to do more work than lower velocity gas (to drive the compressor to higher boost pressure).

In addition, altering the distance from the driveshaft of the turbine wheel influences both the level of torque available to compress air as well as potential shaft speed. As the diameter of the turbine wheel increases (and with the exhaust gas stream directed to hit toward the tips), it produces higher torque on the driveshaft. This is a result of the energy of the exhaust gas acting through a longer lever. Of course, the trade off is lower potential shaft speed, just like lower gearing in your transmission.

One of the primary means of tuning is to vary this cross-sectional area, either by changing the turbine housing or using a variable geometry turbine (VGT), which does essentially the same thing without having to change the housing. Turbines with variable turbine geometry change the cross-section between volute channel and wheel inlet. The exit area to the turbine wheel is changed by variable guide vanes or a variable sliding ring covering a part of the cross-section.

The cross-sectional area of the exducer and the exit port downstream of the turbine wheel influence flow. A larger diameter exducer and exhaust port allows high mass flow on the exhaust side and potentially more mass flow on the compressor side. Keep in mind this is why a free-flowing exhaust system behind the turbo helps make power. In fact, the best exhaust system is one that uses the turbine as the "muffler" with no other restrictions behind the turbine.

Turbine Maps
(If you can find one!)

To match different turbines to various engine combinations, engineers and tuners use factory-supplied maps. These maps describe the flow parameters plotted against the tur-

Exhaust gas pressure is converted into kinetic energy by first directing the exhaust gases at the turbine wheel's circumference, and then turning the gas with the shape of the blades at a constant velocity toward the center of the turbine wheel. It's during this process that kinetic energy is transferred into shaft power, which of course, is used to spin the compressor wheel. The turbine wheel's blades are designed to capture nearly all of the kinetic energy by the time the exhaust gas leaves the exducer. (Photo courtesy of General Motors)

bine pressure ratio. The turbine map shows the mass flow curves and the turbine efficiency for various speeds (shaft RPM). However, to get a good picture of the overall performance of the turbine you can draw a "mean" or average curve.

This information, along with a lot of experience finding out what actually works, allows a good tuner to coordinate the compressor and turbine wheel diameters to get the desired power curve from the engine. The process, in simplified form, involves noting the operating points on the compressor map that correspond to the engine's air demand. These determine the turbocharger speed. The turbine wheel diameter and trim choice is decided by whether or not the turbine efficiency is maximized in this operating range.

It needs to be said however that the mass flow points on the compressor map assume that the engine and turbine choice can generate the desired boost levels within the desired engine speed range. That's somewhat tricky if you're developing a whole new combination or one that's not very common. If you're working with popular equipment such as the Cummins, late-model Ford Powerstroke, and GM Duramax engines, you have much experience at your disposal from the aftermarket companies marketing diesel performance products, so you should use it. The exhaust-driven side of the turbo is analogous to many performance parts in this sense: the theory is very well known, but there is still an art to applying the practice of theory to real world combinations. Acquiring the skill to make artful choices in a turbocharger combination takes experience. I'm presenting the information here so you know enough to shop wisely, and to help you filter the opportunistic marketers from the ones that will actually help you.

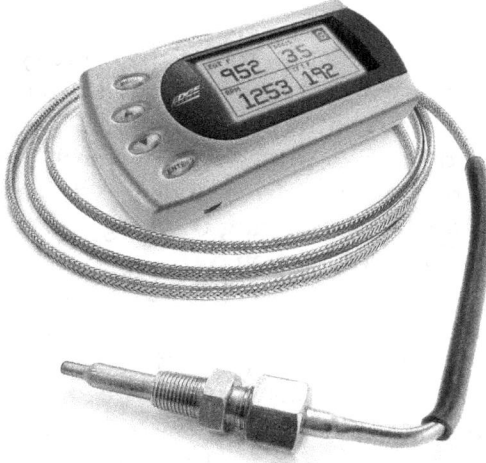

This Evolution tuner from Edge Products has an input for an EGT sensor. It also displays the EGT, so you can keep an eye on it and make tuning changes to help keep it in check. (Photo courtesy Edge Products)

Just remember during the process that the goal of most turbocharger combinations is to create sufficient boost at low to midrange speeds, while having enough exhaust mass flow capacity to hit the compressor map flow points at high boost and RPM. When searching for the right balance, keep in mind that in general, a larger diameter turbine wheel develops maximum boost at a high RPM. An oversized turbine can cause low-speed performance to suffer from excessive turbo lag. On the other hand, a small turbine can spool up quickly at low engine speeds and mass flows, but because it can't flow the mass required for high horsepower, performance falls off.

This reminds me of the luxuries diesels have over gas engines, especially small gas engines. Because diesels make so much torque without much boost, they're more forgiving when choosing a turbo. Keep that in mind when you're making your combination choices.

EGTs: What's too Hot?

The same diesel engine that gives 200-degree exhaust gas temperatures at idle can quickly give 1,300-degree temperatures under load. While cruising, the exhaust gas temperature with a properly sized turbocharger will normally be in the 600- to 800-degree range. This vast change in temperature comes from the way a diesel operates. As we noted earlier, at an idle, the air to fuel ratio may be 50:1, with most of the heat doing work on the piston rather than being rejected to the water jacket and the exhaust stream. Under power, an increasing amount of heat is produced while the air to fuel ratio goes to about 20:1, even under high boost. Additionally, a greater amount of heat is rejected into the water and exhaust stream instead of doing work by moving the piston.

Under normal load circumstances Banks and most other diesel authorities consider 1,250 to 1,300 degrees F a safe turbine inlet temperature range. So even if you're towing up a long grade and you're at full rated power, as long as your EGT before the turbine is within that range, your machine is working properly. If you see temps above 1,300 degrees F, you're probably either running out of air because of altitude or a compressor problem or your fuel system is over-fueling. Operating your engine with EGTs consistently above normal accelerates the system wear, particularly on the turbocharger unit. According to Gale Banks, run over 1,400 degrees F and you're gambling against a stacked deck and it's only a matter of time until you lose. The higher the EGT, the sooner you'll have to pay the bill.

CHAPTER 5

THE FUEL SYSTEM

Diesel fuel systems differ from their gasoline siblings in that they not only deliver varying rates of fuel in response to load, they also perform the timing function as well (there's no spark). The fuel system also has to be designed to help atomize the fuel, since diesel fuel doesn't have the aromatic and light chemical mix of gasoline blends.

Not only is the fuel delivery system much different than a gas engine's, so is the fuel. So to get a broad understanding of how your diesel engine works, we need to understand the fuel.

Diesel Fuel

The process of refining crude oil is basically to heat it up and let it separate into its various compounds. The most volatile component of crude comes off first at the lowest temperature. If you're storing crude oil, volatile compounds will evaporate. If you heat it, you accelerate the process. The first elements are compounds such as butane and propane,

As you're probably starting to see, the fuel system is incredibly important to diesel performance. You can add more boost and a free flowing exhaust, but your fuel system—transfer pump, injection pump, and injectors—needs to be able to keep up. (Photo courtesy of BD Diesel Performance)

HIGH-PERFORMANCE DIESEL BUILDER'S GUIDE   69

but pretty quickly you get the gasoline part of the distillate curve. With more heat you get into kerosene, jet fuel, and finally to diesel.

Thus, petroleum diesel is a "distillate" refined from crude oil. There are various grades or types of distillates, but "Number 2" (No. 2) distillate is the primary source for the motor diesel consumed in the United States. It is also used as a fuel oil for heating buildings and by industry. U.S. petroleum refineries produce an average of 7 to 8 gallons of diesel fuel from each 42-gallon barrel of crude oil.

Diesel has a higher Btu content than gasoline. One British thermal unit (Btu) is enough energy to heat one pound of water one degree Fahrenheit. Years ago, fuel companies decided to charge more money for diesel because it had more energy content. Even though at the time it cost them less to produce than a gallon of gasoline. Then companies decided the energy equivalent or mileage equivalent of gas should set the price, so why not set the price equivalent to gas? Hence, diesel's price has traditionally tracked that of regular grade gas.

More recently, in high-income areas where there are some diesel passenger cars but not enough commercial truck traffic to support competitive diesel prices, they charge more for diesel than even premium gas. In areas with more truck traffic, diesel prices are competitive with gas. So in areas without significant commercial rig traffic, regular diesel drivers are paying too much.

Since the price is manipulated you have to view diesel in terms of cost per mile, not cost per gallon. If you look at miles per dollar instead of dollar per gallon, diesel is more cost effective than gasoline. Gasoline engines are getting more efficient, using cylinder deactivation and other tactics (even direct injection). Some engineers I've talked to tell me cylinder deactivation won't work on a diesel, but I can't see why it won't. It may not show as much of a gain on a diesel engine, but it should improve mileage.

Diesel fuel is heavier than gasoline, has more heat energy content by weight, is extremely detonation resistant, and requires a different mechanism to use in an internal combustion engine. The Btu content of a unit volume (gallon or liter) of diesel fuel is higher than that of gasoline, and the Btu content of No. 2-D diesel fuel is generally higher than that of No. 1-D diesel fuel. The Btu content of No. 2-D diesel fuel is typically about 130,000 Btu/gal. (Photo courtesy of DaimlerChrysler)

Diesel Fuel Contamination

Fuel contamination can cost a diesel owner big money. Diesel fuel injectors can easily cost over $400 each, and the most common cause of diesel injector failure is contaminated fuel. Since injectors are lubricated in part by the fuel, contamination with water, gasoline, or alcohol can cause failure. Fuel contaminated with biomass or particulates can also clog the injectors and cause a failure.

Injectors fail in a variety of ways. They can fail to open fully or open at all, leading to low power and rough running. They can deliver vastly different rates of fuel, destroying the power balance of the engine, increasing wear, and shortening the service life. Sticky, malfunctioning injectors can cause hard starting, a no start condition, or stalling. If an injector sticks open it can lead to damaged pistons and cylinder walls from over fueling, contaminating crankcase oil with fuel, or even hydro-locking a cylinder. A hydro-locked cylinder is catastrophic failure

THE FUEL SYSTEM

The Retail Price of Diesel

The cost to produce and deliver diesel to consumers includes the costs of crude oil, refinery processing, marketing and distribution, and retail station operation. The retail pump price reflects these costs and the profits (and sometimes losses) of the refiners, marketers, distributors, and retail station owners. The relative share of these cost components to the retail price varies over time and among regions of the country.

The price at the pump also includes federal, state, and local taxes. In 2005, Federal excise taxes were 24.4 cents per gallon, and state excise taxes averaged about 21.6 cents per gallon. Some county and city governments also levy additional taxes. The retail price also reflects local market conditions and factors such as the location and the marketing strategy of the station owner. Some retail outlets are owned and operated by refiners, while others are independent businesses that purchase diesel fuel for resale to the public.

The phase-in of the U.S. Environmental Protection Agency's (EPA) ultra-low-sulfur diesel (ULSD) standard of no more than 15 parts per million sulfur by weight for on-highway diesel fuel also has the potential to influence diesel prices. (Reduced sulfur content standards for off-highway diesel fuel begin phasing-in in 2007.)

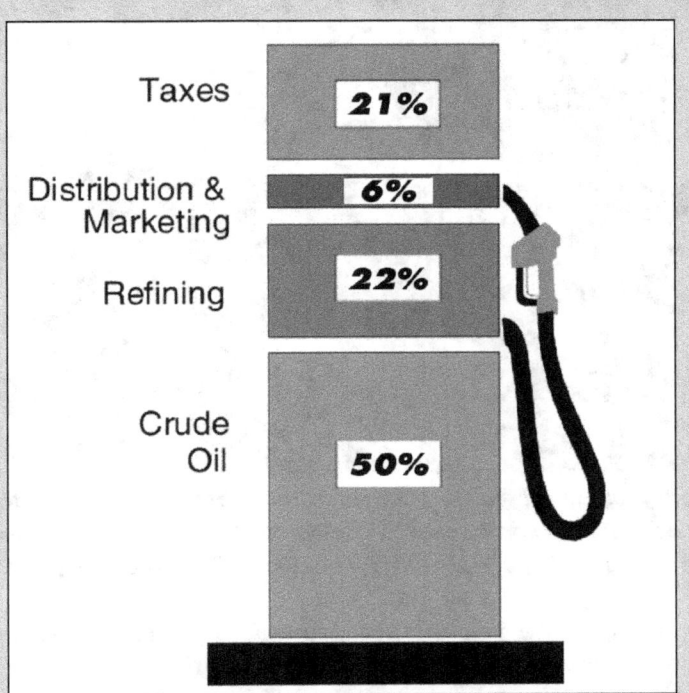

This graphic shows the breakdown of the national average retail cost of diesel fuel according to the Department of Energy. (Photo courtesy of the Department of Energy)

---

usually leading to at least a cracked piston, bent connecting rod, or broken crankshaft.

The trick to avoiding these problems is to take care of your fuel. It's a good tactic to buy your fuel from a source that moves a lot of diesel fuel so you're assured the fuel hasn't been sitting in the tank for too long. You may want to use a fuel conditioner to prevent water accumulation. In addition, you can get fuel conditioners that improve the lubricity to enhance injector life. Of course you have to change your fuel filter and water separator.

If you suspect your fuel is contaminated, remove it ASAP. For contamination with gasoline, do not start the engine. You have to drain the tank and purge the fuel system. Particulate contamination requires you to drain and flush the tank as well as the fuel filter. When purging, flushing, or otherwise maintaining your fuel system, remember to dispose of fuel properly. Don't just dump it on the ground.

[Editor's Note: As fuel injection pressures rise (to assist in meeting emissions requirements), the clearances of injection system parts become much tighter and more accurate so the pressurized fuel doesn't just leak out. These tight clearances make it more critical to remove small particles of contamination. Where 10-micron filters were good in the past, finer filters, such as seven- and even three-micron filters, better protect today's engines. This rating means that particles smaller than three microns will pass, but larger contaminants will be trapped. Additionally, higher pressures cause contaminants to blast the parts instead of just floating on by, so better filters are helpful for this reason as well.]

Biodiesel

Biodiesel is the term for a variety of ester-based oxygenated fuels made from vegetable oils or animal fats. Ironically, what is now called biodiesel was in fact the original fuel Dr. Rudolf Diesel designed his new

Today, biodiesel typically comes from soybeans, canola, cottonseed, and mustard seed. There is some research being conducted in the genetically modified crops, as well as using certain strains of algae. (Photo courtesy of DaimlerChrysler)

heat engine to run on. He demonstrated his engine using peanut oil as fuel at the World Exhibition in Paris at the turn of the twentieth century. Of course, modern biodiesel comes from a variety of sources.

Since biodiesel softens and degrades certain types of synthetic and natural rubber compounds, using high-percent blends can cause fuel system components, hoses, and pump seals to fail. Natural or butyl rubbers should not be allowed to come in contact with pure biodiesel.

Biodiesel degrades quickly and easily in the environment, so fuel spills aren't toxic to the environment. However, both petro diesel and biodiesel cloud and gel in cold weather. Since biodiesel is more susceptible to clouding and gelling in cold, users of a 20 percent biodiesel/80 percent petroleum diesel blend (B20) typically experience a decrease of the cold flow properties, i.e., cold filter plugging point, cloud point, and pour point at a few degrees above freezing.

B20 can generally be used in unmodified diesel engines. Biodiesel may be one of the "additives" used to improve lubricity, which will be negatively affected by the removal of sulfur to meet the ULSD standards. Biodiesel production increased from very little 10 years ago to about 75 million gallons in 2005, most of which was produced from soybean oil at about 35 major facilities and sold by 1,400 distributors and 450 retail stations (source: National Biodiesel Board; www.biodiesel.org).

Cetane Number

Diesel fuel's cetane number is somewhat analogous to the octane rating of gasoline. But instead of the fuel's resistance to detonation, the cetane number is a precise rating of the temperature at which the fuel ignites.

Cetane is measured in a special variable-compression-ratio test engine with precisely controlled coolant, intake air temperatures, injection pressure, injection timing, and engine speed. The tester adjusts compression ratio until combustion occurs at TDC with a start-of-injection timing of 13 degrees. For this reason, the cetane number is referred to as a rating of the fuel's ignition delay.

Since the compression ratio under these controlled conditions produces a predictable raise in temperature of the intake air in the diesel engine, designers then have a standard and reference point of how long it takes the fuel to absorb the heat of compression and start to burn. This allows them to design the engine in terms of compression ratio, boost pressures, and injection timing to place peak pressure at the most efficient point on the power stroke.

Higher cetane fuels have shorter ignition delay periods than lower cetane fuels, which is why automakers recommend using a higher cetane-rated fuel when temperatures are below freezing. As an FYI, number-2 diesel has a 15 to 25 octane rating, but don't use the cetane number alone when evaluating diesel fuel quality. API gravity (American Petroleum Institute rating of density versus water), Btu content, distillation range, sulfur content, stability, and flash point are also very important but are of more concern to engineers than to end users. In colder weather, cloud point and low-temperature filter plugging point are critical factors for vehicle owners. However, most of the chemical properties of the fuel have more to do with emissions and how the fuel affects the reliability of the engine components.

There is no benefit in using a higher cetane number fuel than is required by the engine tuning. The ASTM (American Society for Testing and Materials) Standard Specification for Diesel Fuel Oils (D-975) states:

THE FUEL SYSTEM

Unlike regular gasoline, which is sold with varying octane ratings, diesel fuel is rated in centane. Higher centane fuels will have shorter ignition delay periods than lower centane fuels, which will affect the ideal time to start the injection process. (Photo courtesy of BD Diesel Performance)

"The cetane number requirements depend on engine design, size, nature of speed and load variations, and on starting and atmospheric conditions. Increase in cetane number over values actually required does not materially improve engine performance. Accordingly, the cetane number specified should be as low as possible to insure maximum fuel availability."

This quote underscores the importance of matching engine cetane requirements with fuel cetane number. Diesel fuels with a cetane number lower than minimum engine requirements can cause rough engine operation. They are more difficult to start, especially in cold weather or at high altitudes. They accelerate lube oil sludge formation. Many low-cetane fuels increase engine deposits, resulting in more smoke, increased exhaust emissions, and greater engine wear.

Using fuels that meet engine operating requirements will improve cold starting, reduce smoke during start-up, improve fuel economy, reduce exhaust emissions, improve engine durability, and reduce noise and vibration. The specific fuel requirements for your vehicle should be published in your owner's manual.

Flash Point

The flash point is the temperature at which a combustible liquid vaporizes sufficiently enough that it can be ignited. Diesel fuels have a flash point above 130 degrees F, so they are relatively safe compared to gasoline.

Diesel fuels generally contain sulfur of varying concentrations depending on the crude-oil quality and other refining processes. Sulfur is converted into sulfur dioxide (SO) during combustion and has been tied to acid rain. Therefore, sulfur content in diesel fuel is now regulated. The intention is to reduce particulate emissions, which contain sulfates as well as unburned fuel in the form of soot particles.

Injection Systems

In general, diesel fuel systems consist of a fuel tank, fuel lines, transfer pump (sometimes called a lift pump), filters, injection pump, and injection nozzles.

Transfer Pump (low pressure)

The fuel transfer or lift pump is usually electric, powered by either

Energy Content Comparison

	Stoichiometric Air/Fuel Ratio:	Btu Content
Gasoline:	14.6:1	124,000
Diesel:	14.4:1	130,000
Propane:	15.7:1	91,000
Methanol:	6.47:1	62,800
Hydrogen:	34.3:1	113,400/Kg

This chart shows the energy content of diesel fuel compared by the amount of energy stored in one gallon. The higher the fuel's heat combustion, the more power will be derived from each gallon of fuel consumed. Energy content is measured in British Thermal Units (Btu) per gallon and is related to the fuel's specific gravity and the temperature range at which it vaporizes. The Btu content per unit volume increases as the specific gravity increases.

CHAPTER 5

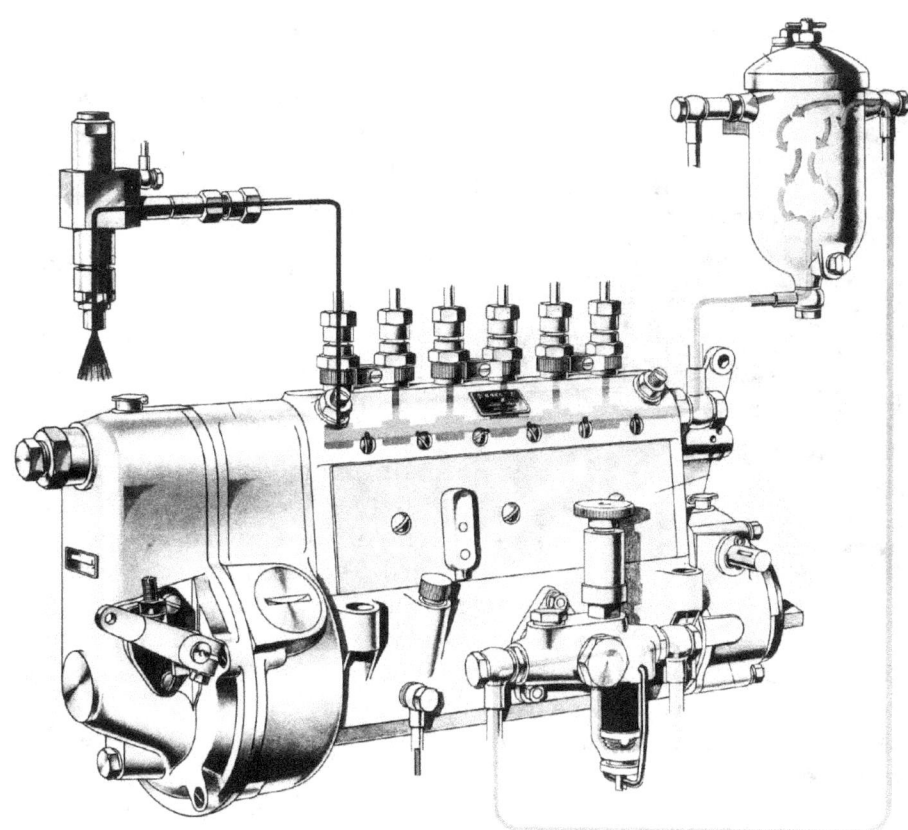

Modern electronically controlled diesel fuel injection systems make smooth, quiet, powerful diesel engines possible. We are just at the beginning of the diesel revolution and there are many tuning and performance discoveries on the horizon. Shown is a technical drawing of a system using an early Bosch inline pump. It's interesting that other than electronic monitoring and control, the basic elements of the diesel fuel system has remained relatively stable. (Photo courtesy of DaimlerChrysler)

engine or battery voltage. It can be located on the outside of the fuel tank in the supply line or submerged within the fuel tank. Some are mounted on the back side of the injection pump. The transfer fuel pump pushes or draws the fuel through a filter to clear it of small particles that could harm the high-pressure injector pump or clog the injector nozzles.

Injection Pump (high pressure)

There are several designs and operating approaches to injection pumps. They supply high-pressure fuel to the injection nozzle in one way or another.

Injection Nozzles (high pressure)

Injector nozzles come in a wide variety of designs and operating principles. The goal of the injection nozzle is to spray the fuel in atomized form into the combustion chamber or pre-chamber of each cylinder.

Cold Weather Starting Aids

Diesel fuel evaporates much slower than gasoline and requires more heat to cause combustion in

The term common rail comes from the use of a common fuel pressure "plenum" or rail. The rail contains pressures on some of the newer systems over 2,000 bar. That's 2,000 atmospheres, or over 20,000 psi. The earlier versions didn't use a mass flow sensor, but did monitor boost and air temp to refer intake density from a series of maps stored in the ECU. The fuel recirculates on the high- and low-pressure sides and typically flows through a fuel cooling system.

---

74 HIGH-PERFORMANCE DIESEL BUILDER'S GUIDE

THE FUEL SYSTEM

Indirect Injection

Before electronic control of diesel fuel injection and the current emissions requirements it was difficult to achieve smooth operation by injecting the fuel directly into the combustion chamber. However, engineers found that by indirectly injecting fuel they could delay peak pressure to a more advantageous crank angle, resulting in more power and smoother operation. This fuel injection tactic is called indirect injection, so named by the method used to introduce fuel into the combustion chamber.

With indirect injection, the fuel is injected into a pre-combustion chamber in the cylinder head, ported into the main combustion chamber. During the compression stroke the compressed hot air is forced into the chamber designed to generate a rapid swirling motion to promote the burning of fuel. When fuel is injected into the pre-combustion chamber energetic swirling air it reacts and shoots into the main chamber generating its own swirl in the main chamber for more complete combustion in the main combustion chamber.

Indirect-injection engines are less efficient than direct-injection engines because the pre-combustion chamber rejects heat into the cooling system, as does the main combustion chamber. In addition, indirect designs require systems for preheating for cold start, though at the time, these tradeoffs were worth the price for the smoother, quieter operation.

---

the cylinders of the engine. The glow plug is one common starting aid. Glow plugs provide a heat source in the combustion chamber to help the fuel to begin the combustion process. Instead of glow plugs, Cummins direct injection engines use a grid style electrical resistance heater in the intake manifold area to preheat the air in cold ambient conditions.

Electronically Controlled Common Rail Injection

The common rail system by Bosch is one big reason modern diesels are so appealing. The technology gives engine developers the ability to reduce exhaust emissions and to lower engine noise. Most of the diesels that you can modify and tune successfully are common rail designs, so extra time is spent on this subject.

Common rail injection generates the injection pressure separately from the injection itself. A high-pressure pump generates high pressure in an accumulator, in this case, the rail. The pump generates from 1,600 bar

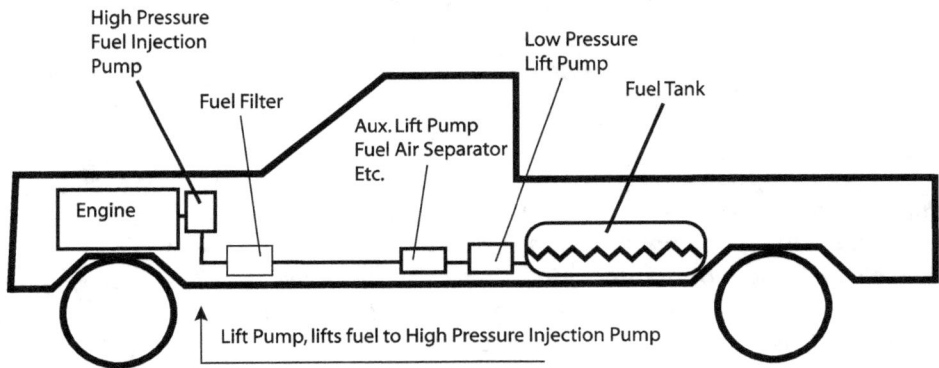

The low-pressure side of any high-pressure diesel injection consists of a lift pump to bring the fuel to the high-pressure pump. Because of the high pressures, the fuel needs to be extremely clean and free of particulate and liquid contaminants such as dirt, algae, and water. The redundant filtering scheme is typical of most diesels.

to 2,500 bar independently of the engine speed and the quantity of fuel injected. The fuel is fed through rigid pipes to the injectors, which inject the correct amount of fuel in a fine spray into the combustion chambers. The Electronic Diesel Control (EDC) precisely directs all the injection parameters, such as the pressure in the rail and the timing and duration of injection, as well as performing other engine functions.

In the first and second generation of Bosch's common rail system, the injection process is controlled by a magnetic solenoid on the injectors. The hydraulic force used to open and close the injectors is transmitted to the jet needle by a piston rod. In the third generation common rail system, the injector actuators consist of several hundred thin piezo crystal wafers. Piezo crystals have the special characteristic of expanding rapidly

CHAPTER 5

Pumps like this Bosch CP-1 electronically controlled high-pressure fuel pump are just one of the many marvels on a modern diesel engine. This cutaway shows the three stages of compression used to control pressure and mass flow to meet engine demands.

The pressure regulator valve diverts fuel to the recirculation line to maintain pressure to the injector depending on engine load demands.

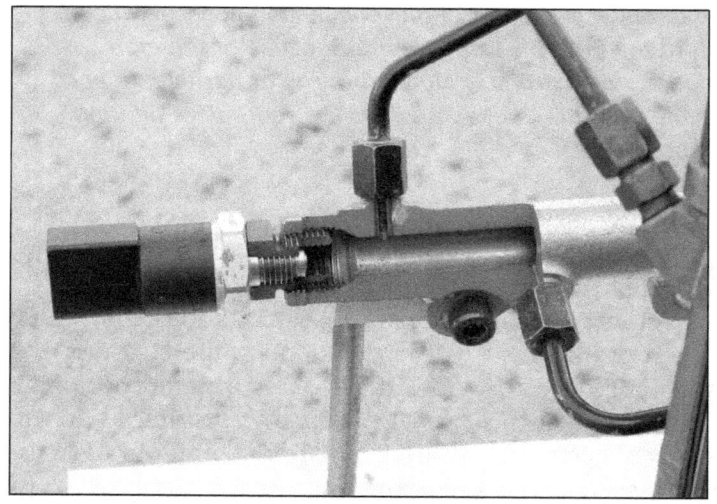

Across the accumulator rail, the rail pressure sensor (black, left) feeds back to the ECU, which controls the rail pressure by actuating the rail pressure regulator.

Here you can see the internal structures of the first-generation Bosch (CRIP-1) injector, the metal sheath glow plug design, and the piston. The alignment of the injector nozzle and the piston as it travels up and down the top of the bore is part of the atomization strategy of direct injection diesel.

THE FUEL SYSTEM

This shot gives you an idea of the scale of the injector nozzle end and the combustion cup in the piston. The angle of the injector is not correct—it should be straight up and centered. The glow plug protrudes from the fire deck at an angle nearly as shown.

able injection geometry, or the ability to shape the rate of injection.

The Future: Rate Shaping

Looking forward, Bosch is developing advanced fuel injection equipment to enhance and refine the advantages of the common rail system with some of the advantages of the unit injection with a distributor pump. Rate shaping would provide:

- fully flexible injection pressure
- maximum required injection pressure, dependant on the specific concept
- flexible timing of multiple injections
- small and stable injection quantities to realize pilot and post injections

These are the properties needed to provide rate shaping fuel delivery within the combustion chamber:

- fast needle opening
- low injection rate during ignition delay
- max allowed injection rate to increase the local air ratio
- strong increase of the injection rate after start of combustion
- high maximum injection rate
- fast rate decrease at the end of injection
- high needle closing velocity

Talking Fuel Injection with Bosch

It took much time on hold and weeks of emailing to arrange a phone

when an electric field is applied to them. In a piezo inline injector, the actuator is built into the injector body very close to the jet needle. The movement of the piezo packet is transmitted friction-free, using no mechanical parts, to the rapidly switching jet needles.

The third-gen's advantages over the earlier magnetic and current conventional piezo injectors are a more precise metering of the amount of fuel injected and an improved atomization of the fuel in the cylinders. The rapid speed at which the injectors can switch makes it possible to reduce the intervals between injections and split the quantity of fuel delivered into a large number of separate injections for each combustion stroke. Diesel engines thus became even quieter, more fuel efficient, cleaner, and more powerful.

For its fourth-generation common rail setup, Bosch is currently exploring designs using even higher injection pressures (more than 2,000 bar!), as well as injectors with vari-

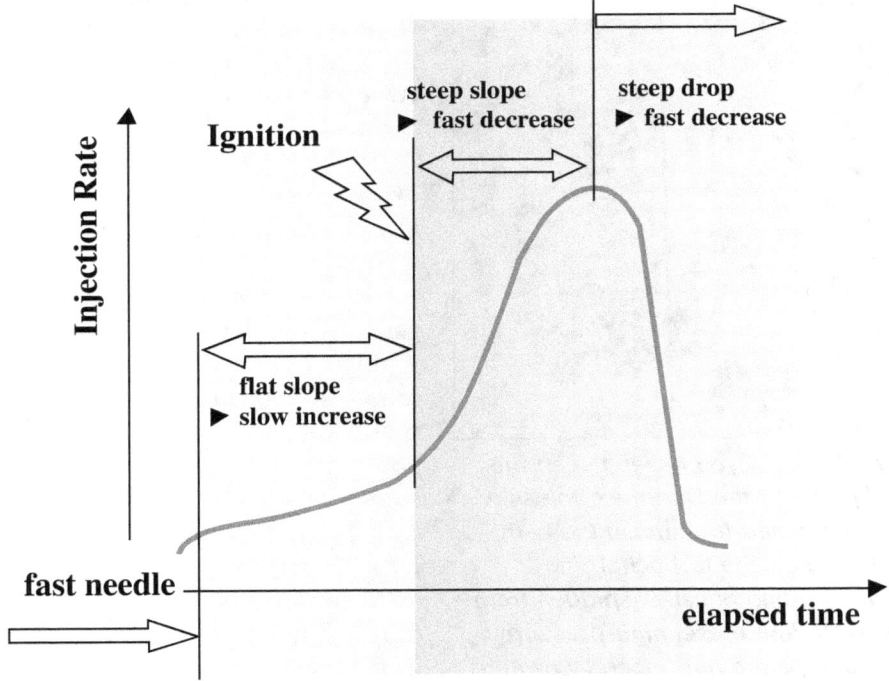

Rate shaping is a promising technique that improves diesel performance and reduces emissions in a wide variety of operating conditions. Instead of turning the injector on and off as current systems do, even though they can pulse several times per power stroke, they are still square waves. Rate shaping refines the pulsing tactic into a more analog delivery that ultimately delivers more fuel, burns it better, produces more power, and reduces emissions.

CHAPTER 5

Bosch Common Rail Injection System Development Milestones

1997: First common rail system in the world for passenger cars
Injection pressure: 1,350 bar
First production use: Alfa Romeo and Mercedes-Benz

1999: First common rail system for trucks
Injection pressure: 1,400 bar
First production use: Renault (RVI)

2001: Second-generation common rail system for passenger cars makes diesel engines even more economical, cleaner, quieter, and more powerful
Injection pressure: 1,600 bar
First production use: Volvo and BMW

2002: Second-generation common rail system for trucks
Injection pressure: 1,600 bar
First production use: MAN commercial engines

2003: Third-generation common rail system with rapid-switch piezo inline injectors for cars
Advantages: up to 20-percent lower emissions, up to 5-percent more power, up to 3-percent lower fuel consumption, up to 3 dB(A) less engine noise
Injection pressure: 1,600 bar
First production use: Audi

If you're lucky you haven't seen the fuel pump of the Duramax unless you've wanted to. It fits in the cam valley below the turbocharging plumbing and is usually hidden from view. Modern diesel high-pressure fuel pumps are not generally owner-serviceable items.

interview with Gary Hirschlieb, Vice President of Diesel Engineering at Bosch. I wanted to get factory-direct intelligence on diesel fuel injection—and what better way than to speak to an engineering representative from the firm that virtually invented modern diesel fuel injection.

▶ **JP: First off, could you give us an overview of how a common rail works, staring with the pump?**
GH: Well, the pumps work by using a piston or plunger in a cylinder to generate the pressure. The area of the plunger and force behind it determines the pressure. The plungers are pretty good size, not huge, but you're not looking to raise the pressure of a lot of fuel.

The fuel pump forces fuel into a rail. The rail has a pressure sensor and other sensors that tell the pump not to generate a maximum amount of flow so you're not wasting power raising the pressure of fuel you don't use. You try to tailor the pump flow at high pressure to the actual demands on the engine.

Common rail is very similar to port fuel injection on gas motors: You have a rail and you have injectors—unfortunately they're not coupled directly to the rail, they have a line between them, and a suite of sensors that allow the computer to determine fuel and injection timing depending on the load on the engine.

The advantage of the common rail is you don't have to have the injection events timed exactly to the crankshaft, tied back through any gear train. The injection event isn't restricted by the crankshaft position—you can inject anytime you choose.

JP: What is the most significant development in common rail systems today?
GH: Higher pressures are the trend to more power better efficiency and Piezo is faster, more precise fuel control and close coupling of injection events. The first-gen common rail used around 5,000 psi max; but the current systems are at 29,000 psi. Forcing the fuel through the small

THE FUEL SYSTEM

The later generations of common rail pumps feature an integrated low-pressure pump that helps bring fuel to the high-pressure mechanism. (Photo courtesy of Bosch)

In 1989, Audi was the first automobile manufacturer to utilize the electronically controlled axial piston distributor injection pump (VP34) from Bosch. This is the forerunner to the VP44 radial piston distributor pump on mid-'90s Cummins-powered Dodge Rams. The VP pumps use a cam plate and a radial piston arrangement that pressurizes the fuel toward the center. A channel running axially to the distributor head directs fuel pressure to the cylinders much like a distributor directs electricity in a gasoline engine. (Photo courtesy of Bosch)

holes in the nozzles really breaks up the fuel well and atomizes it. The electronic control, since it's not tied to the crankshaft, allows us to inject up to five times per combustion event. It's amazing when you're injecting so much fuel in a millisecond or so. But small quantities of fuel in short periods using close coupled injection events one right next to the other are just as impressive. This ability makes diesels very quiet and also allows us to reduce emissions and particulates, plus enable the effective use of after-treatment.

JP: How do the injectors manage the high-pressure fuel pulse?
GH: The electronics in the injectors, whether it's a solenoid or a piezo stack, operate a small valve that controls the high-pressure fluid. It's the fuel under very high pressure that actually lifts the needle inside the valve body off its seat. And it is amazing that it happens so quickly and precisely, but then you also have such high pressure, once you trigger that pressure there is a very fast reaction against the spring that also holds the needle closed.

JP: What's new in nozzle technology?
GH: The R&D on nozzles at Bosch is unbelievable. Part of it is strength of materials because we're raising pressures, so you get high pressures within the injector body around the needle; how you set up the holes, the stagger, the angle, the taper to the inlet and outlet. There are just a ton of processes that go into making and calibrating the nozzles. It's something that is very critical to Bosch.

This is Bosch's EDC16 control unit. The Electronic Diesel Control (EDC) monitors and dictates all the parameters that are important for effective, low-emission combustion. (Photo courtesy of Bosch)

CHAPTER 5

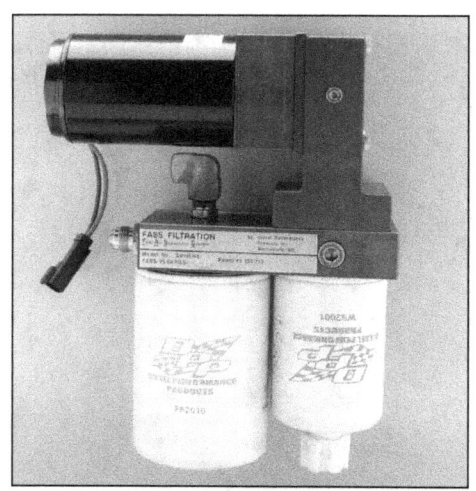

The Fuel Air Separator System, F.A.S.S., from Diesel Performance Products Inc, removes air, dirt, and water from your fuel before it reaches the engine. This improves the cleanliness of the fuel as well as its density, so you get more fuel per injection and thus more power.

BD Performance provides an auxiliary lift pump to replace the stock lift pump, which is barely adequate for the stock engine. When you start adding performance electronics and bolt ons, the stock lift pump can be overwhelmed by fuel demand, placing additional strain on the injection pump. This setup also has a pressure switch that reduces pressure during start up to avoid hard start problems associated with auxiliary lift pumps. (Photo courtesy of BD Diesel Performance)

JP: In the aftermarket, some tuners are using additional pumps to provide more fuel. Any comment on that approach?
GH: We don't condone or recommend that. The nozzles are pretty much sized to the engine as it's set up at a given horsepower, so those tuners would have to work around that. But since they're not concerned with emission, just power, they can choose higher-rate injectors. Bosch has to deal with emissions, durability, transmissions—and the current production drivelines don't support that much power.

The pump and injectors have such close tolerances that an enthusiast couldn't just open it up and gain a 30-percent increase in pressure and flow rate. They're pretty much set. If you drill holes in the injectors you'll get more fuel, not sure what it'll come out like, but...

JP: How much does the common rail fuel pump heat the fuel? Any need for fuel cooling?

GH: Not usually on the light-duty engines. The reservoir of the fuel tank is usually enough to control the fuel temperature.

JP: What do you think about modifying the electronics onboard?
GH: Bosch doesn't condone modified electronics.

JP: Could you comment on any impact ultra-low-sulfur diesel (ULSD) fuels have on the fuel system?
GH: The ULSD 15-ppm lubricity standard is something we've accepted. We would have liked more lubricity, but that's the fuel and we design to the spec. We still have concerns and we're working on it. We're working with ASTM and other professional organizations to modify that lubricity standard.

You have to have the ULSD for the '07 model's after-treatment systems. Bosch doesn't recommend any additive packages and the oil companies do that on their own. The additive package is proprietary art on their side. The aftermarket has products, but we don't get involved in testing or recommending.

Gale Banks on Fuel System Tech

Throttling with Fuel

You may remember from our earlier discussion that diesel engines vary the air density using a throttle, so they vary the fuel ratio to control engine output instead. Diesels are designed to run with air/fuel ratios from 50:1 to 22:1, some even as "lean" as 18:1. When you're idling at 50:1, you can see it doesn't take a lot of fuel for a diesel to idle. This is partly because it's not sucking air past a butterfly and so there's not a lot of intake pumping losses. This is why diesels have such cool exhaust temps at idle and why you need to have the cold start aids such as glow plugs, etc. When you want more power out of a diesel, you just richen it up.

THE FUEL SYSTEM

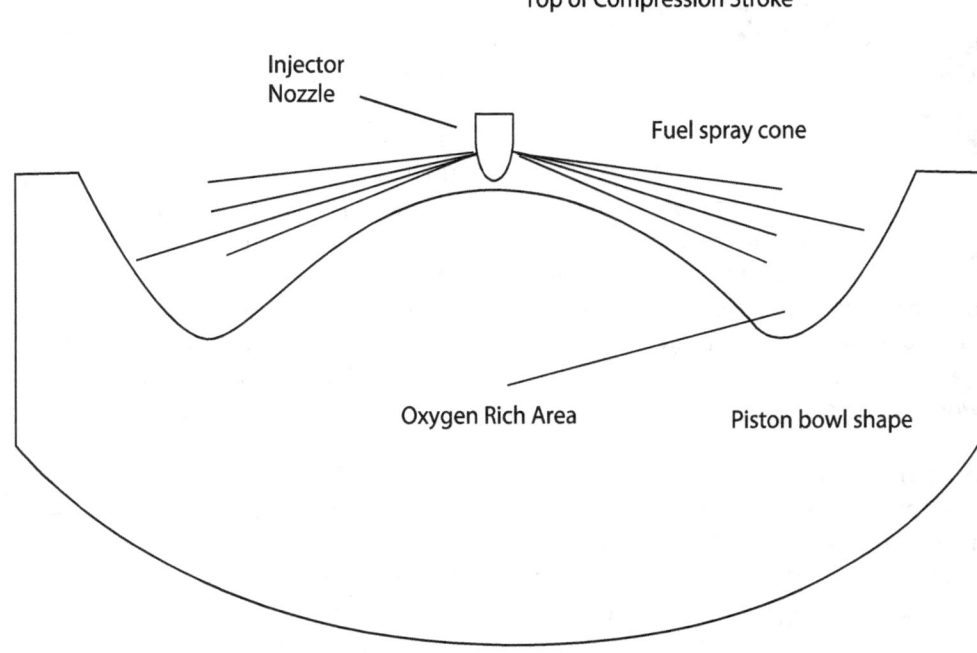

To maximize fuel atomization, the high-pressure injector nozzle sprays the plume at the piston cup edges where most of the oxygen migrates because of the inertia of mass responding to swirl in the chamber.

Direct-injection nozzles spray fuel into oxygen-rich areas of the combustion chamber. They're designed with several holes that spray plumes at a slightly downward angle away from the cylinder head and into the combustion cup. (Photo courtesy of Bosch)

So it might idle at 50:1, but when you start adding fuel to it, it will makes more power up to the point where there is insufficient oxygen for the fuel delivered. When you get to about 20:1, the diesel is probably starting to smoke. When you see smoke from the exhaust of a diesel, it's because it doesn't have enough air for the fuel. If it doesn't have enough air you have to figure out a way to get more air to it.

Swirl, Not Tumble, Helps Atomize Diesel

The way to add air is to pressurize the intake with a properly designed turbo system to increase the air density in the cylinder. However, that's only part of the answer. You also need to add some turbulence in the cylinder to help mix the fuel droplets with the available oxygen. The turbo pressure helps generate turbulence, as do the intake ports and the fuel injection design.

Turbulence is critical for diesel engines, but it's not a tumble like you get with gasoline engines, it's a swirl. The swirl can be clockwise or counterclockwise looking from the top down, depending on the design. The rotation of the air causes it to stratify: the air density near the cylinder wall is greater than that near the center. The injection is targeted into the dense air, injected in a cone with a spread angle of somewhere between 130 and 160 degrees.

The angle of the injection cone is tuned to the bore size, the stroke length, geometric considerations (piston dwell), and the diameter of the piston relative to the diameter of the cylinder—there's just a bunch going on. Suffice it to say, it's all a matter of the diesel fuel particles getting a constant feed of oxygen so they react as completely as possible within the cylinder.

Injection Velocity

Diesel fuel is injected under very high pressure. The industry is going for 2,000 bar: (1 bar = 14.7 psi) so 2,000 bar is approaching 30,000 psi of injection pressure. Such high pressure is necessary because diesel fuel doesn't vaporize as easily gasoline. When diesel burns you don't have the sudden change from liquid to vapor as with gas. It's injected through smaller nozzle holes under high pressure to form a mist of fine particles.

In the older diesels, the particles were comparatively large and the velocity was relatively low. The mass of these larger particles gave them sufficient momentum to keep moving through the air up to the point most of the fuel reacted with the

HIGH-PERFORMANCE DIESEL BUILDER'S GUIDE

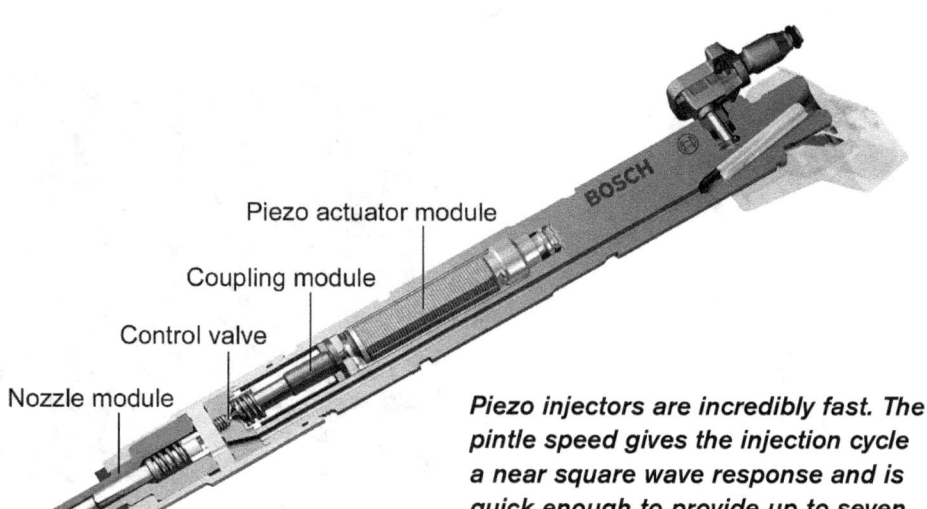

Piezo injectors are incredibly fast. The pintle speed gives the injection cycle a near square wave response and is quick enough to provide up to seven injection pulses per power stroke. (Photo courtesy of Bosch)

oxygen. However, the velocity of the fuel particles in older diesels was not sufficient to completely vaporize and react to the fuel. At some point it stopped moving, stopped burning, and formed a lot of soot.

Complex Nozzles

A modern diesel fuel injector nozzle, you'll see it has several injector holes, usually five or six. The holes are arranged radially to distribute the fuel evenly through the cylinder. The holes are also angled downward toward the piston. The angle varies depending on the design of the combustion cup, the reciprocating component geometry, and even the intake port design.

The velocity of the fuel as it's shot from the injector hole is really the most important factor in how thoroughly the fuel atomizes and mixes with the intake charge air. The fuel's velocity can also reduce the effective cross-sectional area of the hole, which reduces the potential mass flow of fuel. This comes about because as some of the fuel molecules accelerate toward the opening from the sides, they have to make a sharp turn. They separate from the wall of the nozzle hole for a small period before getting caught up in the main flow through the center of the nozzle. This process changes throughout the injection pulse as

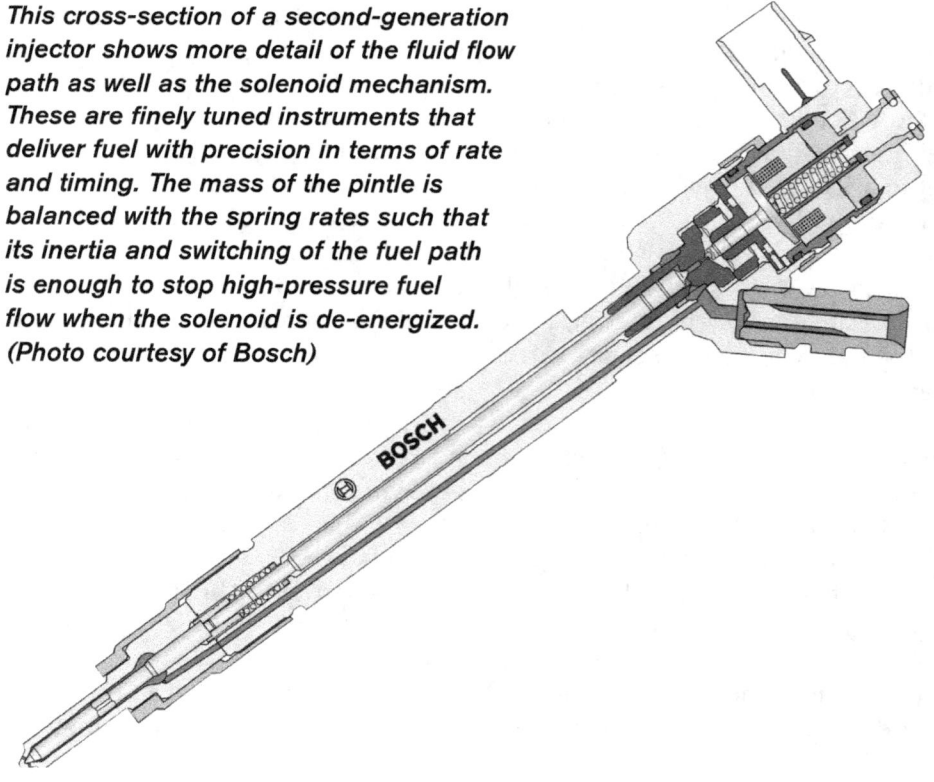

Second-generation common rail designs use solenoid-actuated injectors. Third-gen common rail designs use piezo stacks to actuate the pintle. The fuel flow is shown in red with the injector in the "off" position. When electric current is applied to the solenoid or piezo stack it lifts the pintle allowing fuel to flow around it and through the nozzle into the combustion chamber. (Photo courtesy of Bosch)

This cross-section of a second-generation injector shows more detail of the fluid flow path as well as the solenoid mechanism. These are finely tuned instruments that deliver fuel with precision in terms of rate and timing. The mass of the pintle is balanced with the spring rates such that its inertia and switching of the fuel path is enough to stop high-pressure fuel flow when the solenoid is de-energized. (Photo courtesy of Bosch)

THE FUEL SYSTEM

BD Diesel Performance offers these high-flowing injectors for Dodge Cummins engines and other models. BD matches its injectors with the proper wastegate and tuner to determine proper boost level and air/fuel ratio. (Photo courtesy of BD Diesel Performance)

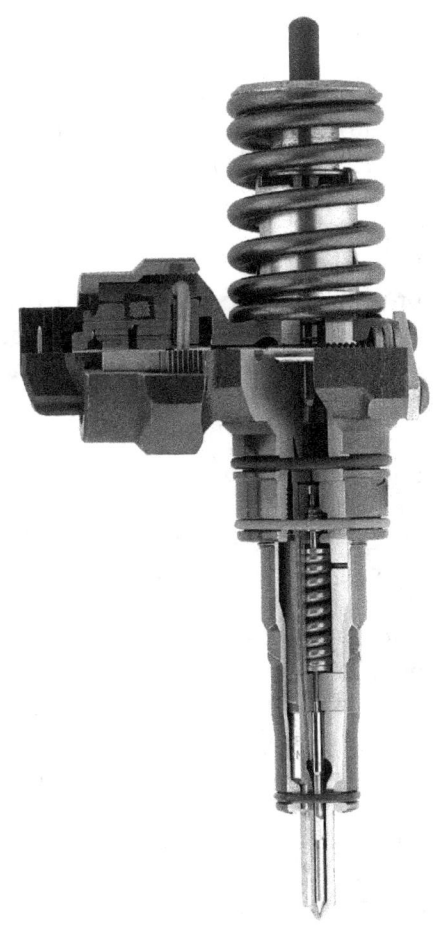

Bosch's unit injector combines electronic control with a mechanical leverage system to provide the injection pressure. This is an early tactic, but a hybrid version of it will probably be used to build rate-shaping-capable injection systems. (Photo courtesy of Bosch)

well as in response to the pressure conditions inside the cylinder.

The turbulence generated in the nozzle opening causes ripples on the fuel jet's surface that grow exponentially as it travels away from the nozzle finally breaking apart into a droplet. These in turn break into smaller and smaller droplets. As the particles break away, they spread out and form a cone. How quickly and how wide the cone forms is also important. This is the process of atomization: The finer the droplets, the better for more complete combustion. These are just a few of the reasons why diesel injectors are so expensive.

Aftermarket Injectors

The aftermarket companies offering increased-flow injectors are increasing the hole size, but they don't have a way to change the spray angle. They just extrude hone the nozzle holes bigger. According to Banks, it's tougher to do than that. "We tried it once when we needed some injectors and Bosch was back ordered. We sent it to Extrude Hone to have them honed out. We put them in the engine and found one that ran way hotter than the rest, which were very balanced. So we took another one of the nozzle tips and cooled it down. Obviously they didn't match. This from the best guys (Extrude Hone) and they only did 10 of them."

You don't get a flow sheet on your injectors from the aftermarket with each nozzle. When the Bosch engineering guys do it we get a flow sheet with each to tell us where we're at in terms of flow and angle. So keep that in mind when shopping.

The problem you get with aftermarket nozzles is their impact upon swirl in the combustion process. When you make the holes bigger to get more fuel, the atomization gets coarse. You get bigger particles so it burns differently. You can get the velocity back up and help that a little bit with more rail pressure, but it isn't what it should be. The answer is more along the lines of having a seven-hole nozzle so you can put more fuel in and maintain proper atomization.

This is where the concept of the combination or recipe is most important. The angle of the spray, the velocity, the size of the atomization, the timing—all of it plays into the design of the combustion cup in the piston. If you don't get it right you can overheat the piston, lose power, or make it smoke excessively.

We monitor the cylinder pressure to make sure that the changes we make to the injector, combustion cup, and swirl are working. Our system measures the cylinder pressure 1,444 times per revolution. Currently we're just monitoring one cylinder, but if you're getting really refined you do all eight cylinders.

Energy is released by the fuel and imparted into the piston every quarter of a degree. Four samples per degree multiplied by 360-degrees equals 1,444. Every quarter degree of crank angle we're measuring the

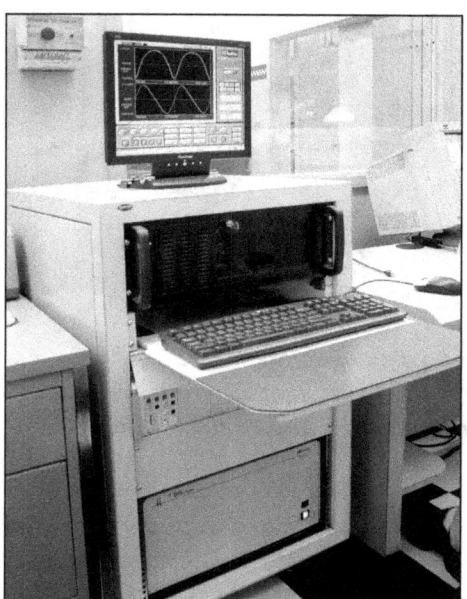

Monitoring the cylinder pressure throughout the load and RPM range is key when developing any engine part. Banks uses a system that measures the cylinder pressure 1,444 times per revolution. With this data, Banks can monitor the energy released by the fuel and imparted into the piston every quarter of a degree, which tells them if the part or modification is working correctly or not.

cylinder pressure. We know the geometry of this engine, the stroke length, the bore diameter, the length of the connecting rod, the distance from the centerline of the wrist pin to the top of the piston. Therefore, we can calculate, given a certain torque output at a certain RPM, how much energy the fuel has to put into that piston to move it that quarter degree. So we can look not only at this peak cylinder pressure, which guys talk a lot about because it has to do with kicking out the head gasket, as well as engine durability. You also can look at the rate of energy released from the fuel and the use of that energy. If you get more energy into the piston then you've done the job right.

You can also look at the emissions and what's called brake specific fuel consumption (BSFC). The BSFC is the ratio of how much fuel you're putting in and how much energy you are getting against the piston. Knowing the BSFC can tell you whether or not you're burning the fuel correctly. Diesel engines are running in the range of 0.380 to 0.420 BSFC. Gas engines run on average 0.5 BSFC. If you run an engine at one speed you can really optimize the efficiency. The fact that you have to run it at various speeds with current transmissions means a compromise as it sweeps through different engine speeds.

Tuning the Fuel Injection Cycle

Other than increasing boost pressures, all the electronic tuners on the market essentially tune the fuel injection cycle. With a turbo diesel, the wastegate is computer controlled, so you crank up the boost and add fuel electronically. Of course, the fuel side is more complicated than with a gas engine. For a diesel engine, the fuel injection system is also the ignition timing, plus since diesel fuel requires specific combustion chamber turbulence, you have to tune for changes to the engine combination that affect the intake charge air. The current tuners control the start of injection, i.e., the ignition timing, the duration of the injection, and the injection pressures. You can accomplish a lot by altering these three variables, as anyone familiar with aftermarket tuners can attest.

The start of injection, not the pilot injection, begins near the end of the compression stroke and continues into the power stroke. The fuel starts burning almost immediately (there is some lag time).

Since fuel is power, increasing the quantity of fuel injected increases power up to a point. There are three ways to increase fuel delivery:

1. Increase pressure: Given the same injection time, higher injection pressure delivers more fuel. Extra pressure also has the advantage of atomizing the fuel better, which tends to allow it to release more of its heat in a usable portion of the power stroke.

2. Lengthen pulse width: Given the same pressure, you deliver more fuel with a longer pulse width. There is a limit to this tactic because there is a limited window of time and piston position in the bore where the fuel's heat can be efficiently used to make mechanical power. You have the option of advancing the timing slightly *and* increasing pulse length. This shifts the peak pressure a little, but not too much because the piston is traveling down the bore, expanding the volume and decreasing the temperature and pressure.

If you inject too long, the fuel at the tail of the injection pulse is considered excess fuel. Its burn rate is slowed because the temperature is lower, the volume of the cylinder is larger, and the crank angle is not as advantageous. The bottom line is that there's still enough oxygen to create lots of heat, but the heat can't be turned into work efficiently, so instead, the heat energy goes into the pistons, coolant, down the exhaust pipe, etc. That's why the EGTs increase so dramatically when you add too much fuel or inject it too late in the cycle. This leads to a lot of heat and smoke with little increase in power.

THE FUEL SYSTEM

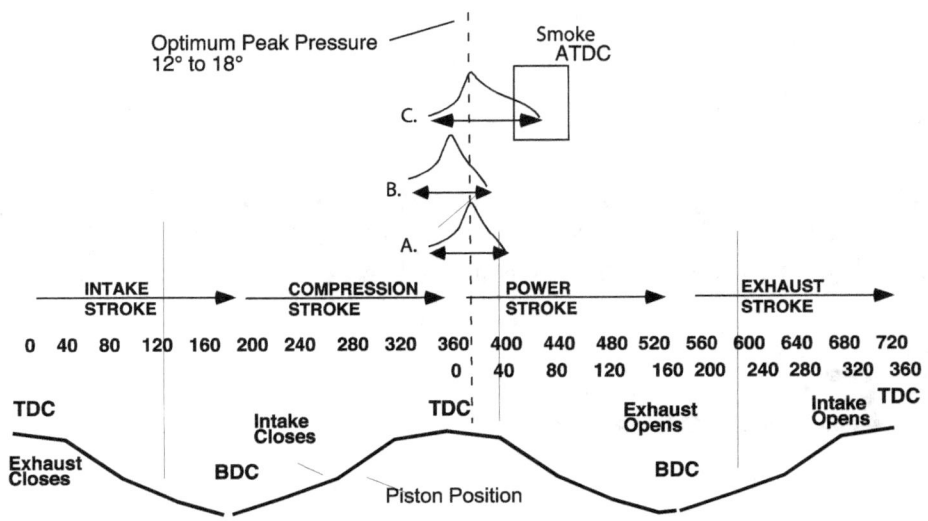

Here we analyze the limits of the combustion process and the piston-to-valve clearance imposed on the injection cycle. The diagram shows the narrow window in crank angle degrees to get the charge air in, compress it, heat it, and heat it further by injecting diesel fuel. Higher-RPM flow is reduced by the lack of overlap dictated by the thin piston-to-head clearance. The smoke window also shows what happens if the fuel is injected too long, or too late. The fuel will burn while it's in the exhaust tract. With diesel, there is always air to react with fuel since you're never able to get on the rich side of stoichiometric.

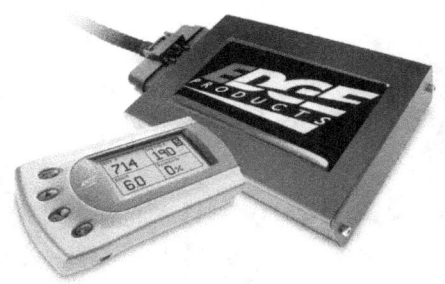

Engine tuners like this Edge Juice with Attitude increase performance and efficiency by controlling boost and fuel injection timing. This setup also serves as the boost and EGT gauges, and has the ability to derate your engine based on EGT, boost, and transmission slip levels. (Photo courtesy of Edge Products)

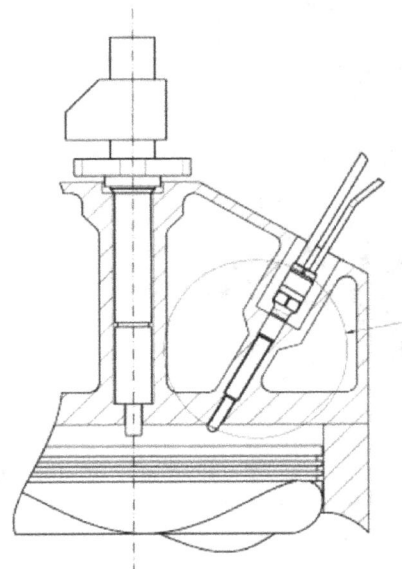

Siemens' pressure-sensing glow plug is a new technology that will put the final touch on the suite of emissions control strategies. It will allow exceptional power and the precision required to make that power without unintentionally making more pollution. Your diesel control computer will be able to tune where and for how long peak cylinder pressure occurs. Cylinder pressure is where the power comes from, and controlling it in the most advantageous and efficient way is what tuning is all about. (Photo courtesy of Siemens)

The reason that diesel fuel burns so hot at this late stage is because there is still plenty of oxygen. The stoichiometric ratio for diesel is 14.4:1. In other words, it takes 14.4 molecules of air to completely combust one molecule of diesel fuel. We're starting to see smoke in the 20:1 to 18:1 range, so there is plenty of oxygen in there to make heat, it's just not contributing to peak cylinder pressure because it's not reacting with the fuel at the right time.

3. Advance injection timing: The limiting factor here again is that you have to time the beginning of the injection pulse to the optimum point in cylinder volume and crank angle for peak cylinder pressure to get the maximum power output and efficiency. The burn rate of the fuel, which is controlled by the compression ratio and the cetane, should affect when you want to time your fuel injection. Higher compression equals hotter temps equal faster burn rate. So as the boost comes up you have to tune the fuel delivery to match the hotter charge air temps.

The trick is to use the electronic tuning tools to meet your power requirements. For example, according to Banks, the stock Duramax responds well to 30-degree duration injection pulses, with a max lead of 10 degrees or so, and no pilot pulse. That's the baseline and you can add from there. Crank up the boost and you can add a few degrees of lead and extend the duration of the injection pulses a few degrees and see how it responds. Aftermarket tuners are set up based on stock components, or certain aftermarket intake and exhaust components, so if you change the combination you may have to tweak the tuning.

CHAPTER 6

EXHAUST

A turbocharged engine is force-fed air, which produces a lot of turbulence and helps atomize the fuel. Since the turbo forces more mass air into the engine, you need to get it out just as quickly. Whether you're using diesel or gas, if you run a turbo, improving the exhaust-side airflow is very important. If you're limited to improving only one side of a turbo motor, it has to be the exhaust side.

On naturally aspirated gasoline production engines, the exhaust valve and port are sized to have a certain intake-to-exhaust ratio. Generally the exhaust valve is 73 to 75 percent the diameter of the intake. The larger intake valve area is to increase volumetric efficiency on the intake cycle. The larger cross section presents less resistance to incoming air at atmospheric pressure (during WOT) and or less (part throttle) than if they were the same size as the exhaust. In addition, the exhaust is forced out of the chamber by the piston, so it can be smaller and still evacuate the mass flow capacity of the intake.

Modern direct-injection turbo diesels have symmetrical intake and exhaust valve sizes. This indicates that the mass flowing efficiency of each side is roughly equivalent. However, the intake has an advantage in that it's pressurized positively, while the exhaust side is pressurized negatively, so to speak. When you force more mass air through the intake with higher boost, you need to get it out. So we need to explore ways to improve the efficiency of the exhaust side, which of course, starts with the exhaust valve.

With a turbo diesel you don't have a throttle blade in the intake tract to cause a restriction. You're also working with a pressurized intake, so you're stuffing a lot more air in through a given size valve and port. For these reasons, the exhaust needs to be larger to keep a mass

EXHAUST

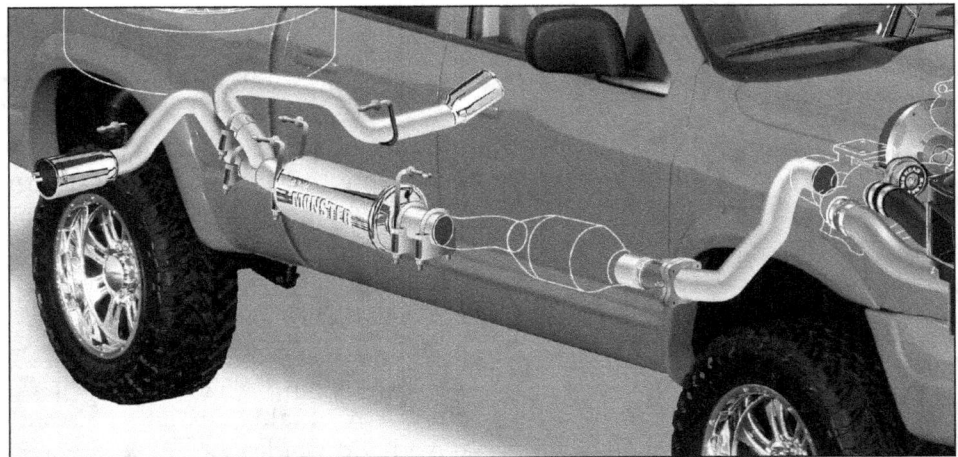

Aftermarket exhaust systems usually consist of larger-diameter, freer-flowing components behind the catalyst (muffler and pipes at left). In addition, you can get better flowing down pipes, which route exhaust flow from the turbine to the catalysts (right-hand side). (Photo coutesy of Gale Banks Engineering)

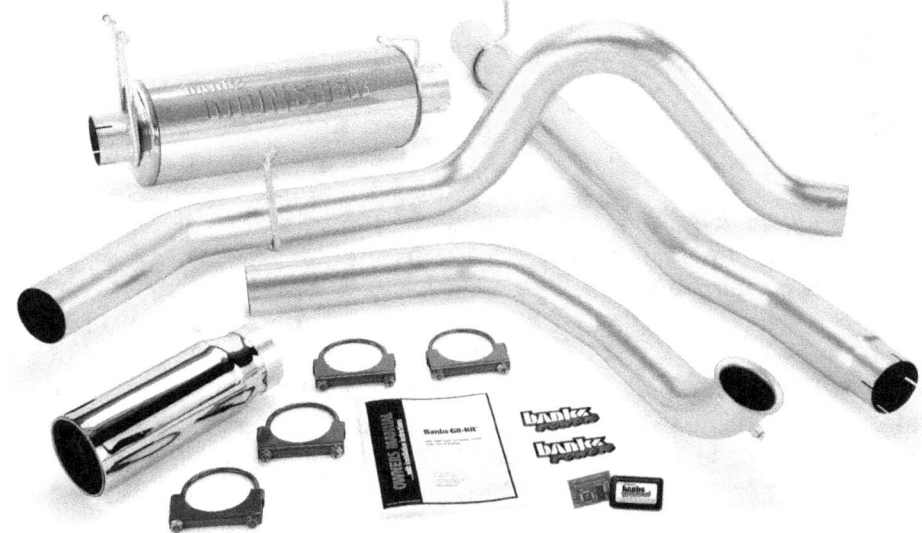

This Banks exhaust kit for the Ford Power Stroke shows excellent build quality, which is something you need to consider when choosing a system. Like many aftermarket exhausts the kit features generously sized, mandrel-bent tubing, a free-flowing muffler, and a polished tip. (Photo courtesy of Gale Banks Engineering)

flow balance. For this reason, the intake and exhaust valves are about the same size on turbo diesel engines. For example, the Cummins B series 6-cylinder, 12-valve engine used in Dodge Rams from 1989 to 1998 model years has 1.77-inch diameter intake valves and 1.65-inch exhausts. A naturally aspirated gasoline engine with that size exhaust valve would have an intake valve diameter of at least 2 inches.

Diesel engine ports are different in that as we saw in Chapter 3, the intake port is designed to turn the charge air to promote swirl in the chamber. The exhaust ports don't need to do that, they just need to flow. In addition, the exhaust gas is pressurized and restricted by the turbo. For these reasons, the exhaust ports don't have the cross-sectional area of the intake. Engine designers use the Bernoulli principle to determine the range of exhaust gas velocity and mass flow requirements. The idea is to keep the mass velocity up so its energy can drive the turbocharger and yet provide enough area to flow the mass required to meet power level specs.

The exhaust system of a turbo diesel consists of several common components, though there is variation between makes and models. Before the turbo, most stock turbo diesels have a log manifold that collects the exhaust of all of the cylinders in the engine bank and then directs it to the turbo. The exhaust squeezes through the turbo, powers the turbine wheel, and then needs to be directed to the atmosphere with the least amount of resistance to mass flow as possible.

After the turbo, a down pipe and other plumbing direct the exhaust to the atmosphere at a point on the vehicle that it doesn't interfere with the health of the occupants or vehicle operation. On big rigs, the exhaust is directed to exit above the vehicle after running through a low restriction muffler. On modern street-driven medium- to heavy-duty pickups and commercial rigs, the exhaust is directed through a catalyst or a series of catalysts before entering a muffler and exiting to the atmosphere to the side or rear of the vehicle.

From a performance view, the goal in building an exhaust system is to increase mass flow through the engine. In other words, the pipes, the header tubes (if you're building headers), the collector, down pipes, catalysts, and mufflers have to be large enough to convey the spent

CHAPTER 6

This Bully Dog exhaust system doesn't have the premium finish of some systems out there, but it's less expensive and still makes great power. Most importantly, you get the mandrel-bent pipes and straight-through muffler. (Photo courtesy of Bully Dog)

so you get a broader power band. Second, it amplifies the effects of upstream flow enhancement such as air filters and intakes. Third, it makes any performance flash programming of the computer more effective by providing the additional airflow required.

Things to look for in an aftermarket exhaust include build quality and material choices with an emphasis on the airflow attributes listed above. A quality exhaust should have good welding at all joints and flanges. Some higher-end and custom-built exhausts use flame welding instead of wire-feed welding. The difference claimed is the flame welds are more resistant to cracking than harder wire welds.

Stainless steel is used to increase service life because it resists the corrosion in harsh environments. If you live in an area where the roads don't get salted in the winter, aluminized steel exhaust systems should last.

Exhaust Manifolds

The exhaust manifold or manifolds carry the exhaust gases between the cylinder head and the turbo (there may also be a pipe or two between the manifolds and the turbo to recirculate exhaust gas). Most stock diesel engines are designed with cast-iron log manifolds for reliability and compatibility with EGR emissions control. On a max-effort engine, you are not worrying about that: You want the most power.

Most stock exhaust manifolds are fine for the stock power levels, but for the ultimate in performance, a tubular manifold or manifolds with equal-length primary tubes and merge collectors allow you to make the most power. The basic exhaust header theory is that pri-

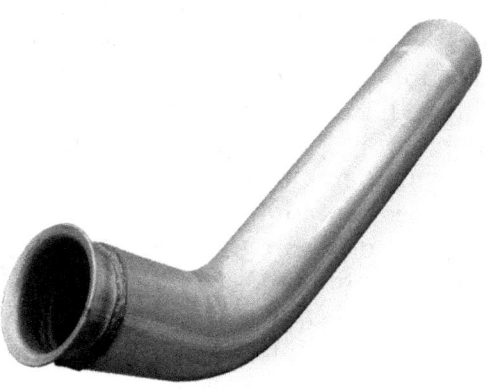

Flowmaster manufacturers this down pipe as part of its 4-inch Duramax kit. Reducing backpressure after the turbine allows the turbo to spool up faster for more power throughout the RPM range. (Photo courtesy of Flowmaster)

gases to the cool, low pressure atmosphere with least resistance to flow. The best-case scenario would be a straight pipe coming off the turbo. But since that's not realistic because of emissions and packaging requirements, you have to settle for a system with the fewest bends. The bends should be smooth and as gentle as possible to get the job done. In addition, the inner diameter of the exhaust tubes should be symmetrical from the transition to the bend to the straight. Exhaust systems that are mandrel bent typically have that quality.

The benefit you get from improving exhaust flow is threefold. First, by reducing pressure behind the turbo it tends to spool up faster,

EXHAUST

Which Stainless is Best?

Many aftermarket stainless steel exhaust systems don't advertise the type of stainless used. Essentially there are two grades used: 321 stainless for the high-heat applications such as turbo headers and aircraft applications, and 304 stainless for the lower temp portions, i.e. cat-back exhausts and mufflers.

321 stainless weighs about half as much mild steel and it's very stable at high temperatures, which is why it's used extensively in aircraft. It also is corrosion resistant. In fact, like most stainless, 321 forms a layer of oxidation that sort of heals itself.

304 is the least expensive and most available stainless steel tubing. It's often used for naturally aspirated headers, as well as mufflers and cat-back exhaust systems. It doesn't have the structural integrity at high temps that 321 does and it's not as light. It does however have the self-healing oxidation quality that makes it great for exhaust systems.

Log exhaust manifolds are traditionally used to mount turbos mainly because they have a long service life. For moderate power levels, that design works fine, but to make serious power through a wide RPM range, you need to reduce the restriction through the entire airflow path. In addition to the diameter and length, the radius of the bends influence flow. Notice the smooth bends leading to the collector on the Banks Type R truck.

Merge collectors feeding into the turbine increase the efficiency of the flow path, which improves spool up and high-end power. You don't find these on too many street trucks, though.

mary tubes should be of equivalent length and diameter leading to the collector. The idea is to power balance the engine by equalizing the mass flow across each cylinder, which requires that the intake and exhaust efficiency be equal across the cylinders. So equal-sized primary tubes promote power balance as well as increase mass flow.

The merge collector is a device that blends the individual header tubes into a single, larger exhaust tube. The smoother the transition, the higher the potential mass flow. The arrangement of the primary tubes in the collector can also influence reversion pressure pulses on other cylinders, reducing mass flow efficiency.

Engineering headers is a complex process that involves a lot of trial-and-error testing. Engine design software can get you close, but to optimize the combination, you need a lot of experience and patience. If you're building a racing diesel engine and you don't have those skills, find the best header available from the aftermarket.

HIGH-PERFORMANCE DIESEL BUILDER'S GUIDE

CHAPTER 6

The exhaust system after the turbine influences system performance. A free-flowing exhaust system increases the pressure differential across the turbo allowing it to spool quicker and generate more work (higher boost potential) on the compressor side. The exhaust system on your street truck probably won't look like this, but you can see how the Banks crew strived for gentle bends and high flow.

Since a diesel is a four-stroke internal combustion heat engine, the kinetic energy and behavior of the exhaust gas is essentially the same as with a gas engine. The velocities won't be as high (unless the boost pressure and air density is high), since the engine speed is not equal to a gas engine. But a good header designer takes that into account when working with the various computer programs that predict design specs. This is still a relatively new area of performance, so the information that is out there is still held close to the vest. On the Banks Type-R Duramax, the diameter of tubing is in the 1-3/4-inch to 2-inch range. These are designed to flow well enough to spool two racing turbos capable of making 44 psi boost.

Regardless of the specific engine combination and power target, the proper primary tube size on a turbo engine will maintain the highest possible exhaust charge velocity and flow the mass you're putting into the engine. The tuning factors you use are the diameter of the tubes and the length. A smaller diameter tube will increase exhaust gas velocity for a given pressure, while a larger one slows it down and lowers the pressure while offering more mass flow potential. As the primary tube grows longer, it moves the torque curve to a lower RPM, while a shorter tube moves it higher.

For turbo motors, you must maintain the velocity by keeping heat loss to a minimum to keep the turbo spinning. Once you get it optimized you are able to use a larger turbo that spools much more quickly.

As a practical consideration for street performance engines, keeping the exhaust gases tight and hot before the turbocharger will be important to optimum functioning of the turbo. The exhaust gases should not be allowed to expand before the turbocharger. Therefore, the exhaust manifold or tubing should be of the same size as the exhaust ports and of a material that retains as much of the heat as possible. The gases should expand for the first time when they are in the turbine section of the turbocharger. Ideally, the exhaust gases will experience a constant cross-sectional area until the constriction just before the volutes of the turbine housing open to the turbine wheel.

Backpressure is certainly an issue, but we need to look at it in terms of before the turbine and after the turbine. Backpressure before the turbine is controlled by the choice of turbine "size," desired intake boost pressure, and wastegate setting (to mention the most important).

If your primary tube diameter is too large before the turbine performance suffers. Exhaust comes in pulses, not a steady stream. If you make the pipe too big, the exhaust will slow down too much and not have the energy to spin the turbine as effectively as a more energetic pulse. So you need to select a primary tube large enough to move the exhaust mass flow, but small enough to conserve the speed and energy of the pulse so it can drive the turbo. If you go too small, the penalty is increased backpressure. The more backpressure, the harder the piston has to work to force the exhaust gases out of the cylinder.

This balancing act is called crossover. Crossover is the point where the backpressure spinning the turbine equals and eventually exceeds the boost pressure. While you can still make good power if the backpressure exceeds the boost, the

EXHAUST

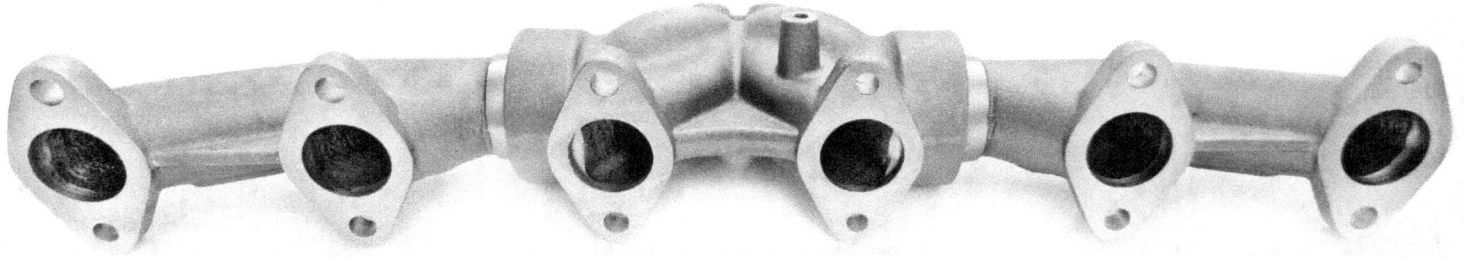

BD Diesel Performance's Dodge Cummins exhaust manifold has expansion joints that allow it to expand and contract as it heats up and cools down, which helps keep it from cracking. It's also pulse tuned for more efficient combustion chamber evacuation and increased power over the stock manifold. (Photo courtesy of BD Diesel Performance)

This Full Bore Duramax exhaust manifold from BD Diesel Performance does away with the dent in the factory driver's side manifold. The result is increased exhaust flow for faster turbo spool and more power everywhere. (Photo courtesy of BD Diesel Performance)

larger the imbalance, the more power is used to drive the turbine, and efficiency drops significantly as the spread increases. The goal for any performance turbo diesel is to have less backpressure than intake pressure. In that case, the engine operates extremely efficiently and can make huge power and have good BSFC.

However, in the real world, backpressure also helps to drive the turbocharger. With typical street setups and turbochargers, there is often a little more backpressure than boost pressure. This condition is not nearly as big a concern on a turbocharged diesel as it is on a normally aspirated gas engine. Diesels have much less overlap engineered into their camshafts, so there isn't the worry of high-pressure exhaust returning to the cylinder and the intake tract. Wastegating the turbo brings in another set of variables. You are bypassing the turbine wheel with some of the exhaust gas. This procedure increases exhaust flow and moderates the driving force on the turbine and hence compressor. However, it also wastes energy available to do work through the turbocharging process, and means that the backpressure must be higher than would otherwise be needed if you hope to continue driving the turbine wheel as it was before the wastegate opened.

You won't generally notice that the crossover balance is off from the seat of your pants (unless it's really off!). This is a design consideration that's sorted out on the dyno or with computer software. We mention it because it is one measure of design elegance. On the dyno, you have sensors measuring backpressure and boost pressure and you're measuring the mass of fuel per horsepower produced. If you ignore crossover, the BSFC goes up, and your engine will use more fuel per horsepower produced than it would otherwise.

After the Turbo

Reducing backpressure after the turbine is just as important. You want the least amount of backpressure on a turbo motor directly after the turbo. To illustrate, think of a child's pinwheel, spinning freely in the wind. Put your hand behind it, slowing and diverting the air flowing through its vanes, and the wheel will almost stop. It's the same for a turbo. If you have high pressure behind the turbo, it will stop or at least spin slower than it would in a low- or no-backpressure environment.

Based on the above, the exhaust after the turbo should be as free flowing as possible. The key mechanism aftermarket exhausts use to reduce backpressure behind the turbo is cross-sectional diameter. This includes your exhaust pipes, the catalytic converter, and muffler. Large

CHAPTER 6

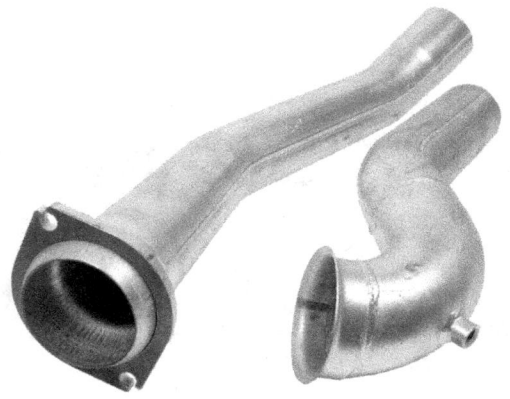

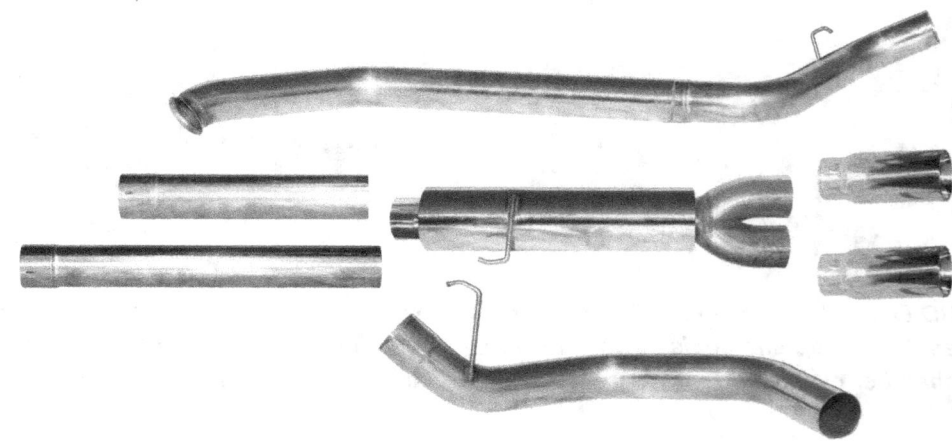

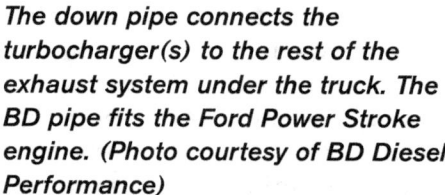

The down pipe connects the turbocharger(s) to the rest of the exhaust system under the truck. The BD pipe fits the Ford Power Stroke engine. (Photo courtesy of BD Diesel Performance)

A good cat-back exhaust system can give you faster turbo spool, more top-end power, and even better mileage. BD and other manufacturers offer high-flowing kits in stainless steel (shown) or aluminized steel. (Photo courtesy of BD Diesel Performance)

exhaust pipe diameter is most important near the turbo, where the gases are hotter. Most of the aftermarket systems use four-inch diameter mandrel bent tubing flowing through a non-restrictive muffler. The systems are laid out to provide the widest radius turns given the confines of the undercarriage it needs to lace through in order to provide the least restriction to flow. The pipes are bigger and therefore flow more mass at an equal backpressure to the stock exhaust, or flow the same mass as the stock unit with less backpressure. There are a few 5-inch diameter systems out there as well, but unless you've added an aftermarket turbo or are running lots of fuel enrichment with nitrous, you don't need to step up to the 5-inch unless you like the looks.

Clogged or undersized converters and restrictive mufflers also degrade a turbo's performance at mid to high RPM. Depending on the severity of the restriction, it can even output at low RPM as well. While you can lose power with oversized exhaust headers before the turbo, the freer the flow after the turbo the better. Even forsaking a muffler won't hurt power—in fact, it'll help. Taking the backpressure off the back of the turbine tends to increase low-end power because the turbo can spool up quicker. If you increase the low end and keep that going to the peak power RPM, even if the gains taper off up top, you're still improving the area under the curve. That means great driveability and excellent towing—and less restriction means better part throttle efficiency, so you get better mileage.

Turbos do not like to have backpressure behind the turbine. They spool faster and build boost quicker with a greater pressure difference across the turbine. So 20 psi measured between the exhaust port and the turbine and 10 psi after the turbine gives a pressure difference of 10 psi. This is preferred to having 25 psi before the turbine and 20 psi after for a pressure difference of just 5 psi. The greater pressure difference before and after the turbo throughout the RPM range is the main benefit of an aftermarket exhaust.

That's not all an exhaust system needs to do, however. It has to sound

Turbochargers use acoustic energy as well as heat energy, so they make a pretty effective muffler. The Banks Type R doesn't use a muffler and yet is reasonably quiet. You may not get away with this on the street though, depending on the temperament of your local law enforcement. Diesel trucks also have to deal with the stigma of being smoke belchers, which may work against you.

good, look good, and last. There are many good exhaust systems on the market; so let your tastes and sound preferences guide you. If you're considering extensive mods, such as intakes, turbo upgrades, and tuners, staying with a single manufacturer can make troubleshooting, dealing with warranty issues, and refining the tuning easier.

EXHAUST

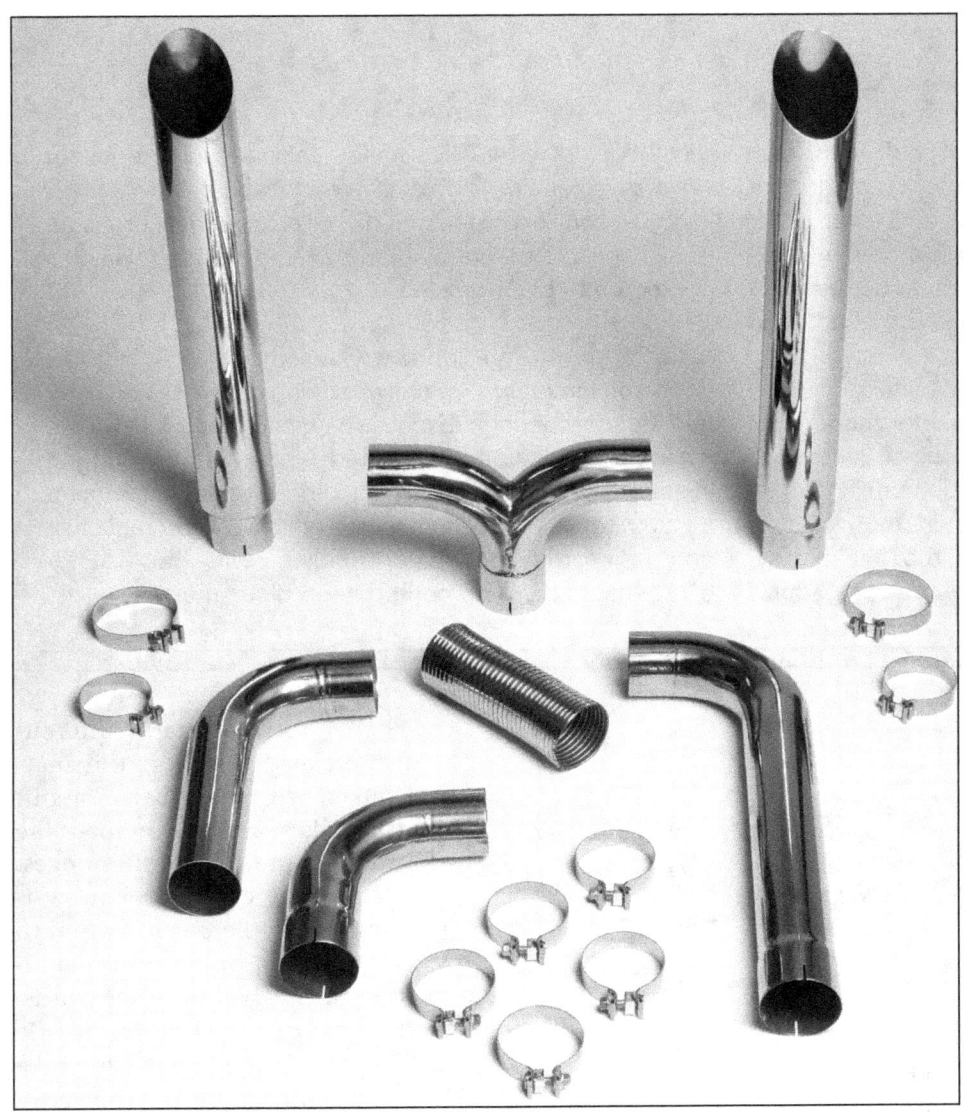

This SMOKERS stack kit is available from MBRP, Inc. These stacks reduce backpressure to speed turbo spool and increase performance, plus they give you that big-rig diesel look. (Photo courtesy of MBRP, Inc.)

Exhaust Brakes

Since diesel engines do not use a throttle blade in the intake, they don't engine brake very well (they don't slow down when you let off the gas in gear). When you let off the accelerator pedal, the intake track does not close to increase the pumping losses of the engine and slow it down. It just freewheels. That's a problem when you need to descend a grade with the vehicle and trailer at the load limit. This is where an exhaust brake can help save your wheel brakes to control your vehicle on extreme grades and for emergency stops. The exception to the rule is in some later-model turbo diesels with variable vane turbine sections, where the vanes can be articulated to become an exhaust brake.

Exhaust brakes get their name because they bolt into the exhaust system after the turbo and before the cat. Exhaust brakes partially close the engine's exhaust when you release the accelerator. This is accomplished using a shut-off valve, literally a throttle blade, in the exhaust system. An actuator closes the valve against exhaust flow, forcing the engine to pump against a restricted exhaust to create braking resistance. In addition to providing engine braking, they are also relatively quiet. You can turn it on or off so you can coast when you want to and brake when you need to. Since exhaust brakes are easy to install and reduce brake wear and maintenance, installing one is kind of a no-brainer.

BD Diesel Performance's exhaust brakes have a huge 3.75-inch inside diameter, which means they won't restrict exhaust flow or power when they're wide open. These brakes mount right after the turbo, replacing the stock elbow and connecting the turbo to the rest of the exhaust system. (Photo courtesy of BD Diesel Performance)

Common Causes of Smoke

White smoke: Caused by unburned fuel passing through the engine. Some white smoke is normal on cold start-ups. Excessive white smoke could be an indication of inoperative glow plugs, loose injectors, low compression from worn rings or bent connecting rods, or coolant leak into the cylinders, which could be caused by bad head gaskets or injector-well sleeves.

Black smoke: Caused by excessive fuel for the amount of air drawn into the cylinders. Some black smoke on hard acceleration or at higher altitudes is normal. Excessive black smoke could result from restricted intake or exhaust, inoperative, leaking, or weak turbo, intake ducting leaks, leaking or worn injectors, fuel return or supply restriction, or a stuck exhaust backpressure regulator valve or solenoid. Problems with the barometric, MAP, injection control pressure (ICP), or exhaust backpressure (EBP) sensors (depending on make and model) can also contribute to black smoke.

Blue or blue/white smoke: Caused by insufficient fuel or oil consumption. Normal when engine is cold or idling for extended periods. Excessive smoke could be caused by air in the fuel, contaminated fuel, loose or plugged injectors, worn or leaking injector o-rings, thermostat stuck open, oil consumption, or plugged crankcase depression regulator valve. Problems with the MAP or ICP sensors can also contribute to blue smoke.

Exhaust brakes are basically throttle blades that restrict the exhaust flow. Make sure the brake you choose integrates well into the rest of your systems and doesn't impose a restriction to flow when it's open. This setup from Banks is quite complete. (Photo courtesy of Gale Banks Engineering)

There are several different exhaust brake designs on the market. I talked with Gale Banks about exhaust brakes and he helped me understand some of the differences. Banks says that entry-level designs tend to use a simple on-off switch to trigger a solenoid or a vacuum actuator to close a valve. In other words, it's either on or off—nothing subtle about it all. Some of these brake designs use holes in the butterfly flap to relieve pressure so the device doesn't overpressure the exhaust side and float the valves. As we noted in the discussion on camshafts, there's not much piston-to-valve clearance to play with. A little float could be costly.

Another factor in exhaust brake design is the amount of backpressure they add into the exhaust system, even while open. Some designs create an exhaust restriction even when not activated, negatively affecting both performance and fuel economy. The key to avoiding that problem is buying a brake that at least has the cross-sectional diameter of the down pipe.

CHAPTER 7

NITROUS AND PROPANE

Nitrous and propane are both compressed gases, but other than that, they're not at all the same. Injecting nitrous oxide into the intake is a means of delivering oxygen to the combustion chamber. You make more power when you add the fuel to match and burn the mixture. Propane, on the other hand, is a fuel in compressed gaseous form. Both are popular power adders for diesel applications, so let's take a look and see how they work.

Nitrous Oxide

Nitrous oxide is a colorless, odorless gas composed of two nitrogen (N2) atoms chemically bound to one oxygen atom (O). The correct abbreviation for one nitrous oxide molecule is N2O. This is where the familiar phrase "N-2-O" comes from when people talk about nitrous oxide. The bottom line is that nitrous is one-third oxygen, and above 575 degrees F the nitrogen and oxygen atoms separate, freeing the oxygen to react with the fuel in the chamber.

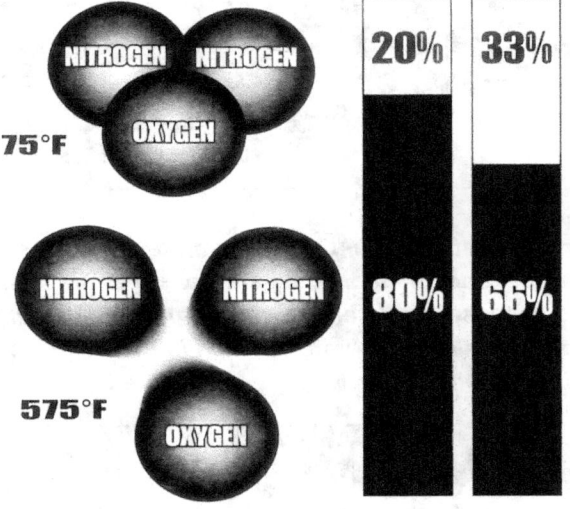

Nitrous oxide is 33 percent oxygen compared to the average atmospheric oxygen content of 20 percent. The oxygen is the active molecule in the air that reacts with fuel to create heat and pressure in the engine's cylinder. More oxygen equals more pressure equals more power.

The turbocharger adds oxygen to the mix by increasing charge density. But with nitrous, the engine doesn't have to expend the work to compress the air. That's done before you put the bottle on the chassis. Nitrous, therefore, is free energy to the engine, and it doesn't need to be intercooled like boosted air. In fact, it's so dense that it really doesn't tax the intake ports so you can get it into the engine very easily. For a turbo diesel, the tricky part is getting the fuel pump to provide enough fuel to match the oxygen density that nitrous and your turbo are able to provide.

It should be obvious that nitrous has serious upside potential with diesel engines. That said, the cool thing about using nitrous with a diesel, in contrast to a gasoline engine, is that there is zero worry

Continued on page 98

HIGH-PERFORMANCE DIESEL BUILDER'S GUIDE

CHAPTER 7

Banks Sidewinder Type D

Gale Banks wants this S-10 to be the quickest diesel pickup truck in the world, and he's not just building a pretty car for a magazine prop. This full tube-chassis drag race pickup truck, dubbed the Sidewinder D-Max Type-D, gets its thrust from a Banks diesel-racing version of a Duramax 6.6L LBZ V-8 with twin turbos and a highly modified Bosch common-rail fuel injection system. Power output is reported to be 1,000+ horsepower with quarter-mile times expected in the 7-second range.

As this book went to press the vehicle was still in development, so we can't confirm the MPH and ETs of the combination. But given Banks' track record there's no doubt it'll be quick. The main reason it found its way into this chapter is the fact that it runs a big hit of nitrous instead of an intercooler. Check it out. (Photos courtesy of Banks)

Diesel drag racing will be much quicker with the Greg Houge-driven, Gale Banks Engineering D-Max Type-D S-10 hooking up torque. The team is looking for 7-second ETs once they get everything sorted out. All diesel projects start somewhere, and a select few end up here.

Force = Mass x Acceleration. Current aftermarket fuel pump technology supports 1,200 hp with the Duramax, which equals a lot of wheel thrust once multiplied by the transmission. Notice the smooth arcs of all the manifolding, both intake and exhaust, as the engine is designed for maximum flow. Using nitrous instead of an intercooler increases mass flow by eliminating a restriction in the airflow path. The nitrous not only cools the intake charge after the turbo but delivers nearly 15 percent more oxygen per unit than the atmosphere.

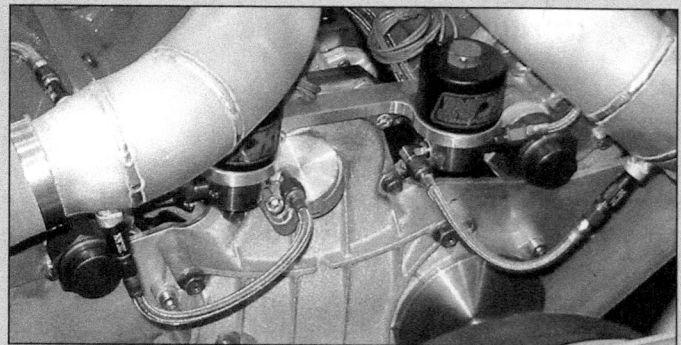

The nitrous system on the Banks Sidewinder is simple and direct. It uses two bottles and two solenoids to control the injection into the intake after the turbo. This position of the injection nozzle works best only if the intake manifold flows equally to each cylinder.

Banks Sidewinder Type D

Gale Banks and driver Greg Houge discuss driver ergonomics (seating, placement of gauges, shifter, steering wheel, etc.).

A pair of Nitrous Express bottles is positioned inside the cage. Each tank feeds one cylinder bank of the Duramax V-8. A key tuning aid for nitrous flow is tank pressure. As the nitrous is expelled, tank pressure falls and nitrous flow falls proportionally. By using two tanks, pressure drop is cut in half so the nitrous flow is more stable than with a single tank.

To move over 1,200 ft-lbs of torque from the engine to the wheels requires a stout transmission. Banks selected a Liberty Extreme manual 5-speed. It uses two gear set shafts astride the input and output shafts to distribute the torque load.

about detonation. You can inject as much nitrous as the engine likes and your wallet can handle. You might not make more horsepower, but the worst that the nitrous can do (besides breaking parts from making too much power) is cool the intake charge air to a point that the compression doesn't raise the temperature high enough to start combustion.

Nitrous and Diesel

Diesels run to the lean side of the stoichiometric air/fuel ratio (14.6:1) even at full power. It's a good rule of thumb that at rated power a diesel is running 20:1 air/fuel ratio, or 20 parts air to one part fuel. As we discussed in Chapter 5, when you add fuel, it starts smoking around 18:1.

Now here's a puzzle: Considering that stoichiometric (14.6:1) is the air/fuel mixture where all the molecules of fuel can combine with all the molecules of the air in the intake charge, why would adding even more oxygen, in the form of nitrous, make more power? After all, we can't even get close to running 14.6:1 with a diesel. How does all this work?

The way fuel is delivered and used in a diesel doesn't allow for the average air/fuel ratio to be measured as accurately as with a gas engine. In a diesel, the air/fuel mixture at full power is not as properly proportioned as is possible with gas engines. Diesel engines inject and atomize the fuel under pressure in several plumes. As the fuel breaks into small particles it begins to react at the surface of each particle with the oxygen in the air. So really there's a stoichiometric boundary layer near the surface of each particle.

The problem is that unless new molecules of oxygen are introduced

NOS put together this nitrous kit specifically for diesel trucks. You can add up to 75 hp with a stock truck, but you can jet in even more power to go along with the extra fuel from your aftermarket tuner. (Photo courtesy of NOS)

ZEX offers three different nitrous kits for GM, Dodge, and Ford diesels. The basic kit uses the TPS signal for activation, the second kit adds a boost switch for timing the nitrous, and the race kit uses two stages to add up to 600 hp. These ZEX kits allow you to take advantage of the extra fuel added by your programmer for even more power, lower EGTs, and reduced smoke. (Photo courtesy of ZEX)

into this area, there is more fuel than can be reacted and then we get unburned fuel coming out the tailpipe as smoke or soot. As we discussed, generating swirl within the combustion chamber is the mechanism a modern direct injection engine uses to present new oxygen molecules to the fuel.

When you consider the average amount of oxygen in the chamber swirling around the injection pattern, it's easier to see a limit to the rate that the oxygen can be fed to the plumes of fuel. Therefore, there is also a limit to the rate of fuel that can be delivered to efficiently react with the oxygen to make heat. The incomplete mixing limits the pressure in the cylinder and the power output. Moreover, during this process there is progressively less oxygen within the swirl, further reducing the effectiveness of continuing to inject fuel.

Introducing nitrous into a diesel engine makes more oxygen available to the fuel. The added oxygen content allows you to tune the fuel delivery rates more aggressively, as you would when adding boost. With more boost, you do get more energy to promote swirl, but if you can triple the oxygen content using nitrous without pushing the turbo to make extra boost, you've got serious potential for a net gain in power.

The effects of the added oxygen on the fuel influence the delay time to ignition: the more oxygen, the less delay; it's like using a slightly higher cetane fuel. Because of the increased density, it's possible to increase the rate of fuel injected on the front end of the combustion period as well as extend the injection event. As with any fuel tuning, you're looking to create the most cylinder pressure in the most advantageous part of the compression stroke.

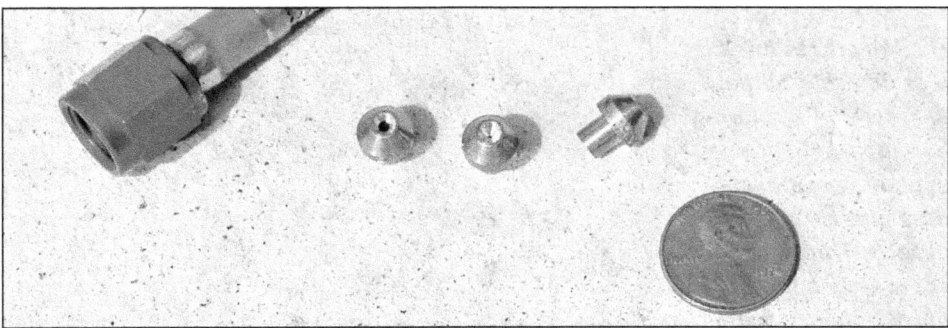

Many nitrous systems use interchangeable jets like these to tune the amount of nitrous (or fuel in the case of a wet system) being injected into the engine. The jets install between the nozzle and the hose and allow a specific quantity of nitrous to flow through. Of course, the other variable is bottle pressure, which will cause more or less nitrous to flow through a given size jet. (Photo courtesy of Travis Thompson)

ZEX Jetting Recommendations

Nitrous Jetting	Est. HP Increase	Tuning
0.030, 0.035	30, 45	stock or tuning
0.040, 0.045	70, 90	tuning required
0.051, 0.055	115, 130	significant tuning & fuel pump

Jetting Nitrous for Diesel

Some nitrous companies out there recommend pretty conservative nitrous jetting. This isn't harmful to the engine, just conservative. Manufacturers also have recommendations for their gas kits, so make sure that's not what you're looking at. Remember that diesels run different air/fuel ratios than gasoline, usually much leaner on fuel, so adding oxygen with nitrous tends to cool EGTs.

Therefore, to increase power using nitrous you need to enrich fuel delivery above that which is effectively burned without nitrous. For example, if your tune were right on with the nitrous, it would probably be rich enough to smoke if you suddenly turned the nitrous off.

Tuning the nitrous system means controlling its flow to match the fuel you're injecting. This is done by using a nitrous jet of a particular size, with a known and stable bottle pressure forcing the nitrous through the jet and into the engine. The trick is to find the right jet diameter to support the power level. Different companies' kits come with different jetting recommendations. I've included a table of recommendations from ZEX. Those recommendations are a great place to start, but you can also fine-tune your setup for the best results. Nitrous Express and other companies also offer progressive controllers that vary the nitrous based on your boost level.

Tuning Tactics

Let's take a closer look and find out how/why to calculate how much nitrous to inject for a given power increase. The estimated Nitrous Jetting chart (page 100) includes some jetting recommendations from NOS

CHAPTER 7

NOS provides this kit that controls bottle pressure with a large heating element and sensors to stabilize pressure as you use the nitrous. This is key in accurately controlling nitrous delivery rates and power output from the engine. It also comes with a remote bottle valve opener to make use safe and convenient. (Photo courtesy of NOS)

The ZEX racer tuning kit includes a heating element to control bottle temperature, a bottle-pressure gauge, blow-down tube to direct an accidental release of nitrous outside the driver compartment, arming and micro switch, braided line, solenoid nozzles, and wiring. (Photo courtesy of ZEX)

for a range of power outputs for their plate systems using gasoline (center column). NOS nitrous systems are calibrated for a nitrous bottle pressure of 950 psi, which requires a bottle temperature around 85 degrees F. The power ratings are just estimates even with gasoline, but we can use these rough estimates to give us a place to start when jetting for diesel.

When tuning the jetting for your diesel, remember that diesels operate well over a wide range of air/fuel ratios. Keep in mind that on the nitrous side, the only damage you can do is put the fire out in the chamber by injecting too much. Tuning the fuel system controls the heat you release in the chamber, which can in theory hurt your engine if you make too much cylinder pressure, or put too much fuel in at the wrong time. See Chapter 5 on tuning the fuel system for more info.

The gasoline recommendations are based on an equivalent air/fuel ratio of approximately 12:1. Diesel engines need an air/fuel ratio of around 18:1 in order not to cause smoke. The difference in airflow is roughly one-third more, so by multiplying the nitrous jetting for gasoline by 1.33, we increased the jet size recommendation by 33-percent. If you increase the jetting by 40-percent

Estimated Nitrous Jetting		
	Gas	Diesels (33%)
A/F	12:1	18:1
100 hp	0.047	0.063
125 hp	0.055	0.073
150 hp	0.063	0.084
180 hp	0.073	0.097
210 hp	0.082	0.109
250 hp	0.093	0.124

you'll be tuned for a ratio of 20:1.

The reader probably notices that these recommendations call for more nitrous for a given power level than the ZEX recommendations. The ZEX recommendations seem conservative to me, probably to reduce adding more nitrous than the fuel will support and thus wasting it. A short chart like the one ZEX supplies with their diesel kits and even the one I generated are guides from which to baseline your tuning efforts. Remember that adding additional nitrous is not going to hurt the engine. You'll only have problems if you add too much fuel at the wrong time and make too much cylinder pressure or EGT. If you don't add enough additional fuel (a much bigger problem with gas engines), you'll just get cooler EGTs. It is possible to cool it enough to stop combustion and stop

Fuel, Air and Nitrous Mass Flow

Using nitrous on a diesel engine requires a different tactic for tuning than a wet system on a gas engine. Instead of adding an oxidizer (nitrous) and fuel at the same time in a specific ratio, as in a wet system, we're adding an oxidizer without fuel, which is referred to as a dry system.

Of course, we still have the ultimate goal of matching nitrous flow with fuel flow. If you know how much extra power you want to make with nitrous and jet accordingly, the next step is to increase the fuel flow to match the additional oxygen carried by the nitrous. The following chart tells you how much additional fuel you need to deliver to go with a nitrous shot of a certain

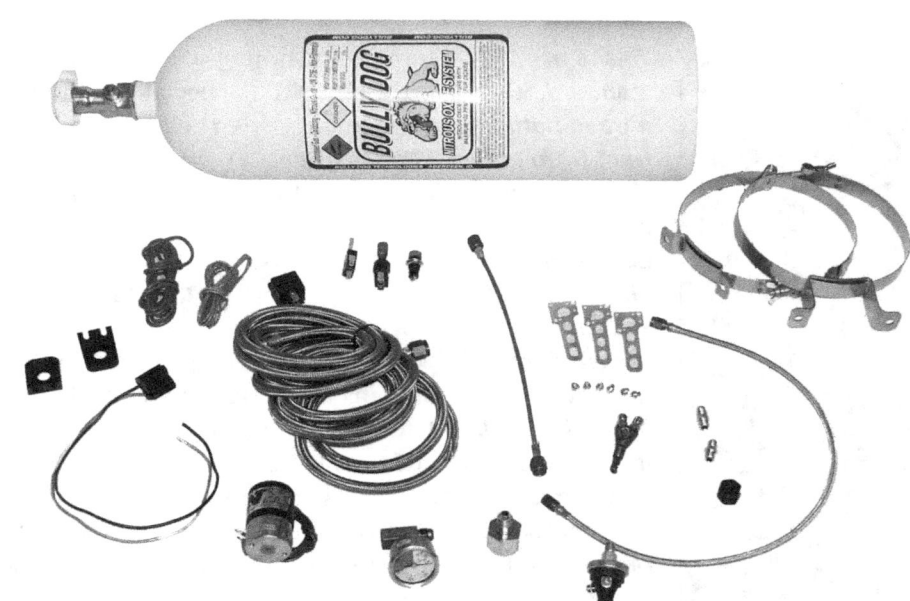

Bully Dog offers 50- and 150-hp single-stage and 200- and 250-hp dual-stage nitrous kits. These kits leave it up to you to tune in the correct amount of fuel. (Photo courtesy of Bully Dog)

Additional Fuel Fequired	
HP	lbs/hr
100	40
125	50
150	60
180	72
210	84
250	100

horsepower level.

The chart above displays the additional fuel required assuming a brake specific fuel consumption (BSFC) rate of 0.4 pounds of fuel per hour for each horsepower hour. For example, to make 100 hp at a 0.4 BSFC means that the engine uses 40 lbs/hr of fuel to generate 100 hp. We've been using 0.4 BSFC throughout the book because it's a good average for diesel engines. At their most efficient, diesels can run at 0.35 to 0.38 BSFC, but in other RPM ranges they may run at 0.45 BSFC. Also keep

This Nitrous Express Boost Reference progressive nitrous controller allows you to adjust nitrous injection based on boost level or RPM. The system can be set up to add up to 200 hp and 340 ft-lbs of torque. (Photo courtesy of Nitrous Express)

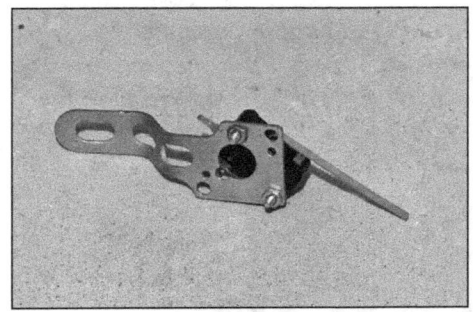

This is a full-throttle switch and its mounting bracket. The idea is to mount this switch somewhere near the fuel pedal or linkage. The switch is tripped when you floor it and the nitrous is injected. (Photo courtesy of Travis Thompson)

in mind that the BSFC value is not the air/fuel ratio, but its magnitude is influenced by air/fuel ratios.

To use this information you need to translate it to your fuel pump. On common rail systems with good aftermarket electronics you can increase pressure and pulse duration to deliver more fuel. You can also tune the timing of the fuel delivery, all with an aftermarket tuner. But ultimately, the fuel flow rate is limited by the capability of your fuel pump and injectors. Some shops offer higher flow pumps and can check pump flow rates on a specialized test bench. Don't try to measure the flow rate at home—the pressures are quite high and you can easily injure yourself.

The fuel pump and injectors aren't parts you can really tweak or

CHAPTER 7

This is a standard 10-lb nitrous bottle from Nitrous Express. It is wrapped with a bottle-heating blanket to help keep the pressure inside the bottle closer to ideal. If the pressure falls too low, less nitrous will be injected for a given size jet, and you won't get the advertised power jump. Keeping the bottle pressure consistent keeps the nitrous flow consistent, which helps you tune the system accurately. (Photo courtesy of Travis Thompson)

This is a liquid-filled bottle-pressure gauge from Nitrous Express. As you can see, the gauge indicates low (white/yellow), ideal (green), and high (red) pressure. Opposite the gauge is a pressure transducer that activates and deactivates the bottle heater to regulate the temperature and thus pressure of the nitrous in the bottle. (Photo courtesy of Travis Thompson)

improve at home, so you have to rely on a shop that specializes in diesel performance. For example, Pacific Performance is very savvy on increasing fuel delivery for diesels.

Nitrous System Components

As mentioned above, nitrous systems are designed as wet flow systems or dry systems. Wet flow systems add extra fuel with a separate solenoid to compensate for the nitrous. Dry systems use the factory fuel injection system to provide the additional fuel. Diesel engines can only use dry systems, since a diesel injects fuel into the combustion chamber after the air is compressed. So we limit our discussion to dry systems (after a quick overview of a wet system) in order to acquaint those unfamiliar with the concept.

Once a wet system is on and flowing, the nitrous oxide and additional fuel are introduced into the intake system and carried to the individual cylinders along with the normal air/fuel mixture. The ratio and quantity of nitrous and additional fuel is regulated by jets within the nitrous and fuel plumbing circuits. The jets, which are precisely sized orifices, allow an exact amount of nitrous and fuel to flow at specific pressures. Typically, the nitrous jetting is based on 850-psi bottle pressure, while the fuel jetting is based on the approximate fuel pressure at the jet, which varies for carbureted and fuel-injected gas engines. Again, wet systems are not used on diesel engines. Dry kits for diesel engines are available from Bully Dog, NOS, Nitrous Express, ZEX, and other manufacturers.

Nitrous Bottles: Never drill, machine, weld, deform, scratch, drop, or modify a nitrous oxide tank or the valve in any way! Although some people have polished their tanks to a chrome-like appearance, even this is not recommended because it removes a non-uniform layer of the tank's material that may or may not affect its integrity. Certainly, never attempt to subject a nitrous tank to any type of plating process, as this can affect the strength of the tank's material.

Never overfill nitrous tanks. That little extra bit will put you and others at great risk for injury. More often than not, when the cylinder warms up, the pressure goes above

Pictured is a Nitrous Express nitrous nozzle (left) and purge valve (right). The pressure in the bottle forces nitrous through the line up to the solenoid. When the solenoid is activated, it opens, allowing nitrous to pass through the rest of the system to the nozzle and into the engine. Adding a purge valve gives you the option of priming the system by bringing a fresh supply of nitrous up to the solenoid so it's ready to go the instant you hit the button. This increases consistency for drag racing and gives you a harder hit. (Photo courtesy of Travis Thompson)

the limit of the safety relief disc and you lose all the nitrous you just paid for anyway. Don't do it.

Aside from the above safety warnings, size is what should concern you when choosing a nitrous bottle. The most common sizes are 2, 5, 10, and 15 lbs. There are also lighter-weight tanks available at a price. Of course, the benefit to having a larger nitrous bottle is more hits between refills, plus less of a pressure drop during a run/pull.

Hoses: A high-pressure hose gets the nitrous from the bottle to the rest of the system under the hood. This is a special hose that has a Teflon inner liner and a braided-steel outer covering. The ends are power-crimped. Don't replace this hose with a standard neoprene-rubber-lined braided-steel hose, especially one that has screw-together-type ends. These types of hoses cannot take the high pressures of nitrous, and they will become very brittle at the extremely low temperatures of liquid nitrous.

Filters: Among the most important components of a nitrous system are the nitrous (and fuel) filters. Because of the pressures involved, the diameter of the jet orifice is very small. It doesn't take much debris to clog the jet. If the nitrous jet gets clogged, typically, it's not catastrophic, though you'll lose power dramatically.

Solenoids: The solenoids are the next step as the nitrous flows. Since diesel engines use dry nitrous systems, all they need are the nitrous solenoid and a means to activate it. Gas engines using wet systems require a second solenoid for the fuel.

Solenoids are basically the valves that control the on/off operation of the nitrous system. These electromechanical valves use 12 volts to create a strong magnetic field to

Nitrous filters are designed to keep debris from clogging your jets. Installing a nitrous filter between the bottle and your jets keeps your machine running strong and your tune spot on. (Photo courtesy of NOS)

This is a dry system nozzle. It shoots the nitrous against a surface to atomize the nitrous into a fine fog for better performance. Most manufacturers recommend mounting the nozzle early in the intake tract. (Photo courtesy of NOS)

pull open a small plunger, which allows the pressurized nitrous to flow through. The solenoids are designed so that the bottle pressure assists in keeping the valve closed. The arrangement works similar to a ball covering the drain in a bathtub. As the water gets deeper the pressure on the ball increases, thereby increasing the sealing action. In a solenoid, the magnetism created by the wire windings of the coil must be strong enough to pull open the plunger.

Injecting Nitrous: There are various schemes for introducing nitrous to the engine. Most of them have been developed for gasoline engines and have the complication of adding fuel. For diesels, you don't have to add fuel so the standard dry manifold systems on the market are a good place to start. Just remember two things: nitrous-to-fuel ratios are different for diesel engines and gas engines, which we discuss above; and any fuel enrichment has to be controlled through the engine management system via a tuner.

Presently most diesel nitrous systems are using a nozzle at a single point of injection near the beginning of the intake tract. The reasoning is to give the nitrous as much time as possible to cool the intake air and mix in homogenously. A case could be made to use individual injectors near the intake, usually called a direct-port system. The advantage of a direct port system is the ability to tune the power balance in each cylinder by jetting the nitrous nozzles. This would work as long as you weren't injecting so much nitrous that the intake charge did not reach a sufficient temperature to ignite. If you position the injector nozzle close enough to the valve, you can nearly inject the nitrous in liquid form, which can potentially put the fire out, or more accurately doesn't let the fire get started.

Propane: Is it Worth the Effort?

If you're considering a propane system on your diesel as a performance adder or a mileage booster, you'll probably want to hear what I learned from Gale Banks on the subject. But isn't propane one of the more common and affordable alternative fuels? Doesn't using it do good things for the environment by burning cleaner and reducing the use

This Digital Propane Injection (DPI) system from MSD uses a computer to monitor engine parameters so it only injects propane under ideal conditions. (Photo courtesy of MSD)

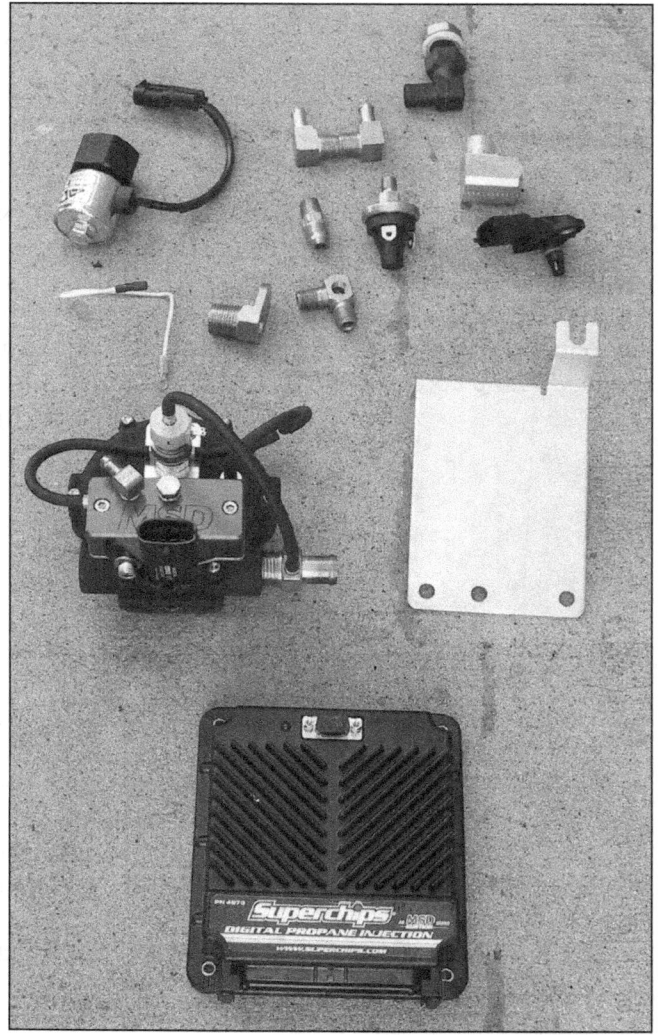

of dirty diesel fuel? Why exactly does this diesel expert reject such a useful technology?

To understand the positives and negatives of using propane, we need to evaluate the costs and benefits of using it in a diesel engine from engineering and economic perspectives.

MSD has one of the better-engineered propane systems on the market. It states accurately how propane works in a diesel using the extra air present in the combustion chamber. Elsewhere we discuss diesel engines at full power rating, without smoking, run around a 20:1 air/fuel ratio. So there is always air, or more precisely oxygen molecules, available to combine with the propane to make heat and cylinder pressure and, therefore, power.

One of Banks' criticisms of propane is that when you're using two fuels (diesel and propane), it's difficult to control the fuel burn rates to tune the optimum timing of peak cylinder pressure. Here's a quick review of the science that supports his view.

When you fumigate the intake with propane, it's drawn into the chamber, compressed with the air, and in a properly functioning engine, doesn't ignite until the diesel is injected. The reason it doesn't ignite before the diesel is injected is because the auto-ignition temperature (the minimum temperature required to ignite a substance in air) of propane is 842 degrees F, while number 2 diesel fuel ignites at just 494 degrees F. This is what makes using propane in a diesel possible.

The air is compressed a specific amount in a diesel on the compression stroke. This thermodynamic process raises its temperature to over 500 degrees F, and when the high-pressure diesel is sprayed into the chamber, it ignites, further raising temperature and pressure to a point where they ignite the propane, which further raises temperature and pressure, forcing the piston down the bore.

At first glance, the fuels seem to work in harmony, even considering the auto-ignition temperature of a substance decreases as pressure increases and/or oxygen concentration increases, as occurs with higher boost values from the turbocharger. For the most part, the ratios of each fuel are regulated to use only the available oxygen in the chamber. When the fuels begin to compete for the oxygen, the propane will use it first, leaving a lot of unburned diesel in the chamber. It's this condition that forces the diesel fuel into detonation.

It may surprise you that a diesel can detonate, but it can and does occur when the engine is mistuned. Tuning to use two fuels with different auto-ignition temps and different octane ratings is tricky when you start pushing the engine tuning to use diesel ratios beyond the smoke threshold of 20:1.

As Banks says, smoke is fuel and therefore power you can see but can't use. So if it's coming out the tailpipe, the engine is not consuming the fuel in the chamber. If you're only burning diesel fuel that's just

NITROUS AND PROPANE

MSD offers these propane systems for Cummins, Duramax, and Power Stroke (shown) trucks. The systems computer is programmed for your specific engine combo, so there's no jetting or guesswork needed. (Photo courtesy of MSD)

wasteful and dirty tuning. When you combine propane and its 110-octane rating with diesel's 15 to 25-octane rating, you're set up for a bad case of detonation if conditions in the combustion chamber are right (or wrong).

What happens is the propane, because it's in vapor form already, is dispersed throughout the combustion chamber and reacts more quickly with the available oxygen molecules once combustion begins. The first part of the diesel cycle goes okay; the diesel fuel is injected and starts to react at the lower temperature. But as soon as the temp is high enough the propane starts grabbing the oxygen generating a lot of heat and pressure quickly. This happens so quickly in fact that the diesel being injected doesn't have a chance to burn correctly, it just collects in the combustion chamber. The fast burn of the propane raises the pressure high enough to surpass the detonation limit of the unburned diesel fuel, causing it to ignite in pockets within the combustion chamber. The flame fronts collide at inopportune times (detonation). This is not a controlled compression ignition and will hurt your engine.

Cost Per Btu

Now let's analyze the economics of using propane. One of the reasons why you may want to install a propane system on your diesel is to conserve diesel fuel. The idea is to use propane to augment the diesel fuel. Now this would make sense if propane were less expensive per Btu than diesel and the cost to install the equipment was recoverable in a reasonable time. Unfortunately, that is not the case. According to the U.S. Department of Energy's *Clean Cities Alternative Fuel Price Report* of June 2006, one gallon of number 2 diesel costs $2.98; one gallon of propane costs $2.08. But because propane has less Btu per gallon than diesel, you have to buy $3.21 worth of propane to equal the energy in that $2.98-gallon of diesel.

So that means you have to pay for the system, and then install it or pay extra for the installation. All that and you still have to pay more per Btu than you do for diesel. It just doesn't add up to an economic advantage. Plus you have to consider the loss of stow space, load carrying capacity, the added complexity, and required system maintenance.

In summary, the correct engineering approach when you need more fuel is to add diesel and inject it properly. However, I can see a place for propane as a power adder for a moderate power increase once you've reached the limit of your diesel fuel system and aren't ready to upgrade properly. Given the above, it does seem like you'd be better off spending your money on adding more diesel into the mix.

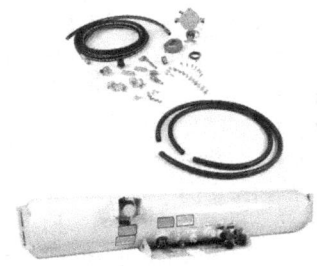

Bully Dog's propane system is of similar construction and complexity to a nitrous system, however, it delivers fuel (propane), not oxygen (nitrous) to the engine and therefore requires a different tuning approach. This setup uses a dual-stage regulator to draw propane from the tank and fumigate the intake for more power. (Photo courtesy of Bully Dog)

CHAPTER 8

DRIVELINE

The driveline consists of the transmission, driveshaft, rear end, and axles. You can also argue that the wheels are part of the driveline. For our purposes we consider the drive wheels as part of the driveline insofar as tire diameter influences gearing.

Unfortunately, when adding power to your diesel vehicle, you can't afford to leave the driveline out of your plans. Even though diesel-powered trucks come with heavy-duty driveline components, it's just too easy to make enough torque to take out the stock transmission. Even with stock power ratings, many late-model diesels make enough power that the engine management computer "de-rates" or reduces power between shifts, and only allows full power once the computer senses that the trans is not slipping. Therefore, you'll have a much better experience with modifying your diesel if you understand how the components work together to manage and transfer the torque to the ground.

Bully Dog debuted its Super High-Output Transmission in '07 featuring more clutch packs and new pistons. If swapping in a fully built tranny isn't your style, you can always upgrade along the way. (Photo courtesy of Bully Dog)

For the most part, the driveline components are designed to meet the performance of the stock engine rate. All the driveline components will fail if you deliver a forceful enough blow without any give or slip. To keep your driveline reliable with extra torque from the engine, you have to consider adding components that are designed better and/or built from stronger materials. In addition, knowing how the driveline works allows you to use the engine's power more judiciously and thus increase the performance of your vehicle without causing damage.

106　HIGH-PERFORMANCE DIESEL BUILDER'S GUIDE

DRIVELINE

Fortunately for diesel enthusiasts, transmission upgrades are available for all the popular transmissions. This trio of cutaways (from the top: GM Allison, Ford, Dodge) comes from BD Diesel Performance, who offers deep finned pans, converters, valve bodies, and other transmission upgrades. (Photo courtesy of BD Diesel Performance)

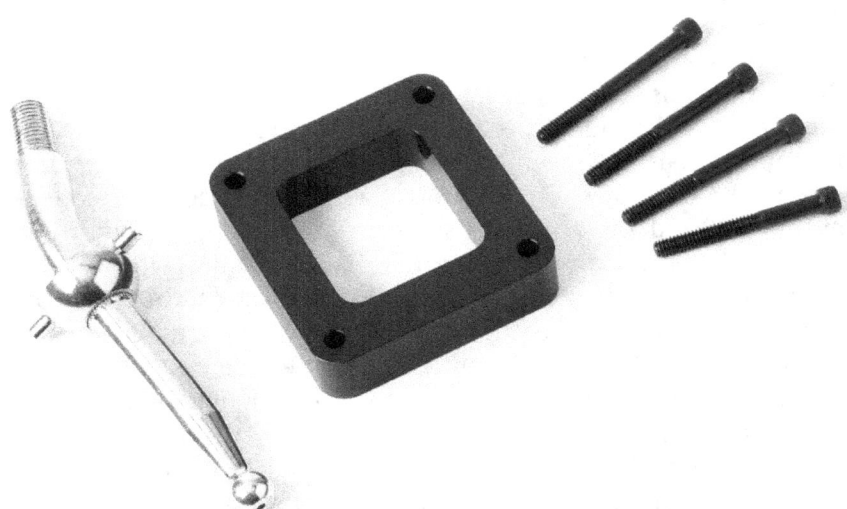

If you want your diesel pickup to shift a little more like a sports car, check out one of these short shifters from BD Diesel Performance. They shorten shift throws by about 20 percent. (Photo courtesy of BD Diesel Performance)

The purpose of the transmission is to connect and disconnect the power flow from the engine to the rear end and eventually to the rear wheels. It also provides a means to multiply engine torque and power for acceleration, increased load capacity, grade climbing, and vehicle speed. Of course, the transmission also provides a means of changing the rotational direction of the power flow so that the vehicle can be driven in reverse.

Manual Transmissions

In general, the automatic transmissions need significant upgrades to be reliable with a bunch of extra power. However, manual transmissions used in diesel pickup trucks are usually pretty strong. You may find a difference though given your driving style or the type work you do with your truck. If you're already started upgrading your manual-trannied diesel, you may have realized that the stock clutch does slip if you try to put too much power to the ground.

Clutch

The clutch is composed of two driving parts, the pressure plate and the flywheel, and one driven part, the clutch disc. The pressure plate is bolted to the flywheel with the clutch disc sandwiched between. The clutch disc is connected to the splined input shaft of the transmission. The clutch engages when the two driven plates squeeze the driven disc, which then transmits the rotational power from the engine into the transmission.

With manual-transmission-equipped diesel rigs, the clutch can be the weak link in the driveline chain. It's designed that way because it's better to have a clutch slip than to break the transmission. However, if you install harder gears, stronger shafts,

HIGH-PERFORMANCE DIESEL BUILDER'S GUIDE

This is a heavy-duty clutch kit from South Bend Clutches that uses an organic friction material. They are rated to hold 350 to 400 hp and 700 to 900 ft-lbs of torque depending on the model. (Photo Courtesy of Diesel Dynamics)

This heavier-duty South Bend clutch features a more durable Feramic metal friction material. This one can handle in the neighborhood of 550 hp and 1,100 ft-lbs of torque. You can bet this clutch will be a little more grabby than stock. (Photo Courtesy of Diesel Dynamics)

and an aftermarket clutch, a manual trans is the choice for ultimate power transfer. That is true in spite of the fact that the various stock transmissions have different weak points. For example, the Ford transmissions for the 7.3 and 6.9 liter have an issue with the pilot bearing. The 6.9-liter tranny also has problems with the springs in the clutch disc. This is not to pick on Ford, since breaking or losing a spring on the clutch is a common failure on many stock clutches.

If you're at the limit of your stock clutch's capacity you'll need to get one that can hold more force. There are several good clutch makers out there, including South Bend Clutch in Indiana, that provide units to hold the extra force. When shopping around, you should know a little about how the clutch operates and holds the torque so you can make an informed decision.

To that end, here's the basic equation that tells us how much torque the clutch can hold before slipping:

$$(PNRCF)/12 = T$$

Where:

T = **Torque in ft-lbs**
P = **Pounds per square inch (pressure plate clamping force)**
N = **Amount of friction surfaces (each clutch disc has two)**
R = **Mean effective radius (swept area of the disc)**
CF = **coefficient of friction**

Before going further, lets explore the fundamentals of clutch operation. When you let the clutch pedal out, the diaphragm is putting maximum force on the disc, pressing it against the flywheel and the pressure plate. That means the disc and the splined transmission input shaft are the only components connected to the drive wheels and engine. The contact between the flywheel, which is bolted to the crankshaft, and the input shaft, which goes through the center of the disc, are the important areas of the clutch.

The equation indicates that the torque capacity of the clutch is dictated by the force, in pounds per square inch (psi), applied by the pressure plate, multiplied by the size of the swept area of the disc's friction face (which is not the entire area of the clutch disk). The flywheel's swept area value is multiplied by the number of clutch discs. For example, a twin-disc clutch has four friction surfaces (two for each disc), which doubles the torque capacity of the clutch. This is why multiple-disc clutches work so well for high-torque applications. Next, multiply the swept area by the coefficient of the clutch material, the product of which is divided by a constant (12).

From this equation, it follows that the things you can change to increase the torque capacity of the clutch are: 1. the clamp pressure of the pressure plate; 2. the surface of the clutch material (increase swept area); 3. the number of discs involved; and 4. the coefficient of friction of the clutch materials.

If the clutch you're looking at follows the physics discussed above, you're probably dealing with a reputable clutch maker. If not, you need

DRIVELINE

BD Diesel Performance manufacturers the FleX-Plate for Dodge Cummins 5.9-liter engine. The FleX-Plate is SFI approved, twice as thick as stock, and can handle 1,500 ft-lbs of torque. (Photo courtesy of DB Diesel Performance)

This cutaway of a Rockland Standard Gear Tranzilla T-56 shows some of the inner workings of a heavy-duty performance transmission. Rockland claims it can handle up to a 1,000 ft-lbs of torque. To triple the load capacity of a stock Tremec T-56, RSG installs 9310-alloy gears cut with a 22-degree Helix angle, teamed with a tough 9310 main shaft. (Photo courtesy of Rockland Standard Gear)

to keep shopping.

Following that logic, if you check out South Bend Clutch, you'll see that all of their products conform to the physics above. They have double-disc clutches with materials and clutch disc designs for sled pulling as well as street use. They sell clutches that'll handle up to 1,000 hp and support the higher clamping force packages with upgraded clutch pedal hydraulics. They also have input and output shaft upgrades.

Power Flow

In a manual transmission, the input shaft connects to a clutch gear that meshes with a counter gear shaft assembly. The rotation of the input is opposite that of the counter gear. In neutral, only the clutch and the counter gear are engaged, not the

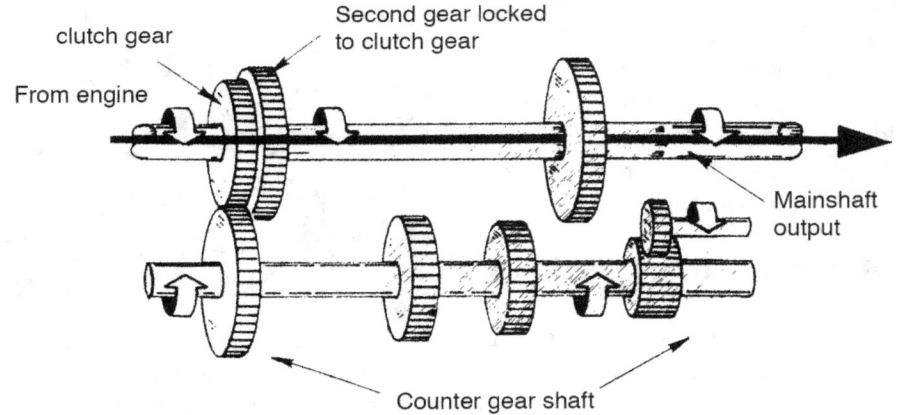

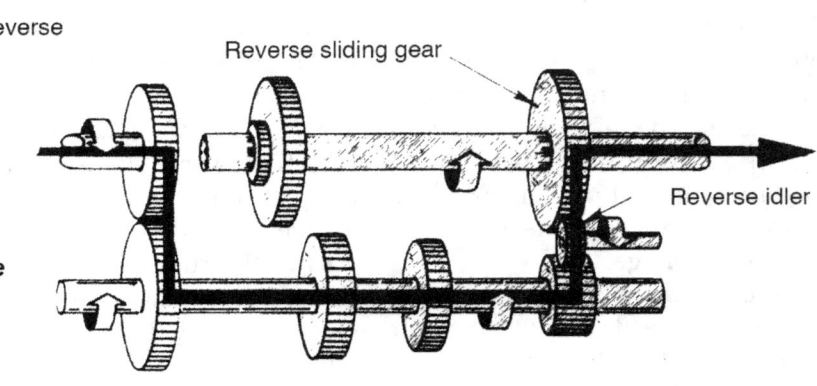

This diagram shows the power flow of a manual transmission in various gears. Notice how much stress is placed on the gear meshing points and the shafts. These are the prime areas that need reinforcing to build more torque capacity. (Photo courtesy of General Motors)

HIGH-PERFORMANCE DIESEL BUILDER'S GUIDE

output shaft.

In first gear, a large-diameter gear on the output shaft meshes with a smaller gear on the counter shaft. This arrangement multiplies the torque and transmits the power to the output shaft. Second gear uses the same principles, just with different gears for less torque multiplication for more distance per revolution, which is why it's harder to start out in second, but you can get up to a higher speed than in first.

That scenario is repeated until top gear, which is direct drive, meaning input rotation matches output rotation. Overdrive means output rotation is greater than input rotation. In direct drive, torque output equals engine input minus any inefficiencies, which on average are about 7.5 percent with a manual transmission, meaning that 92.5 percent of the energy input reaches the output shaft. The actual efficiency rates vary according to use, temperature, and of course, transmission. In addition, I'm splitting the difference between the trans and rear end, each of which loses some energy.

Automatic Transmissions

Most modern automatic transmissions are refinements of the traditional torque converter and hydraulically shifted 3-speed planetary gear-set combination. The shift points are controlled by engine load and vehicle speed by means of sensors and actuators tied into the engine management system. In addition, on newer diesel transmissions, slip sensors are employed to protect the transmission from damage.

Slip sensors work by comparing input shaft speed to output shaft speed calculated to an expected value given the current gear ratio. If

American Gear & Transmission offers a new heavy-duty replacement for the NV4500 5-speed transmission found in many Dodge trucks. This tranny comes with stronger gears and dual-cone synchronizers in first and second gears for smoother shifting. (Photo courtesy of American Gear & Transmission)

Towing is almost as demanding on the driveline as drag racing. If you're wheelin' a heavyweight rig, you'll need to enhance your transmission, and sometimes even your driveshaft and rear end. Bully Dog offers a turnkey performance built Allison 1000 with upgraded C1 through C4 clutch packs plus the main pressure and backflow valves. It also offers a super strong converter that uses dual-discs for the lock-up clutch. (Photo courtesy of Bully Dog)

the input shaft speed is too high, there's slip somewhere in the system, and the computer cuts fuel to reduce torque. This allows the friction materials in the trans to grab again once they can handle the torque load. Once the friction materials grab effectively, they can hold more torque. It takes less force to keep two surfaces sliding past each other than to get them sliding (think about keeping a burnout going versus getting one started!).

A planetary gear set consists of three main components—the sun gear, the planetary gears and carrier, and the ring gear. Each component can be the drive, be held stationary,

DRIVELINE

The Allison 1000 transmission mated to the 2006 and newer Duramax-equipped GM 2500 and 3500 pickups is a seriously stout stock transmission. When you start making more power you need to at least reprogram the computer to give it higher line pressure to provide more clamping force to the clutch packs. Banks, Bully Dog, Edge, Hypertech, and others can help you out in that department. (Photo courtesy of General Motors)

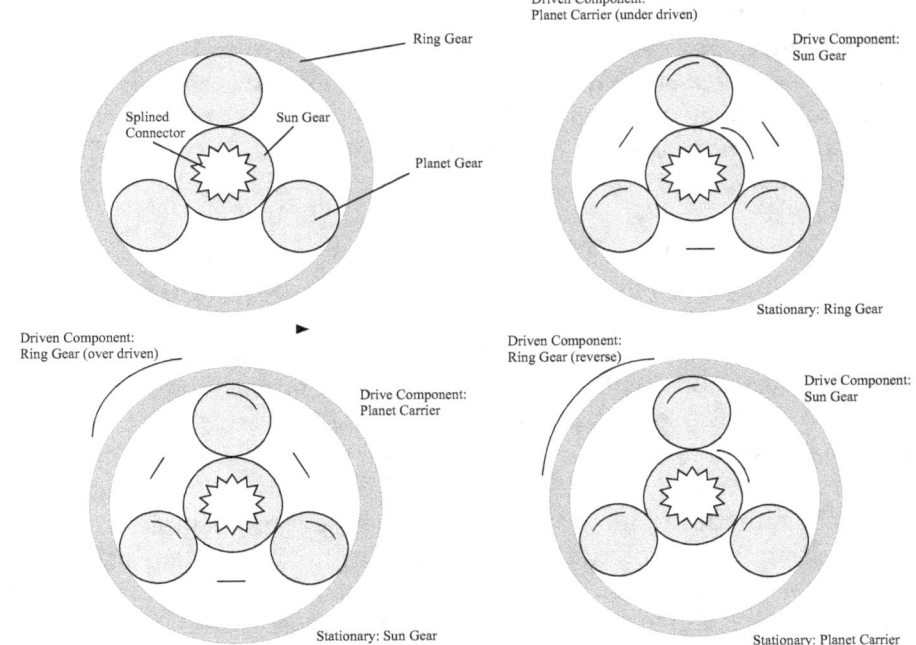

A planetary gear set consists of three main components: the sun gear, the planetary gears and carrier, and the ring gear. Each component can be the drive, it can be held stationary, or it can be driven. By holding one element stationary, then putting power to another, you can manage the direction of power flow as well as the power multiplication and potential output speed and power.

or be driven. By holding one element stationary, and then putting power to another, you can manage the direction of power flow, as well as the power multiplication and potential output speed and power.

Most automatic transmissions use bands to grip the ring gear and hold it stationary, while the clutch discs are pressurized to hold the planetary gears stationary. The sun gears are splined to an output shaft that can be the drive component or be driven, allowing the output of one other planetary gear set to manage another.

As cool and complicated as this design is, it does have weakness as far as transmitting power. Ultimately, the amount of force the trans is able to transmit is limited by the friction that stops the components of the planetary gear sets from rotating when you don't want them rotating. The way you increase the friction is by increasing the pressure and the coefficient of friction between the band or clutch material and the planetary gear set components. That is essentially what a transmission upgrade kit does.

Considering how much power diesel engines pump out, it's quite impressive how well modern automatic transmissions transfer power. They do need some protection, and that is why most have sensors to detect slip and derate the engine.

We won't cover a complete performance build of any one transmission, but let's go over the basics. Just as with a manual transmission, to hold more force you have to use stronger materials for the gears, input, and output shafts, as well as durable, higher-friction materials for the clutches and bands throughout the transmission. The same goes for the torque converter, though the housing material's strength is key to containing the pressures possible transferring and

HIGH-PERFORMANCE DIESEL BUILDER'S GUIDE

multiplying 1,000 ft-lbs of torque.

Let's first look at how the transmission multiplies the torque and power of your engine and allows you to use it conveniently and safely. For the most part your stock driveline and related components are well engineered for the average user. It's important for manufacturers to design a product that fills the needs of the broadest segment of users at the lowest cost to produce. The key to keeping customers happy is not having major components fail, so the transmission is built to perform reliably with the stock power rating. This includes protecting the transmission from input-shaft-bending, clutch-ripping torque that's all too easy to generate from a modern, four-valve per cylinder, common-rail-injected, electronically controlled diesel.

Sensing Slip

Modern vehicles sense transmission slip using a suite of sensors to monitor the engine and the transmission. Gale Banks believes that technology is most developed in systems using the Allison transmission behind the Duramax. The system monitors engine speed, current gear, and transmission input and output shaft speeds. This allows the computer to know if the torque converter is slipping and by what percent, or if the torque converter clutch is locked and whether or not it is slipping. By comparing input and output speeds, the system can tell if the clutch pack for that gear is slipping. Once it sees a predetermined percent slip, it pulls fuel out of the engine to lower output and prevent you from killing the transmission (and taking it back in for warranty work!).

Ford has this technology on its Torqueshift transmission. Early mod-

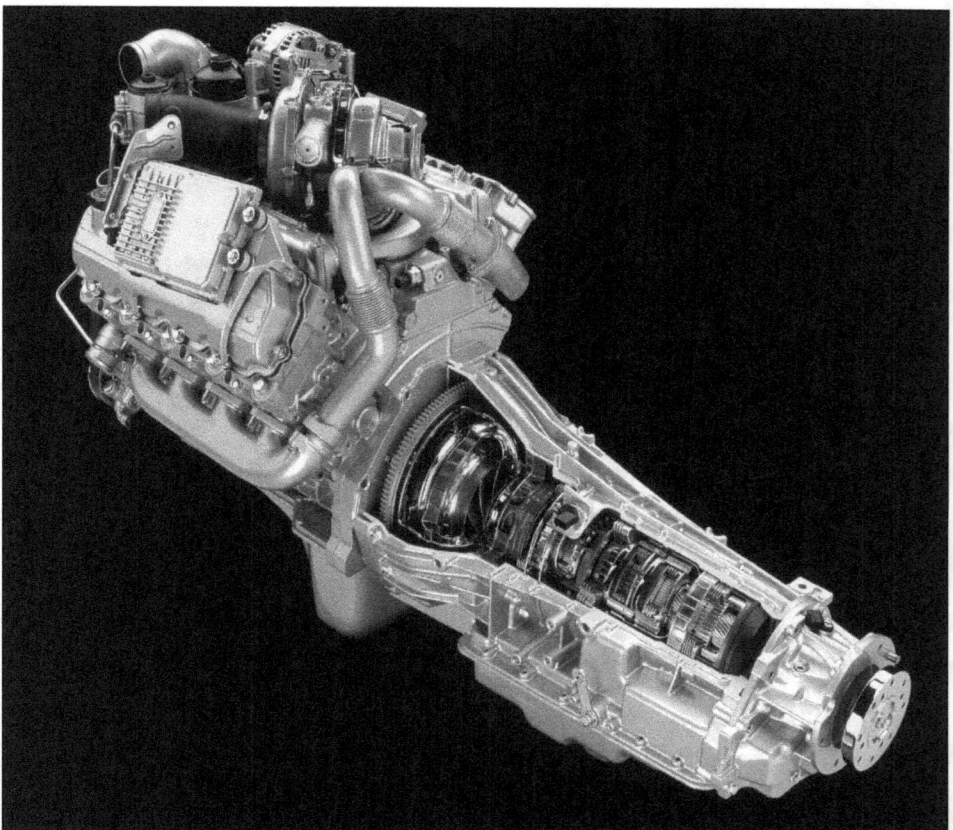

Here's a cutaway view of the Ford TorqueFlite 5-speed automatic behind a 7.3-liter Powerstroke. You can get a sense that this older TorqueFlite won't handle the torque that some of the newer trannys do. The narrow case indicates the girth of the planetary gears within. A larger diameter makes room for larger gears that have more leverage and more surface area for the clutch packs. (Photo courtesy of Ford)

els monitor only engine and output shaft speeds, and so cannot isolate slip in specific gears. The new Torqueshift ('06–'07) has everything the Allison does. Dodge will certainly have it on its 48RE 4-speed automatic overdrive transmission.

Banks Command Centers and power tuner interfaces allow you to control other aspects of the driveline, such as the transmission clutch engagement and line pressures to help you protect your transmission. Most of the other programmers on the market, such as those offered from Hypertech, Edge, EFIlive, HP Tuners, and Bully Dog, have similar abilities, such as the ability to raise line pressure and hold more torque.

Gearing

Because of the flat torque curve of a diesel engine combined with a limited RPM range, the driveline gearing is much different than that usually paired with an equal-sized gas engine. For example, the Cummins in the Dodge Ram makes over 350 ft-lbs when idling, but has a limited engine speed of around 3,200 rpm. This means that you need gears chosen to not only multiply torque but to provide vehicle speed at a relatively low RPM. Let's face it, a 3,200 rpm redline means the engine's cruise RPM is only half of that, and

DRIVELINE

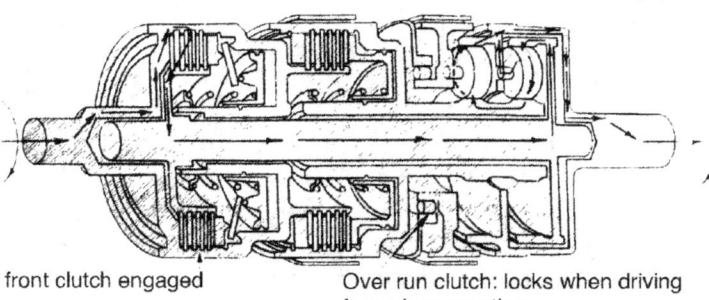

front clutch engaged — Over run clutch: locks when driving free when coasting

Power flow: first gear

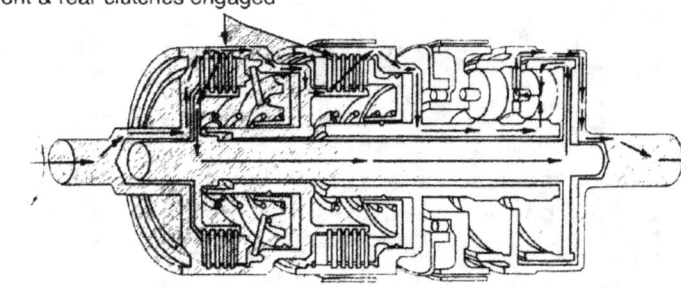

Front & rear clutches engaged

Power flow: high gear

Comparing the power flow through an automatic in different gears gives you an idea of how the bands and clutch packs are used to hold the various components of a planetary gear set. This is done to manage torque output and vehicle speed. (Photo courtesy of TorqueFlite)

In this exploded view of a 5.9-liter Cummins Banks' billet torque converter we can see the engineering that increases the load capacity. The forged steel multi-disc clutch housing is much stronger than the stock unit and can hold more pressure and therefore more torque. The turbine and impeller are redesigned to increase strength and efficiency. (Photo courtesy of Gale Banks Engineering)

you're not going to be rolling much faster than a farm tractor with a 1:1 top gear running through a set of 4:10 final drive gears at 1,600 rpm.

So a diesel needs gears. Dodge offers a 6-speed manual with its Cummins and a 4-speed automatic. You really need six speeds with a manual because it doesn't have the advantage of the torque multiplication of a torque converter. The automatics behind the Ford and GM diesels are 5-speeds. A 5-speed automatic is a better choice for a diesel than a 4-speed automatic, because a 5-speed is better able to use the available engine power, under the curve so to speak, over a wider vehicle

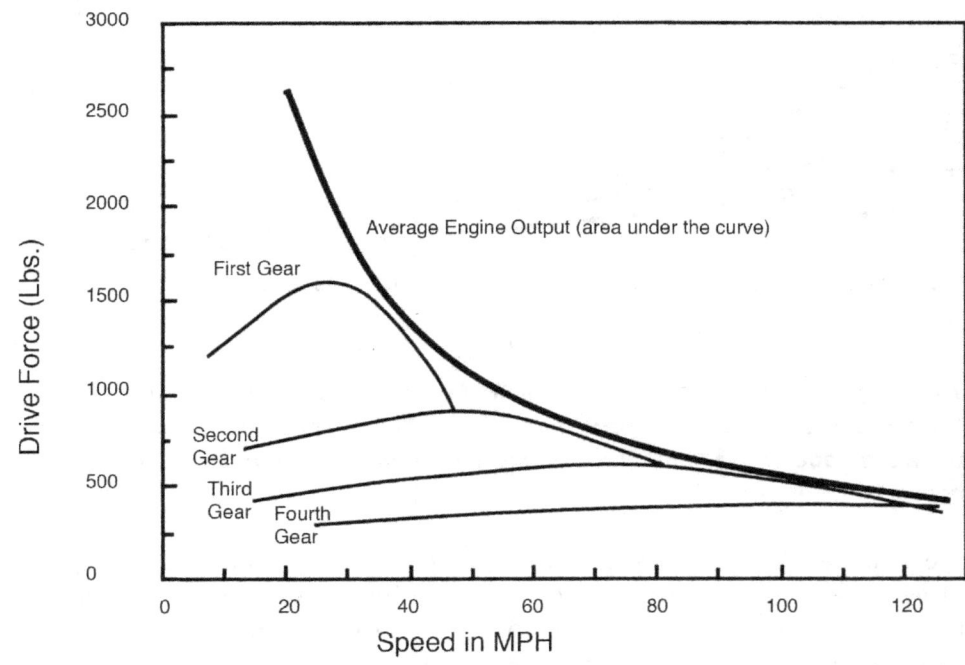

By presenting the torque multiplication compared to vehicle speed for each gear and stacking them together, we can get an average output and a reasonable map of the vehicle's performance potential.

Diesel Torque Curves

Pickup truck diesels are typically designed with flat torque curves. This design gives less torque at peak than the engine might otherwise make, and also gives a horsepower curve that rises with RPM, similar to that of a gasoline engine. The reasoning is that the drivetrain components cannot handle the massive torque that the diesel engine could be designed to make, and that horsepower, being a function of torque and RPM, can be increased to the desired level with RPM, without needing to design in too much torque. It is also easier to control emissions if less torque and fueling are brought in at lower RPM.

Traditional diesels, in contrast, typically are of "high-torque-rise" design. That means that as RPM is dragged down with a load, torque increases substantially, down to the RPM of peak torque (which is often lower in the RPM range). Such diesels have flatter horsepower curves, and are therefore less sensitive to gearing. Their HP does not drop so much as RPM decreases. By its very definition in physics, HP gets the work done. People talk a lot about the torque of the diesel, when it would be more accurate to talk about the high horsepower at low RPM that results from the high torque. If a gas engine makes the same HP at double or three times the RPM, it can pull a heavy load, so long as it can be geared to stay in its power band, and can hold up to the strain. Of course, it will probably get much poorer fuel mileage than a diesel, and obviously won't have the flexibility of the diesel's broad torque band.

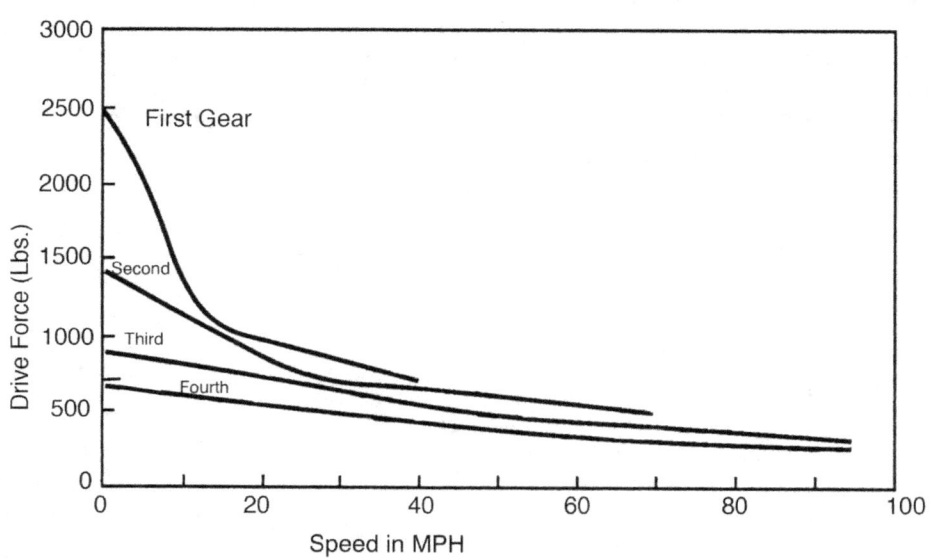

This diagram shows the torque multiplication curves of an automatic transmission. Notice that torque is multiplied the most at zero speed. This is the advantage of the fluid coupling and torque multiplication that a torque converter offers.

speed range. The transmission is a set of gears (levers really) that multiply torque and convert engine speed to road speed. Higher gears (less engine RPM; more wheel RPM) let the vehicle go faster than it could otherwise.

Gearing is like a lever arm. The lower gears (numerically higher, with higher torque multiplication) position the fulcrum away from the engine, so to speak. So the engine spins more revolutions per foot traveled, just like the longer side of the lever arm travels farther to multiply the force on the other side of the fulcrum (like a long-handled wrench or ratchet). As the transmission shifts to higher gears, the fulcrum moves closer to the engine, i.e. the distance traveled per RPM is greater than before, but with less torque multiplication, and on it goes for each gear.

The point of the fulcrum analogy is this: as you move the fulcrum closer to the engine side, i.e. the side you're pushing on to raise a load, it requires much more effort. The transmission experiences the same reverse force multiplication. The driveline components after the transmission (the U-joints, driveshaft, axles, and rear gears) experience stress between the fulcrum and the load that is being lifted. So if the engine and transmission generate more torque, all these parts need to be able to transfer the power and force without bending or breaking. This is not an easy task, which is why most diesels come with relatively heavy-duty components.

The upshot of this is that the

DRIVELINE

Swapping in an aftermarket valve body, like this one for the Allison transmission from BD Diesel Performance, gives you increased clutch clamping force, prevents slipping, and improves the durability of your transmission. (Photo courtesy of BD Diesel Performance)

stress of the force of accelerating the vehicle, or maintaining road speed against a grade, is far greater for the transmission in higher gears than in lower ones. This explains why the clutch is more likely to slip in top gear than in lower gears and why the aftermarket is offering multi-disc clutches in its lock-up converters.

Those are the components under the most stress in the transmission. They tend to fail first and most often, so there is more demand for replacement parts and upgrades. That's why the torque converter is the aftermarket's favorite upgrade component for automatic transmission diesels, while stronger clutches are popular for manual transmissions.

The driveshaft and U-joints and final gear components are in the middle between the torque multiplication of the engine and the contact patch of the tire. These are relatively easy to replace, so people often consider replacing these items with stronger units if you've added power. At what power level you need to upgrade your driveline components depends on how strong your stock components are and how you use your vehicle. Don't be surprised if things start to wear down once you're making a ton of extra power. You can work with a local driveline shop; if that's not an option you have to find one that'll work with you through the mail. Inland Empire Driveline Service in Ontario, California, is a good place to start your shopping.

Gearing and Performance

In addition to managing internal forces, driveline gearing can aid or inhibit performance. Gearing that increases torque multiplication improves acceleration rates and tow weight ratings. Factory diesel gearing is not optimized for quarter-mile acceleration. Instead, it's optimized for tow rating, fuel efficiency, and believe it or not, emissions.

As for quarter-mile performance, there are a couple of equations that Chrysler factory drag racing engineers developed in the '60s and '70s that provide a good estimation of the optimum gearing for quickest ETs. Even though gasoline engines and diesels have much different power curves, in the final analysis, Newton's second law governs acceleration: mass multiplied by acceleration equals force.

Mass x Acceleration = Force

In John Lawlor's *Auto Math Handbook*, he notes that Larry Shepard, a former engineer for Chrysler's Mopar Performance, developed a couple of useful formulas that help determine optimum gearing for quarter-mile acceleration. To use the formula, you need to have a realistic estimate of the potential speed your vehicle can achieve in the quarter. Fortunately, the "Dodge Boys" came up with that as well.

Geoffery T. Fox articulated the experimental work in an article in 1973 in the *American Journal of Physics* titled "On the Physics of Drag Racing." In it he detailed the physics of drag racing based on Newton's Laws. The equations took forms useful to drag racers, in that instead of describing a universal relationship between mass, acceleration, and force, they isolated horsepower, speed, and time to distance with the following equations:

$HP = (mph / 230)^3 \times weight$
$MPH = (hp/weight)^{1/3} \times 230$

CHAPTER 8

$ET = (weight/hp)^{1/3} \times 6.269$

Here's how the horsepower equation works out on our trusty Duramax crew cab example:

Stock power: 360 hp @ 3,200 rpm
Weight: 5,600 lbs

Substituting the horsepower and vehicle weight in the mph equation we get:

$MPH = (360/5,600)^{1/3} \times 230 = 92.14$

With that, we can use Larry Shepard's formula to find optimum gearing for quarter-mile acceleration:

Optimum gearing = tire diameter/335 x rpm/mph

Tire diameter is 30 inches, so:

$(30/335) \times (3,200/92.14) = 3.11:1$

The stock Allison transmission gear ratios and effective ratios (which equal transmission gearing multiplied by the rear end gears) for

Allison Gear Ratios

Gear	Ratio	Effective
1	3.1:1	11.563:1
2	1.81:1	6.7513:1
3	1.41:1	5.2593:1
4	1:1	3.73:1
5	0.71:1	2.6483:1
Rear End	3.73:1	

each gear:

When we do the math, we find that a 3:11:1 gear ratio is called for. But when we check the chart we find that we're not even close with the stock setup. Fourth is too low; fifth is too high. We could change gear ratios in the transmission (expensive), or change the final drive ratio (moderately expensive but pre-

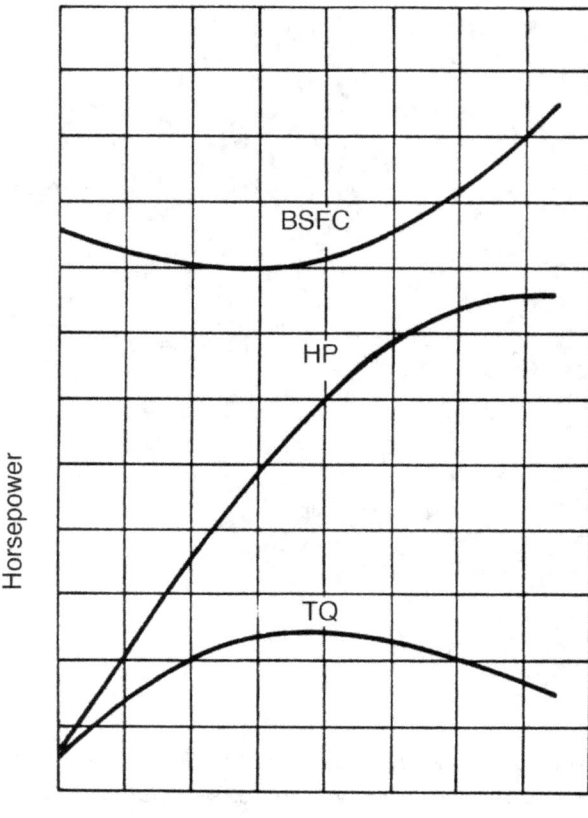

When making gearing choices, you want to consider the power band and fuel consumption curves. This is a theoretical curve, but you can put one together for your combination on a chassis dyno if you really want to get your combo right. The idea is to run your truck at an RPM where you make good power without wasting too much fuel.

ferred). Finally, for a temporary tuning tactic for recreational drag racing, we can change tire size.

Playing with the above formula reveals that a 35-inch-tall tire requires a 3.63:1 gear ratio, which is very close to the gearing in fourth at 3.73:1. This means you should reach your highest speed in fourth gear at the finish of the quarter-mile.

Gearing and Fuel Efficiency

Unfortunately, choosing gear ratios to get the best quarter-mile performance does not give you the best fuel efficiency. The performance ratio increases the work output of the driveline by keeping the engine in its power band. When an engine operates in that manner, it's using all the fuel it's capable of using. It's not sipping fuel just to overcome friction and road loads.

The gearing choice that gets the best fuel economy will keep the engine at a point that its brake specific fuel consumption (BSFC) is lowest. BSFC is usually expressed as pounds of fuel per horsepower hour. This unit means that under the operating conditions the engine is using one-pound of fuel every hour to generate one horsepower. Diesel engines tend to have the least BSFC near the torque peak. Therefore, gearing choices should be made to keep the engine at the RPM where it uses the least amount of fuel to generate the required power to maintain vehicle speed.

How you use your vehicle, normal cruising speed, and the size of your tires are the most influential in determining the gearing for best fuel mileage. The stock Duramax's torque peak is 650 ft-lbs at 1,600 rpm, so you should get the best mileage possible for the gearing at that RPM.

Obviously, you get the best mileage in the highest gear, since the vehicle's distance traveled per engine revolution will be greatest. So the mileage gearing priority has to be given to top gear.

The equation for choosing the most efficient cruising speed given the most efficient RPM is:

Ideal cruising speed = RPM x tire diameter/gear ratio x 336

The constant 336 is the simplification of the equation to factor out the need to multiply engine RPM by 60 to get the revs per hour. Here's how GM arranged it on the stock Duramax crew cab:

Ideal cruising speed = 1,600 x 30/(.71 x 3.73 x 336) = 53.94 mph

We can say therefore that the GM engineers chose the truck's driveline ratios to make the truck most fuel efficient at 54 mph. That's a very good choice because above 55 mph, aerodynamic drag grows increasingly strong requiring more fuel to push through the air, which further decreases fuel efficiency. In addition, since the torque peak is at this speed and RPM, the truck will have the best towing performance here as well.

Gearing and Emissions

While we're talking about gearing, we have to discuss its effect on emissions. As we discussed above, the drivetrain's torque multiplication is analogous to a lever arm and a fulcrum. Higher gears, those ratios giving more distance per engine revolution, move the fulcrum toward the engine. So while the distance traveled per engine revolution is greater, so is the force needed to move the lever. This is another way of saying there is less torque multiplication.

The lower level of torque multiplication not only stresses driveline components, it also feeds back into the combustion chamber in the form of higher cylinder pressure for a given output. NOx formation is the chemical byproduct of diesel combustion most sensitive to cylinder pressure. For example, an SAE test performed at the Fiat Research Facility in Turin, Italy, found that changing the final drive ratio from 2.6:1 to 2.8:1 resulted in a significant increase in NOx, in contrast to HC and CO, which showed only a very slight increase.

At the time of publication, there are no emissions testing programs required for diesels. However, if diesels keep taking market share, it wouldn't be surprising to see some sort of emissions testing become mandatory. If that occurs, gearing may be one of the things tested. This could be a nightmare scenario, especially if you lift and upgrade your rig with over-sized rolling stock and other goodies. The upside is that nobody thinks this will happen in the next few years.

Fluid Cooling

If you upgrade your engine to make more power, accelerate quicker, or pull a heavier load up steeper grades, your driveline will generate more heat because it's not 100-percent efficient. The driveline loss (work not used in force multiplication) is a measure of the energy turned into heat instead of driving the vehicle.

If left unchecked, the heat in the transmission and rear end will cause the fluids to overheat and eventually lose their lubricating qualities. So if you're in a situation where you're putting more heat into the transmission or rear end than

A deep-sump transmission pan like this Ford pan from BD Diesel Performance gives you extra fluid capacity to keep temps down. The finned aluminum construction dissipates more heat than the stock pan and is more structurally rigid. (Photo courtesy of BD Diesel Performance)

they can reject on their own, you have to change your mix of components. Sometimes solving your problem is as simple as upgrading the lubricating fluids to meet the operating conditions, while sometimes you'll need to retro-fit or fabricate a heat exchanger/fluid cooler.

If you've opted for the full towing package with all the trans and oil coolers and whatever else needs to be cooled, you're probably okay in this area provided the added cooling capacity is up to spec for your towing/performance needs. If not, you can go to the aftermarket and add even more cooling capacity.

Transmission and rear end heat exchangers can be as simple as a finned transmission pan or rear end cover, or as elaborate as a fluid-to-air radiator. It depends on how hard you're running and where. Remember, high altitude work requires more cooling capacity because there is less air mass to carry away the heat. Finned covers work by conducting heat from the fluid to the atmosphere. The fins increase the surface area in contact with air moving over them to better transfer the heat.

CHAPTER 8

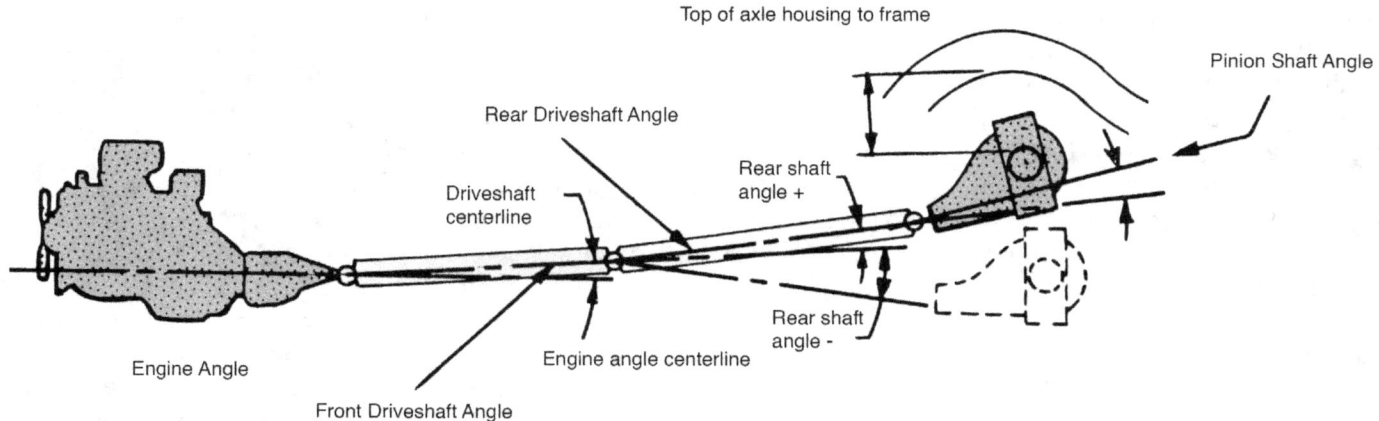

When you lift, lower, or otherwise modify your truck's suspension, you need to be aware of the proper driveline alignment. Each manufacturer has specific driveline angles, so you need to get them from a factory manual or from a reputable shop.

Radiators do the same thing. The tubes have a lot of thin fins that serve to contact the air to transfer heat by conduction.

Driveline Alignment and Balance

This chapter closes with a few comments on alignment and balance. The balance part should be intuitive: If all the little imbalances and tolerances in your driveshaft assembly aren't held within a very narrow range, it's going to vibrate—sometimes violently enough to rip itself apart.

What's a little less understood is the alignment of each driveline component. For example, the pinion angle typical of most trucks does not align the driveshaft. Nor does the transmission centerline align with the centerline of the driveshaft. Why? Because as the system is loaded, i.e. you're in gear and accelerating a fully loaded rig up a grade, the torque moves these components around. In response, engineers have found the amount that the driveline components deflect under the normal power curve and use. They position the components so that when they deflect under load, they become aligned in a way that produces the least amount of vibration and transfers power most efficiently.

Therefore, after increasing engine output, it's not that uncommon for the driveline to produce vibrations that it didn't before. The solution varies, but can include shimming the components a few fraction of a degree, installing stiffer engine and transmission mounts, using different rate springs and shocks, repositioning driveshaft support mounts, rebalancing the driveshaft, and more. This is an area that can drive you crazy, especially since each truck is different.

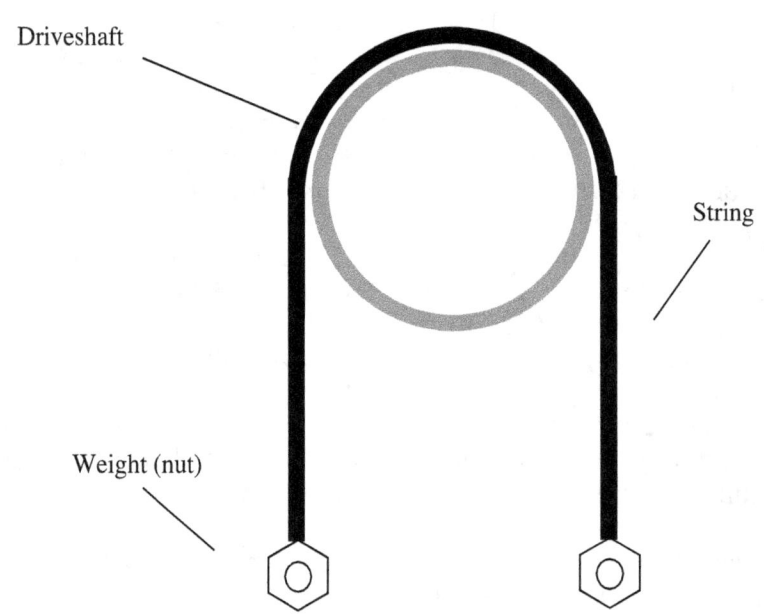

Checking to be sure your driveshafts are straight or properly aligned can be difficult. One easy inspection method is to tie a weight to each end of a string. Make several units. Hang them over the shafts and use them as plumb lines to judge the alignment of the driveshafts.

Advice from Around the Industry

As I've been detailing throughout this book, getting more power from your diesel engine requires moving more air mass and more fuel mass through the engine. Burning more air and fuel generates higher cylinder temperatures and pressures for higher engine power output. Fortunately, aftermarket support for today's turbo diesel engines makes building power almost too easy: super efficient intakes, exhaust, intercoolers, programmers, fuel pumps, injectors, and turbos. There's more and more available every day. All it takes is money, the correct parts, and knowing how to tune it.

To further reinforce the points I've made in this book, I posed a series of questions about the proper sequence of upgrading a turbo diesel to Petery Treydte, Director of Technical Communications at Gale Banks Engineering; Justin McCarthy, Technical Manager of Bully Dog Technologies; Brian Roth of BD Power; Matt Bozarth of ATS Diesel; and Max Lagod, owner owner Hypermax Engineering. For the most part the industry is in agreement as to the overall approach to building power. However, there are some divergent opinions on the order of upgrades, and in the area of modifying turbochargers. I'm of the opinion that each of the sources I consulted is knowledgeable and credible. The differing views probably arise from each firms experience with various combinations and approaches. I suggest you shop intelligently and ask a lot of questions before you buy. In the meantime, here are their comments:

JP: What is the most cost and performance effective sequence for upgrading a turbo diesel engine?

Peter Treydte, Gale Banks Engineering: Diesel upgrades have become a very personalized arena and everybody has an opinion about the best methods and products to use to improve the performance of their vehicle. There are many issues that can affect an individual's choices regarding the order in which modifications should be done, including: budget, performance improvement, impact on fuel economy, and even the make of the vehicle.

Generally speaking, a ram-air intake is a good first modification to make because it's relatively low cost, easy to install, and gives a moderate improvement in fuel economy and power. Improving airflow into the engine is logically followed by a free-flowing Monster Exhaust to allow the air out of the engine. After these two modifications, a Six-Gun tuner is the next logical step. An increase in airflow means that fuel can now be safely

To borrow a line from a legendary off-road documentary, on any Sunday you can find daily driven pumped-up diesel rigs drag racing at a Diesel Hot Rod Association (DHRA) event. (Photo courtesy of DHRA)

Sled pulling competition is a popular venue to prove your truck's power and your driving skills. Building a high-performance sled puller is different than building a 100-percent street truck, so make sure you look before you leap. (Photo courtesy of DHRA)

Advice from Around the Industry continued...

added to the engine for dramatic power increases. Those that are serious about achieving the maximum potential from their engine should next consider an intercooler upgrade for increased air density.

Turbocharger, injector, and fuel pump upgrades should only be considered by serious racers and are the most costly upgrades. These types of modifications require customized fuel tuning for optimum results.

Justin McCarthy, Bully Dog Technologies: My order of preference is electronics, intake, exhaust, injectors, fuel pump, and then intercooler. Combinations producing less than 600 hp generally do not need an intercooler upgrade and turbo upgrades are usually not needed at power levels below 500 hp. Electronics, intakes, and exhausts are the most cost effective parts for your daily driven truck. If you want to build a truck for sled pulling or drag racing, then you'll need to upgrade injectors, turbo, fuel pump, as well as adding a heavy-duty transmission, larger head bolts, and propane or water methanol injection. After those components are installed and tuned, you could add the intercooler.

Max Lagod, HyperMax Technologies: I tell my customers the first 100 hp is relatively inexpensive; it's the second 100 hp that costs real money. We have a good reliable package for the Ford 6-liter engine that includes an exhaust, an electronic module, and a bigger intercooler. That puts them in the range of 485 hp. The next phase is to enhance reliability. The Fords don't have the best track record for head gaskets. So we have performance head gasket sets. Next is stepping up on the injectors and a turbo upgrade then you have a package that's reliable while making power above the 500-hp level. Realistically, a 6-liter can make 625 hp with an electronics package, turbo upgrade, injectors, intercooler, and exhaust. But then you need to get a transmission that can handle that.

Matt Bozarth, ATS Diesel: The best route to go when adding performance is to start with base components that will help to support the upgraded power. This would mean that a good course of action might be (in this order): exhaust system, intake kit, turbo kit, intercooler, fuel system upgrade, electronic tuner/module, and fuel injectors. Having too much fuel or too much power without the supporting pieces makes for unusable performance, not to mention blown-up stock parts.

Brian Roth, BD Power: As with a gasoline performance engine, the best first steps are the simple ones that lay the foundation for getting more air/fuel into the engine, and more exhaust out. We recommend starting off with our X-Intake cold-air intake package and one of our X-Hale performance exhaust systems. The next popular step is to add a performance module, like our X-Tuner for the Dodge-Cummins or Ford Power Stroke, and our Intimidator module for the Duramax. Once you start changing the stock fuel curve, we highly recommend the use of a monitoring system, such as our X-Monitor or new X2 monitor.

JP: Does make and model year influence the sequence?

Peter Treydte: The order of modification upgrades may vary slightly depending on the year and make of the vehicle, but the general guidelines are predominately accurate. For instance, the factory intercooler on a 1998–2002 Dodge is a relatively good design from the factory and upgrading it may not be cost effective except for the most extreme racers.

At drag strips around the country, the diesel-powered tow rig is more likely a race vehicle, too. Mild Mustangs and Camaros hate lining up against well-tuned diesels. (Photo courtesy of DHRA)

Advice from Around the Industry continued...

Justin McCarthy: You cannot add engine electronics to some of the older models, other than that the sequence above would stay the same.

Max Lagod: All of the 6.0-liter Fords are the same. I tell my customers if you've installed a chip and you start bumping the power up, you should at least put a pyrometer in the truck to keep track of the exhaust temp, which is the number one killer of these engines. If you don't do anything else, at least you can see that towing that trailer with your foot to the floor is causing the exhaust to heat way up. I've been keeping our customers with our Mach 7 module in the range of 1,200 to 1,300 degrees Fahrenheit by defueling at 1,300. That seems to be the magic number to keep the exhaust valves, pistons, and turbochargers alive. Above that, the turbos start glowing and eventually pieces start coming off them and out the tailpipe. Even with the older 6.9- and 7.3-liter IDI engines, we set them at 1,250 degrees and they tow all day.

The older IDI engines are all mechanical upgrades. We sell turbo kits to get the air to the engine. We add fuel by turning the right screws on the mechanical fuel pump.

Matt Bozarth: The sequence can vary somewhat from truck to truck and year to year. For example, the automatic transmission on a later-model Dodge (2003+) or on a Duramax will handle slightly more horsepower and torque than an older Dodge or Ford truck. With 6.0-liter Power Strokes, ATS utilizes our E-Power tuner along with the transmission upgrades since it also remaps the transmission parameters for improved shifting and pressure control.

Later trucks may need different fuel system modifications versus an earlier model. With earlier 12-valve Cummins trucks, the P7100 pump can be modified to flow large quantities of fuel, whereas the common rail motor will need our Twin CP3 system to match the fuel volume.

With some trucks such as the 6.0-liter Power Stroke, the need to upgrade the turbo can present itself much earlier. Many times the turbo update is essential due to failure of the stock variable turbo.

Brain Roth: An engine is an engine—it doesn't care how the fuel is delivered so long as it gets there. However, the method changes. For example, earlier Cummins engines would employ modifications to the injection pump such as our Fuel Stop Plate, (instead of an X-Tuner) as well as 3,000-rpm governor spring kits. For some extra performance above the electronic modules, we also offer larger injectors that flow more fuel.

The black smoke mean lots of fuel available for a steep hit of nitrous. You often see the smoke clean up just after the launch when a diesel drag racer hits the nitrous button. (Photo courtesy of DHRA)

If you have a Cummins, we would also recommend our Pulse cast iron exhaust manifold, and if you have a Duramax, we would recommend our Full Bore driver's side exhaust manifold that replaces the pinched-down factory unit.

JP: When are turbo upgrades necessary?

Peter Treydte: The need for turbocharger upgrades is partially dependent on the age of the vehicle and partially dependent on the needs of the vehicle owner. Older trucks such as early model Dodge Cummins and Ford Power Strokes used non-wastegated turbos that might benefit from a smaller turbine housing and the addition of a wastegate. Later-model trucks with variable geometry turbos may not need to be upgraded for most purposes. Hardcore racing enthusiasts are often looking toward compound turbo systems to build massive amounts of boost.

Advice from Around the Industry continued...

Justin McCarthy: The turbo is one of the last things to mess with. If anyone is looking for a really good setup with out spending a whole lot of time and money, you should just look at engine electronics, an air intake, an exhaust, with a little bit of transmission modifications—that is what most people are looking for.

Max Lagod: The variable geometry turbocharger on the Ford 6.0-liter is tough to match. You get the best of both worlds: a tight housing for good bottom end throttle response; but when you're making lots of horsepower, the vanes open up to reduce back pressure. Some guys don't like them because they say they stick, but my experience is that if you don't run them real hot for a long time, they don't stick.

Where I find I can offer my customers a performance gain is with work on the compressor side. We have a custom wheel and housing we're developing that provides the airflow rates to handle upgraded fuel delivery rates above 500 hp.

Matt Bozarth: When performing more than a mild upgrade, the turbo does become ineffective. When the turbo was originally matched to the factory truck, airflow and map ranges were determined based on stock fuel and power output. With increased power it becomes important to complement the extra fuel with more air.

Brian Roth: First off, above a 100- to 120-hp increase, we always recommend transmission modifications. In most instances, we have found that the torque converter clutches will begin to slip, resulting in torque converter shudder. We recommend a BD-modified valve body and a BD heavy-duty torque converter minimum. If you plan further mods later on (and most people do), we recommend a complete transmission assembly, along with our torque converter. In Dodge applications, the stock flex plate should be replaced with our billet steel Black FleX-Plate, which can handle up to 1,500 ft-lbs of torque. A lot of enthusiasts don't realize that even a mildly modified Cummins can crack or disintegrate the stock flex plate.

Only after reinforcing the driveline do we recommend turbo upgrades. BD offers single- and twin-turbo systems for the Dodge Cummins, our SuperMax single turbo upgrade for the Duramax, and our PowerFull single turbo upgrade for the 6.0 Power Stroke are our most popular systems.

We feel it is very important for enthusiasts to understand that an upgraded turbo is probably the best thing you can do for your engine. Adding more fuel to a diesel engine (with a module, injectors, or both) has the opposite effect compared with a gasoline engine; adding more diesel alone causes it to run hotter with higher EGTs. The stock turbo is at or near its performance threshold from the factory, so it simply can't move enough air to compensate for the added fuel. By adding a larger turbo, airflow can keep pace with the added fuel. EGT's go down, and power levels go way up! Not only that, but exhaust smoke on acceleration is dramatically reduced (because the added fuel can actually be burned now) and fuel economy typically increases as well. Contrary to popular belief, a larger turbo won't affect low-speed drivability, if it is engineered for diesel applications like BD/BorgWarner turbos. These units use BorgWarner's extended-tip technology that helps the turbo spool up quickly at low RPM, and deliver strong mid and top-end power as well. A turbo diesel can perform as well on the track as it does towing a trailer when set up properly with the correct combination of parts.

JP: Do you recommend modifying the wastegate, housing, compressor wheels, or turbine wheels?

Peter Treydte: Each engine configuration may have different needs and therefore different upgrades may be effective. For instance, the 1989–1993 Dodge Cummins utilized a non-wastegated turbine housing with a relatively large turbine housing. The Banks Quick-Turbo provides dramatic improvements in acceleration by using a smaller, wastegated turbine housing. The 2000–2003 Ford Power Stroke has a compressor wheel that goes into a surge condition with relatively minor power modifications, a condition that is remedied by using the Banks High-Boost compressor wheel. Each turbo is unique to its application, and therefore there is not one specific "fix" that works for all cases.

Advice from Around the Industry continued...

Diesel engines out-torque gas engines, but diesel drag racers haven't figured out how to make them quite as quick as their spark-ignited cousins—yet. This awesome Sheid Diesel dragster ran the quarter mile in 7.55 seconds at 183 mph. (Photo courtesy of DHRA)

Justin McCarthy: Upgrade the whole turbo.

Max Lagod: I recommend the compressor side upgrades we talked about earlier.

Matt Bozarth: The recommended upgrades depend on what truck is being modified. On 1995.5–2002 7.3-liter Power Strokes, an upgraded compressor housing can make an amazing difference. With most other trucks the difference in performance is negligible until the complete turbo is upgraded, such as one of the Aurora Series turbos. Going this route provides better performance in all areas such as: airflow volume, reduction in EGTs, stronger bearings, better flowing housings, and improved compression ratios.

Brain Roth: Modifications to stock turbos are available, but the improvements are very small. Turbochargers are a matched set of components, and when you change one part of the puzzle to gain in one area of the curve, you can lose it elsewhere. Not to mention the fact that turbochargers use very small tolerances and are very sensitive to dirt—so if someone "modifies" your turbo with a different housing, etc., you could be opening yourself up for big-time trouble. It's much better, and safer, to go with an engineered turbo system.

Diesel drag racing is truly a grassroots, "run what you brung," sport. Check out the DHRA sidebar in Chapter 10 for a little more info. (Photo courtesy of DHRA)

CHAPTER 9

GM DIESEL ENGINES

GM's first attempt at a passenger car diesel was a dismal failure. In the late 1970s, GM designed a diesel engine based on the venerable Oldsmobile gasoline-powered 350-ci small-block. The structure couldn't take the pounding of early diesel technology. Two major limitations were the cast crankshaft (GM had dropped the Olds forging facility in 1967) and the use of only four head bolts around each cylinder, which wasn't too bad for a non-turbocharged diesel, but the lack of a turbo seriously limited power output. I'm not aware of any aftermarket support for this engine.

1982 to 2000: 6.2- and 6.5-Liter Turbo Diesel

The company's second attempt came in the early '80s with the 6.2-liter diesel engine. The 6.2-liter naturally aspirated diesel V-8 was built by GM's Detroit Diesel division and was introduced in the 1982 model year in C/K pickup trucks, as well as later in the infamous military Hummer H1.

In 1992, GM increased the size of the 6.2 to 6.5 liters and added a turbocharger, but the 6.2 liter was still produced until 1993. The 6.2- and 6.5-liter diesels were optional from 1982 through 2000 in the full line of Chevrolet and GMC C/K series pickup trucks, Suburbans, full-size Blazer/Jimmy, Tahoe/Yukon, vans, and motor homes.

The 6.5 liter was used through 2000 in GM light-trucks, when it was replaced by the new Duramax line. It's interesting that the 6.5-liter turbo

Duramax engines have proven quite powerful and modifiable. Their modern injection and electronic systems make it easy for owners to add a little more fuel using an aftermarket tuner. (Photo courtesy of DHRA)

GM DIESEL ENGINES

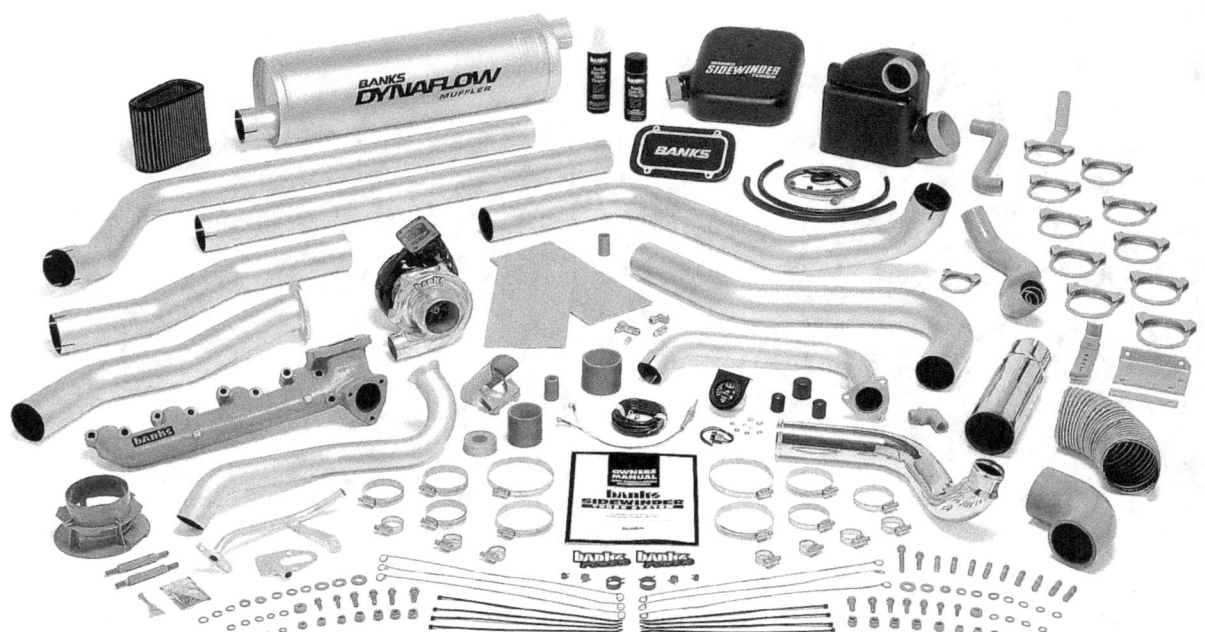

Banks offers a turbo kit for the 6.2-liter diesel. The engine powered a variety of GM pickups and trucks from 1982 to 1993 when the 6.5-liter turbo diesel variant came on line. (Photo courtesy of Gale Banks Engineering)

diesel remained in production for use in the Hummer H1 military vehicles. Because of the huge production numbers and relatively low cost, the 6.5 liter has historically been a popular power unit for custom applications, low-production models, or small-market off-road vehicles and the like.

The 6.5 liter also powered a range of light commercial trucks from 1996 until it was replaced with the new Duramax 6.6-liter in 2001. The later years of the 6.5 saw a turbocharged version available in the GMC Sierra and Chevrolet Silverado. The 1999 L65 turbo diesel produced 215 hp at 4,300 rpm and 440 ft-lbs of torque at 1,800 rpm. It used an electronically controlled high-pressure rotary injection pump with a max engine speed of 3,400 rpm. It was equipped with a catalytic converter, EGR, and PCV emission controls. You could choose between a manual 5-speed and the 4L80-E 4-speed automatic transmissions.

The primary weakness of the 6.2 and 6.5 seems to be the bottom ends. The main bearings fail and the

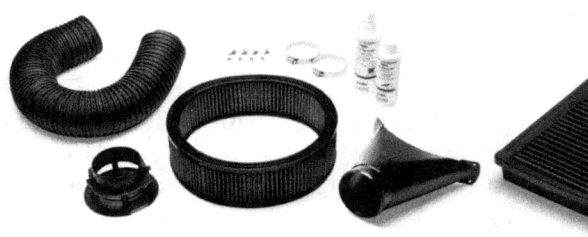

Diesel engines always benefit from a free-flowing intake. Banks engineered this one for the 6.2 liter. It's designed to mount on the nose in a forward facing high-pressure area to deliver a dense charge to the engine. (Photo courtesy of Gale Banks Engineering)

crankshafts go out, especially if you add a bunch of extra power. However, engine remanufacturers offer upgrades in this area that include redesigned and more robust main caps, stronger ARP fasteners, etc.

These engines use Stanadyne injection pumps, with recommended replacement at 80,000-mile intervals. The 6.2 liter used a mechanical lift pump; the 6.5 used an electromechanical one. Later-model 6.5-liter diesels have an electronic control module mated to the

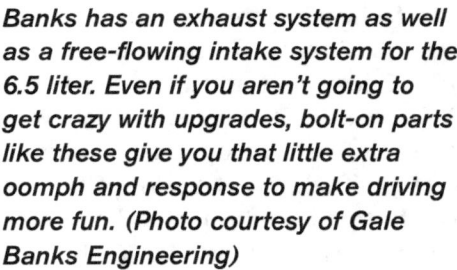

Banks has an exhaust system as well as a free-flowing intake system for the 6.5 liter. Even if you aren't going to get crazy with upgrades, bolt-on parts like these give you that little extra oomph and response to make driving more fun. (Photo courtesy of Gale Banks Engineering)

side of the injection pump. The electronic control module is not reliable however the aftermarket replacement units are much better.

2001–2004: Duramax LB7

The Duramax diesel engine family comes from a joint venture between GM and Isuzu Motors, DMAX Ltd. GM's relationship with Isuzu began in 1971 and was

CHAPTER 9

For the 2004 model year, the LB7 Duramax 6600 6.6L diesel V-8 was rated at 300 hp at 3,100 rpm and 520 ft-lbs of torque at 1,800 rpm. The LB7 came in 2001 to 2004 GM light heavy-duty trucks. It did not use EGR but did have catalytic converters where required. (Photo courtesy of General Motors)

This 7.8-liter inline 6-cylinder is the first diesel engine produced by the joint venture between GM and Isuzu. The 7800 was introduced in 2000 medium-duty trucks, and comes in 200-hp/520-ft-lb or 275-hp/860-ft-lb versions. (Photo courtesy of General Motors)

strengthened in 1997 when GM announced that Isuzu would develop diesel engines for GM. The Duramax Diesel family is domestically sourced, being produced in a DMAX, Ltd. facility in Moraine, Ohio.

Starting with the 2001 model year, Chevy Silverado and GMC Sierra 2500 and 3500 pickup trucks were available with an optional Duramax Diesel 6600 LB7 V-8 engine. The new V-8 featured an iron block and aluminum heads. It produced 300 hp and 520 ft-lbs of torque. The 6.6-liter engine came mated to a 5-speed automatic transmission designed specifically to handle the power and torque of the diesel engine.

The new Duramax engine came with Bosch common-rail direct-injection and four valves per cylinder. It provided Silverado/Sierra customers with best-in-class power, performance, fuel efficiency, reliability, and durability. GM also claimed best-in-class NVH characteristics, virtually eliminating the noise, shake, and roughness often associated with diesel powerplants.

The Duramax Diesel 6600 was actually the second in a growing family of GM-branded Duramax engines. The first was the Duramax Diesel 7800 introduced in GM's 2000 medium-duty trucks.

Most of the diesel engines installed in light-duty trucks have to be restricted in terms of output because the automatic transmissions cannot handle the increased power and torque. That is not the case with the Duramax 6600, with its 5-speed Allison 1000 Series automatic transmission.

The 1000 Series is a fully automatic, electronic 5-speed with overdrive. It offers planetary helical gearing similar to that now used in Allison Transmission's popular World Transmission. It also uses a torque converter with lockup clutch and integral spring damper, and fully electronic controls.

2004–2006: Duramax LLY

The Duramax LLY overlapped production with the LB7 in 2004, as well as with the LBZ in 2006. It is important to note that all these Duramax engines are based on the same basic block and architecture, though each new model received some refinement and reinforcement. For example, the LLY shares much with the higher-output LBZ, which began to be available in late 2005 in heavy-duty Silverados and Sierras. The LLY and the LBZ both featured:

- Revised high-pressure fuel system with new injectors
- Fast-heating glow plugs
- Higher fuel pressure with new pump
- Compression ratio lowered from 17.5:1 to 16.8:1
- Cooled exhaust gas recirculation (EGR) for all applications
- New E35 engine control module

GM DIESEL ENGINES

Duramax Diesel Engines

Engine	Years	Horsepower	Torque	New Feature
LB7	2001-2004	300 hp @ 3,100 rpm	520 ft-lbs @ 1,800 rpm	common rail, Allison 5-speed auto
LLY	2004-2006	310 hp @ 3,000 rpm	590 ft-lbs @ 1,800 rpm	variable vane turbo
LBZ	2006-Mid-'07	360 hp @ 3,200 rpm	650 ft-lbs @ 1,800 rpm	Allison 1000 6-speed auto
LMM	Mid-'07-On	365 hp @ 3,200 rpm	660 ft-lbs @ 1,600 rpm	new emissions standards

*Note that all engines in the above chart are 6.6L V-8s featuring iron blocks and aluminum heads with four valves per cylinder.

The LLY and LB7 overlapped production in the 2004 model year. The LLY was used in the 2500 HD and 3500 Silverado and Sierra beginning January 2004. It was rated at 310 hp at 3,000 rpm with an automatic. The LB7 was rated at 300 hp at 3,000 rpm in the 2500 HD and 3500 Silverado and Sierra. The LLY used EGR and catalytic converters to pass 2007 EPA diesel emissions requirements. (Photo courtesy of General Motors)

In 2006, the Chevy Express and GMC Savana full-size vans offered the Duramax 6600 LLY as an option. In these vehicles, the Duramax was rated to 250 hp at 3,200 rpm and 460 ft-lbs of torque at 1,600 rpm. In the 2500 HD and 3500 Silverado and Sierra, it was rated at 310 hp at 3,000 rpm (with automatic transmission only, beginning January 2004), while the 3500 Silverado and Sierra LB7 was rated at 300 hp at 3,000 rpm.

The Kodiak and TopKick medium-duty trucks also had different ratings, adding to the confusion.

Beginning in 2006, Duramax diesels got new and improved injectors. Each state-of-the-art high-pressure injector has its own solenoid to manage fuel spray, with seven spray points in each injector tip for better fuel vaporization. The solenoid-type injectors reduce the amount of fuel leakage between pulses. They allow more precise fuel control, with more consistent performance.

2006-Mid 2007: Duramax LBZ

The LBZ is rated at 360 hp at 3,200 rpm and 650 ft-lbs at 1,800 rpm. The LLY and the LBZ are essentially the same engine, though the higher-output LBZ has a number of upgrades detailed below. However, the '06 LLY received a few of these upgrades as well.

Strengthened Base Engine Hardware

The cylinder block casting and machining was changed to strengthen the bottom of the cylinder bores to support increased horsepower and torque. The main bearing material was upgraded for increased durability. The piston pin bore diameter was increased and the connecting rod "I" section is thicker. In addition, the LBZ's cylinder heads were revised to accommodate lower compression and reduced cylinder firing pressure.

Lower Compression Ratio

Through a revised piston design, the compression ratio was lowered from 17.5:1 to 16.8:1 to improve the operating smoothness of the engine and enable the significantly increased power output.

Improved Variable-Geometry Turbocharger

The Duramax 6600's improved-performance turbocharger is the core of the most technically advanced turbocharging system in existence. Introduced in January 2004, this intercooled turbo was integrated into the engine V, rather than mounted outside of it like an air conditioning compressor or other accessory. This reduces noise and vibration and limits external plumbing. The turbo still has cooling jackets integrated into the engine cooling system to limit coking (carbon buildup) and enhance durability. In 2005, a variable-geometry turbo was introduced. The variable-geometry turbo's key distinction is a turbine with self-adjusting vanes and a sophisticated electronic control system that automatically adjusts boost pressure and exhaust backpressure based on the engine's requirements. For 2006 this turbocharger has been enhanced for increased aerodynamic and mechanical efficiency.

In the Duramax's variable-geometry turbo, a series of vanes direct exhaust gas at the turbocharger's turbine blades. These vanes can be

CHAPTER 9

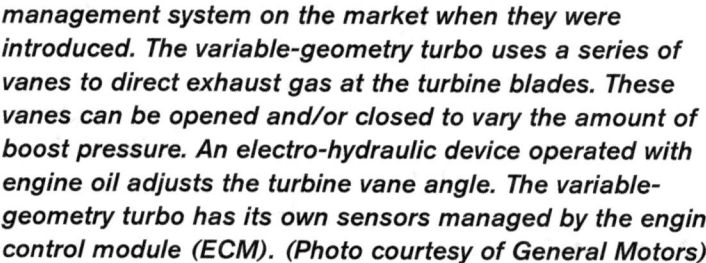

The LLY and LBZ Duramax featured the most advanced variable-geometry turbocharger and engine management system on the market when they were introduced. The variable-geometry turbo uses a series of vanes to direct exhaust gas at the turbine blades. These vanes can be opened and/or closed to vary the amount of boost pressure. An electro-hydraulic device operated with engine oil adjusts the turbine vane angle. The variable-geometry turbo has its own sensors managed by the engine control module (ECM). (Photo courtesy of General Motors)

Externally, the LLY is virtually indistinguishable from the high-output LBZ. This unit as shown would be outfitted with a manual transmission. The differences are internal and are in the always important tuning. (Photo courtesy of General Motors)

opened and or closed to vary the amount of boost pressure. An electro-hydraulic device operated with engine oil, similar in concept to a camshaft phaser, adjusts the turbine vane angle. The variable-geometry turbo has its own sensors managed by the engine control module. A solenoid controls oil pressure against a piston that operates a small cam, which works on a unison ring that moves the turbine vanes simultaneously. As the cam turns, it varies the angle of the blades relative to the turbine wheel. The crucial advantage: With the moveable blades, boost pressure can be controlled independently of engine speed.

The variable-geometry turbo presents a number of benefits over a conventional turbocharger. Boost can be controlled more precisely, with a greater range of modulation. The Duramax's turbo eliminates the need for a wastegate, which is often the first turbocharger component to fail as mileage accumulates. Because the variable-geometry turbo can essentially change resistance and adjust the amount of exhaust backpressure, it also eliminates a separate exhaust pressure regulator, which was previously used to manage engine or compression braking (like an exhaust brake).

Maximum boost in the Duramax remains 20 psi. Yet boost pressure can be varied more subtly over the engine's RPM range. This presents itself to the driver as more immediate engine response, with virtually no turbo lag. Equally important, the ECM measures a number of parameters, from operating temperature to engine speed to fuel injection timing to load demands, when managing the turbine vanes and controlling boost, so the turbocharger operates more efficiently in all conditions. Combined with improvements to the fuel system, the variable-geometry turbocharger allows the Duramax to deliver more power with lower exhaust emissions and no decrease in overall fuel efficiency.

Exhaust Brake

Another new feature of the '06 LLY/LLZ is the ability to use the variable-geometry turbocharger for exhaust braking. This additional functionality is available in the Kodiak and TopKick models and replaces the need for add-on exhaust brake hardware. The braking is controlled by a signal from the ECM and can be activated by

Continued on page 130

The Banks Duramax Type-R Road Race Pickup

You're looking at the most advanced Duramax diesel-powered racing machines on the planet—and it's a truck. The Banks Type-R's Duramax LLY diesel engine makes 650 hp and around 800 ft-lbs of torque with a 5,500-rpm redline. It's been highly modified to increase power over a wider and higher RPM range and to survive the internal pressure of generating 800+ ft-lbs of torque for a 24-hour endurance race.

To increase both cylinder pressures and engine speeds, the engineers at Banks had to re-engineer the Duramax's bottom end and the valvetrain. Diesel engines are limited in duration and lift because of piston-to-valve clearance, so one way to get more flow is to open the valve quicker. The crew at Banks replaced the Type R's stock valvetrain with lighter and stronger components to keep the valves under control at the radical valve acceleration dictated by the revised camshaft. The oil passages were gun-drilled, the lifter bores were shimmed, and rocker shafts were designed to use roller lifters.

Reducing the crankshaft's weight without sacrificing strength is also key to a high-revving diesel. The crankshaft in the Type-R engine was lightened by knife-edging the counter weights and strengthened by contouring and shot-peening the surface to neutralize stress risers and harden the surface. Banks selected 4340 billet-steel H-beam connecting rods and forged pistons custom-designed to produce a 14.5:1 compression ratio. The bottom end is buttoned up with a purpose-built billet aluminum dry-sump oil pan. The pan is designed as a structural member to reinforce and stabilize the main bearings. The oil pan's shallow design permits mounting the engine low in the chassis to lower the race trucks center of gravity.

The excellent 4-valve design of the stock Duramax cylinder heads generate enough airflow and swirl that even in stock trim, they made 460 hp and more than 850 ft-lbs torque from 2,500 to 3,800 rpm. With the torque level achieved, the trick was to increase the mass flow and horsepower without losing the torque or causing excessive smoke. With enough port work and flow bench time, the Banks team increased flow 30 percent on the intake side and 50 percent on the exhaust, both at 0.500 inches of valve lift. The heads also received larger 33-mm stainless steel intake, inconel stainless exhaust valves, and manganese bronze self-lubricating valve guides. (Photos courtesy of Banks)

The Banks Duramax Type R blasts off turn three up a steep incline into turn four at Willow Springs International Raceway during a test session in June, 2006. The Type-R pickup also ran a 1:59 lap during testing at the 2.8-mile Buttonwillow Raceway in California.

The Duramax sits back approximately 18 inches compared to a stock pickup. It's also positioned one-inch to the right of the centerline of the vehicle. The billet aluminum dry-sump oil pan allows the engine to be placed very low in the chassis. The essential airflow components are the twin Garret ball-bearing turbos with electronically controlled wastegates, Banks Big Hoss intake and of course the heads and cam are buried somewhere in there, too.

Type-R continued...

Finally, the Type-R's twin-turbo system consists of a pair of Garrett turbochargers capable of producing a 4:1 pressure ratio for up to 44-psi boost. The pressurized intake charge runs through air-to-air intercoolers, one for each turbo. These Garrett ball-bearing turbochargers were selected because they spool quickly and match the flow demands of the power curve smoothly. The turbos receive exhaust energy through Banks-designed stainless-steel tube headers with boost control via dual electronically controlled wastegates.

Racing engines are cool as heck, and diesel racing engines are even cooler, but there's a whole lot more going on in this truck. Consider all the body, drivetrain, and suspension work it takes build a truck that can put down 800 ft-lbs of torque for a 24-hr race. It will be interesting to see how this thing does once the banks crew gets everything sorted out.

The only stock component in this picture is the GMC grille assembly. The Banks Power Sidewinder D-MAX Type-R road racing truck rolls on Bogart wheels shod with Goodyear Eagle 25.5x12-17-inch racing tires in front and 28.5x14.5-17s on the rear. Its wheelbase of 110-inches is about nine-inches shorter than a stock short bed. The Type-R has a full belly pan that helps generate low pressure and down force by keeping the airflow laminar. At the tail, tunnels and a roll pan release the air upward adding more down force and helping to reduce drag.

the driver.

Fuel System

The new LBZ fuel pump increases fuel pressure from 23,000 psi (roughly 300 times greater pressure than the typical gasoline injection system) to 26,000 psi, and the fuel lines and rails have been strengthened for the higher pressure. The system still operates on the direct injection principle which, other things equal, allows more complete combustion than indirect injection and decreases specific fuel consumption as much as 20 percent. The changes improve both operating and packaging efficiency and contribute to the increase in power.

For 2006, the LBZ/LLY injector tips have been rotated approximately 35 degrees compared to those on the previous injectors. This re-orientation points one of the seven spray holes directly toward the glow plug, improving the cold-start performance.

Each state-of-the-art high-pressure injector has its own solenoid to manage fuel spray, with seven spray points in each injector tip for better fuel vaporization. The solenoid-type injectors reduce the amount of fuel leakage between pulses. They allow more precise fuel control, with more consistent performance under hot-fuel conditions, and greatly reduce the potential for clogging due to fuel contamination. Moreover, they increase maximum fuel delivery by roughly 10 percent, meaning more power when you need it.

Glow Plugs

For 2006, LBZ/LLY new fast-heating glow plugs reduce pre-start heating time without increasing draw on the battery. The glow-plug element has been redesigned to more efficiently convert electricity to heat. Moreover, the glow-plug controller is specifically calibrated for the Duramax 6600's new engine control module and allows pulse width modulation, which manages current more like a rheostat than an on-off switch. Combined with the re-oriented fuel injector tips, the new glow plug system reduces pre-start heating time by as much as 50 percent and reduces cold-start cranking time.

Cooled EGR

All Duramax 6600s built since January 2004 are equipped with EGR systems for reduced emissions. The 2006 LBZ/LLY system features a different EGR valve and higher capacity cooler. The EGR system recycles some exhaust gas back into the intake stream to cool combustion and reduce oxides of nitrogen (NOx) emissions. The system features a unique cooling process that increases its effectiveness. The EGR system includes: plumbing that carries some

GM DIESEL ENGINES

The Duramax's compact, exceptionally rigid cast-iron engine block provides the foundation for smooth, low-noise operation. It features induction hardened cylinder bores (a technique borrowed from larger diesel engines and exclusive in the pickup class) and four-bolt, crossed-drilled bearing caps. A die-cast aluminum lower crankcase strengthens the engine block and serves as the lower engine cover, keeping weight to a minimum. The forged steel crankshaft is surface-hardened by nitriding. Aluminum pistons minimize reciprocating mass and improve efficiency. Each piston has a small hole cast in its skirt, allowing jets to spray cooling oil through a cast channel and up toward the bottom of the piston bowl, where most heat is generated. An integrated oil cooler improves load performance. (Photo courtesy of General Motors)

The Duramax four-valve aluminum cylinder heads deliver strength greater than or equal to cast iron, and with considerably less weight. Several features make it easier to service. Its compact size leaves more space around the engine when it's installed in the vehicle. The timing gears are at the front of the engine for easy access, and in heavy-duty pickups, you can reach the fuel filter simply by leaning into the engine compartment. (Photo courtesy of General Motors)

exhaust gas from the turbocharger outlet to the intake ports, an EGR control valve, and a stainless steel cooling element. Returned exhaust gas passes through a spiraled passage in the element, where the temperature of the gas is lowered before it returns to the combustion chamber.

Intake Air Heater

This heating element in the intake ductwork warms incoming air for short periods, typically after cold starts and under light load, and helps to eliminate emissions that are visible as a white puff of smoke. This offsets the effects of the compression ratio reduction.

E35 ECM

The Duramax 6600's new E35 LBZ/LLY ECM is a diesel-specific engine controller. It has double the memory of its predecessor and increases clock speed to 56 MHz, providing one of the most sophisticated engine control systems in the industry. The E35 allows more software switches, or calibrations that turn on, turn off, or adjust various engine management operations, from fuel delivery to cooling to cruise control operation. More switches mean more control, and the E35 allows management of new systems such as the variable-geometry turbocharger, fast-heating glow plugs, and cooled EGR.

Another feature of the new ECM is the ability to adjust the fuel injection quantity on a cylinder-by-cylinder basis. Each injector is coded with its own fuel flow characteristics from the factory. This data is then stored in the ECM to allow more precision in fuel delivery to each cylinder.

Mid-'07–On: Duramax LMM

The new 6.6-liter Duramax LLM comes rated at 365 hp at 3,200 rpm and 660 lb-ft of torque at 1,600 rpm, despite some new emissions equipment. It carries over much of the LBZ hardware, with the exception of the following:

- New fuel injectors improve combustion characteristics and are ULSD safe
- Durability enhanced variable-geometry turbocharger
- Larger EGR chamber
- Closed crankcase ventilation system
- Diesel particulate filter system
- Intake throttle to control combustion temperature
- Electrically variable engine cooling fan
- Increased engine control processing power

CHAPTER 10

FORD DIESEL ENGINES

1983–1994: 6.9/7.3L IDI

The early Ford diesels were naturally aspirated indirect-injected designs. These were decent work truck engines. They had good torque, but not a lot of horsepower potential. That wasn't what they were designed for. These early engines used a Stanadyne injection pump, which is very affordable to replace.

The turbocharged version of the 7.3 liter, which came along in 1993, was basically the same diesel engine but with a turbo added to make extra torque. However, there is still not a lot of performance potential for these engines because of the limited ability to introduce more fuel and the indirect injection design.

1994–2003: 7.3L Power Stroke

Ford had Navistar International Corporation redesign the earlier 7.3-liter V-8. The Power Stroke version of the 7.3-liter engine was introduced midway through the 1994 model year. It was essentially a top-end redesign that added four-valve per cylinder heads and direct injection. The new setup still used the unit injector fuel delivery system, but the engine was very well developed and made good reliable power for a work truck. The fuel system can be reprogrammed to deliver some additional performance, but it is far more limited than later common-rail designs.

The later version of Ford's 6.0L Power Stroke diesel generates 570 ft-lbs of torque, which is great for spinning the tires. The new 6.4L makes even more horsepower and torque, plus it runs cleaner and quieter. (Photo courtesy of DHRA)

The Power Stroke turbo diesels use a hydraulic injection system where fuel is delivered to the injection pump via a mechanical lift pump. The injection pump controls engine output and RPM by means of a governor that limits fuel to the injectors. The accelerator mechanism works by changing the governor settings, allowing more fuel to the injectors, thereby increasing

FORD DIESEL ENGINES

Ford Diesel Engines

Years	Displacement	Horsepower	Torque	Features
1983–1987	6.9L	170 hp	-	IDI
1988–1991	7.3L	180 hp	-	IDI
1992–1994	7.3L	185 hp	360 ft-lbs	IDI
1993–1994	7.3L	190 hp	395 ft-lbs	Turbo IDI
1994.5–1996	7.3L	210 hp	425 ft-lbs	Power Stroke turbo
1999–2003	7.3L	250hp @ 2,700 rpm	500 ft-lbs @ 1,600 rpm	Power Stroke turbo
2003–2007	6.0L	325 hp @ 3,300 rpm	570 ft-lbs @ 2,000 rpm	Power Stroke variable vane turbo
2008–On	6.4L	350 hp @ 3,000 rpm	650 ft-lbs @ 2,000 rpm	twin-turbo Power Stroke piezo fuel injectors

This 2000 model year version of the 7.3-liter Power Stroke diesel engine is turbocharged and intercooled, and rated at 250 hp at 2,700 rpm and 500 ft-lbs of torque at 1,600 rpm. It has a 10,000-lb towing capacity, and 30 percent better fuel economy than Ford's 5.4-liter Triton V-8. (Photo courtesy of Ford)

This 7.3-liter cutaway model shows the airflow path on the hot and cold sides of the turbo system. Notice the intake port profile. It looks like a high-flowing port on a performance engine. (Photo courtesy of Ford)

The Banks Six-Gun is both a tuner and an all-in-one gauge package. It adds power, plus allows you to monitor your EGT, boost, and the amount of additional fuel in real time. (Photo courtesy of Gale Banks Engineering)

engine speed. Since the governor is RPM sensitive, for any given accelerator angle, the governor increases fuel to maintain engine speed in response to additional loads such as grades or headwinds.

Inside the injection pump, a transfer pump increases the fuel pressure inside the hydraulic head to 60 to 120 psi. Excess fuel passes to the governor housing to lubricate and cool the injection pump en route to the fuel tank. The injection pump hydraulic head distributes the fuel to each injector, using the pressure to open the injector and inject fuel. It does this by sending the fuel to a plunger-type intensifier pump before sending it through a shaft through the distributor rotor to each individual injector line.

When the fuel pressure in the injectors gets above 1,400 psi, the pressure overcomes the spring's

The 7.3-liter injector uses hydraulic pressure that is then amplified in the injector to ram the fuel into the cylinder at high pressure. The timing is controlled via the engine management computer energizing a solenoid in the injector. A second solenoid closes the injector valve. (Photo courtesy of Ford)

*The RFI intake from Bully Dog replaces the restrictive factory intake with a metal heat shield and reusable cone filter. A high-flowing intake like this one will give your Power Stroke more horsepower and torque, especially when paired with some extra fuel from a tuner.
(Photo courtesy of Bully Dog)*

resistance inside the injector, forcing the valve pintle off its seat, allowing the pressurized fuel to pass through the nozzle into the cylinder. Once the fuel pressure drops, the internal spring re-seats the pintle, sealing the injector in preparation for the next injection cycle.

One of the more common problems with diesel fuel injection systems that operate at these pressures is that air trapped inside the fuel lines compresses and does not allow the pressure to rise high enough to unseat the pintle. This causes many performance and starting problems. Unfortunately for enthusiasts, there isn't much in the way of aftermarket support for these engines, though Banks makes a turbo kit and a transmission commander. This engine does respond to programming in more fuel delivery. Air intakes, a programmer, and exhaust work are in order to make a quick hauler quicker. Check with your favorite aftermarket manufacturer to see what else is out there.

The 7.3-liter Power Stroke engine powered the 1994-1/2 to 2003 F-Series trucks as well as the 2000 to 2003 Ford Excursion. It was also available in 1994-1/2 to 2003 Ford Econoline vans and school buses.

2003–2006: 6.0L Power Stroke

Ford continued its relationship with Navistar with the 6.0-liter Power Stroke turbo diesel. The engine is a four-valve per cylinder pushrod V-8 producing 325 hp at 3,300 rpm and 560 ft-lbs at 2,000 rpm in early production. That was increased to 570 ft-lbs at 2,000 rpm later in 2005.

This engine is not as successful as the engine it replaced, as it has been plagued with extremely high warranty claims. By 2005, Ford had issued at least 77 technical service bulletins, advising mechanics how to diagnose and fix various problems, barely three years into the production run. Compare that with the eight service bulletins for GM's Duramax Diesel V-8 and none for the Cummins in the Dodge Ram, each with about the same production time. However, in spite of the warranty claims, Power Stroke-equipped Super Duty trucks continue to sell well for Ford.

Most of the reliability issues with this engine revolve around leaking fuel injectors and broken turbochargers. With nearly 80 technical service bulletins issued, owners spend a lot of time at the dealership. Still, when it's running right and backed with the optional TorqShift 5-speed automatic transmission, the

The 6.0-liter Power Stroke produces 325 hp at 3,300 rpm and 570 ft-lbs of torque at 2,000 rpm with four valves per cylinder and a variable-geometry turbocharger. The design uses a cast-iron block and heads, and has a maximum engine speed of 4,100 rpm. (Photo courtesy of Ford)

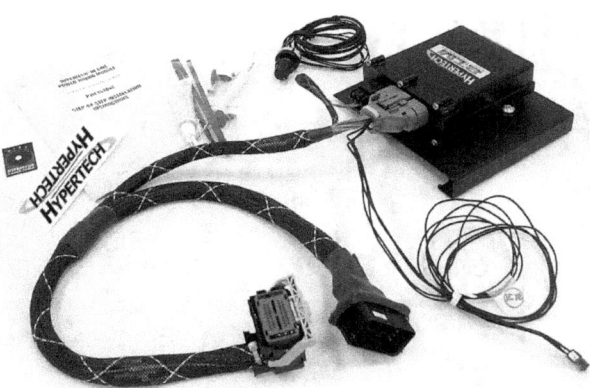

Hypertech's Power Tuning Module (PTM) plugs right into the Ford 6.0-liter wiring harness under the hood. Select from three stages of power boost using the selector dial, which can be mounted in the passenger compartment. Besides engine parameters, the PTM also allows you to dial in firmer shifts. (Photo courtesy of Hypertech)

6.0-liter is a great driving, hauling, and towing machine.

The 6.0-liter has a cast-iron cylinder block and heads. Cast iron is more efficient thermodynamically, but is also heavier than aluminum. The 6.0-liter also has a split crankcase with the upper portion consisting of the cylinders and the top of the mains. The lower portion consists of the skirt and the lower main bearings. The oil pan is also a two-piece design. An aluminum oil pan and windage tray assembly bolts to the lower oil pan sump. The engine oil cooler is integrated with the oil filter base and is found in the valley of the block instead of at the side.

The 6.0-liter drives the camshaft and high-pressure oil pumps off the crank with gear sets found on the rear of the engine. This arrangement puts the high-pressure oil pump activating the injectors under the turbocharger. The "timing cover" on the front of the engine houses the water and engine oil pumps.

The 6.0-liter, as the 7.3-liter before it, uses electronically controlled high-pressure engine oil to provide the injection pressure. The injectors use a solenoid, which when energized, open to allow the high-pressure oil to provide the pressure to inject the fuel. This setup is quieter than the 7.3-liter. Injection timing and duration is controlled electronically through an engine management computer and sensor suite.

The 6.0-liter Power Stroke uses a variable-geometry turbocharger to manage boost and backpressure by varying the area of the turbine. This enhances engine performance in a wide variety of conditions. Electronic control of the turbine area can perform much like a wastegate but with more efficiency and control.

As with most electronically controlled turbo diesels, the 6.0-liter uses mass airflow, boost pressure, manifold absolute pressure, intake air temperature, and manifold air temperature sensors. It's also one of the few systems that uses exhaust backpressure to determine how to adjust the turbine vanes.

The current Power Stroke uses cooled exhaust gas recirculation (EGR) to reduce NOx. It introduces cooled exhaust gas into the high-pressure side of the intake at cruising speeds to lower the combustion temperature. To

The DHRA

If you're reading this book, odds are you want to instsall some performance upgrades for your diesel truck. But what next? How about getting active in a local diesel club or joining the Diesel Hot Rod Association (DHRA)?

DHRA drag racing classes include E.T. Bracket Racing, Quick Diesel Index, Pro Street, and Exhibition. Check out the DHRA rulebook if you want info on how to set your truck up for a specific class, but even mildly modified trucks can compete in the Bracket class. (Photo courtesy of DHRA)

Work Stock class pullers must run stock-appearing body, drivetrain, engine, and turbocharger. The next class up, Street Diesel, allows single turbos with up a 2.8-inch inducer size. (Photo courtesy of DHRA)

The DHRA has a number of events across the country. Diesel owners can test their trucks in drag racing or sled pulling, or just show up and have a good time. Besides testing your truck's traction and power, drag racing gives you a chance to polish your reaction time and driving skills. Sure diesel trucks are heavy, but as you know, they make boatloads of horsepower and torque. You'll probably be surprised how even a mildly modified truck can perform on the strip.

If sled-pulling is more your thing, the DHRA has four classes: Work Stock, Street Diesel, Super Street, and Modified Diesel. Here again, mildly modified trucks can compete in the Work Stock and Street classes, but check out the DHRA rulebook or website (www.DHRAonline.com) for more details. All DHRA events are also just a great place to meet a bunch of like-minded diesel performance enthusiasts, and maybe get some ideas for how to modify your own truck.

do this, the exhaust backpressure needs to be higher than the intake manifold pressure. The computer trims the VGT blades to balance backpressure with EGR needs.

It's interesting that the 6.0-liter engine originally used a pilot injection tactic. On each compression stoke, the engine management computer energized the injector for the pilot pulse, turned it off, and then had to energize it again. The advantage of

Most people would frown at smoke like this on the street, but on a competition vehicle, it's not that uncommon. With all that extra fuel, the driver of this Ford is probably going to add a nitrous shot after the launch. (Photo courtesy of DHRA)

pilot injection is less engine noise and improved emissions. However, the injectors didn't seem to handle the duty cycle that well and it caused hot restart problems and rough running. The pilot injection was changed in later programming.

In response to all the problems with the new 6.0-liter, International almost completely redesigned the Power Stroke's fuel system, replacing or redesigning hundreds of parts. That reportedly solved some problems, but did not cure them all. International contends that the engine can be repaired and made reliable, but Ford canceled the program and designed the 6.4-liter replacement engine in-house.

2008–On: 6.4L

Ford's new 6.4-liter diesel meets the most stringent emissions standards in the world, while producing 350 hp at 3,000 rpm and 650 ft-lbs of torque starting at 2,000 rpm. A tough, cast-iron block and heads provide a strong, durable foundation for making power and torque. A new cylinder head and piston bowl design work with the high-pressure common rail fuel system for more efficient combustion, and for increased power and cleaner emissions. The pistons mount to the forged-steel crankshaft with larger, stronger rods that feature an increased rod bearing diameter. The pistons are galley-cooled, providing optimized operation and increased durability.

Compound Turbos

Ford's new sequential turbochargers provide improved response throughout the entire powerband, including better low-end performance. Tests have shown zero-to-60 times of more than a second faster than the outgoing 6.0-liter.

The compact, powerful new Ford 6.4-liter produces 350 hp at 3,000 rpm and 650 ft-lbs of torque starting at 2,000 rpm while reducing particulate output by up to 97 percent. It features common rail direct injection with peizo injectors and a sequential compound turbocharging system. (Photo courtesy of Ford)

The two turbochargers work in tandem. The small, electronic-controlled, VGT comes on at low RPM to provide extra boost at takeoff. As RPM increases, the larger fixed turbo joins the smaller turbo to boost power through the middle of the torque curve. The larger turbo takes over at higher boost, and the system can make up to 42 psi.

Fuel System

The new 6.4-liter is fed via a state-of-the-art, high-pressure common rail fuel injection system. The fuel is pressurized to 26,000 psi (1,800 bar) and injected into the cylinders through piezo-electric injectors. The latest in injector technology can deliver up to five injections per combustion cycle to better control emissions, provide instant response for optimized acceleration, and improve cold start down to -20 degrees Fahrenheit.

Emissions

Dual 440-mm EGR coolers feature an air oxidation catalyst that literally scrubs the exhaust gasses from the air to protect coolers against fouling and the EGR valve against deposits. The highly efficient exhaust system also includes a diesel particulate and oxidation catalyst to meet new stiffer emissions standards.

CHAPTER 11

DODGE CUMMINS DIESEL ENGINES

The Cummins B-series 5.9L I-6 engine architecture is derived from a joint effort between Case and Cummins to build a diesel engine with wide commercial applications. Its over-built block structure with seven mains was designed to go the distance. These engines have been known to run over 1,000,000 miles, and as heavy-duty emissions-certified engines (unique among pickup truck diesels) they have a "design" lifetime for emissions purposes of 350,000 miles. The super industrial strength of the B's bottom end has made it a choice for competition diesel engine builds. It also uses six evenly spaced head bolts around each cylinder and thick cylinder walls to withstand the tremendous cylinder pressures that result from heavy fueling and high boost levels. The Cummins B-series engines are used in a wide variety of vehicles including commercial trucks, buses, and military vehicles. The basic architecture is also shared with a 3.9-liter inline four-cylinder engine.

The cast-in intake manifold on the head of the Cummins is a significant restriction in the airflow. It also does not distribute the air evenly and therefore throws the power balance off. Banks machines them off in order to install a Banks manifold that flows more air and distributes it more evenly between cylinders.

1989–1993: First Generation

The 5.9L Cummins was first used in the '89 Dodge Ram pickup with 160 hp at 2,500 rpm and 400 ft-lbs of torque at 1,600 rpm. It used the Bosch VE Rotary injection pump through the 1993 model year. It

138 HIGH-PERFORMANCE DIESEL BUILDER'S GUIDE

DODGE CUMMINS DIESEL ENGINES

Cummins 5.9L I-6 Engines

Engine	Years	Horsepower	Torque	Feature
First Gen	1989–1993	160 hp @ 2,500 rpm	400 ft-lbs @ 1,600 rpm	
Second Gen	1994–1998	175 hp	420 ft-lbs	5-spd
		160 hp	400 ft-lbs	automatic
	1996–1998.5	215 hp @ 2,600 rpm	440 ft-lbs @ 1,600 rpm	5-spd
		180 hp @ 2,600 rpm	420 ft-lbs @ 1,600 rpm	automatic
ISB Upgrade	1998.5–2000	235 hp @ 2,700 rpm	460 ft-lbs @ 1,600 rpm	24-valve head,
		215 hp @ 2,700 rpm*	420 ft-lbs @ 1,600 rpm*	electronic fuel system
High-Output	2001–2002	235/245 hp @ 2,700 rpm	460/505 ft-lbs @ 1,600 rpm	5-spd/6spd**
Third Gen	2003–On	250 hp @ 2,900 rpm	460 ft-lbs @ 1,400 rpm	common rail injection
High-Output	2003–2004.4	305 hp @ 2,900 rpm	555 ft-lbs @ 1,600 rpm	
High-Output	2004.5–2007.4	325 hp @ 2,900 rpm	610 ft-lbs @ 1,600 rpm	
B6.7L	2007.5	350 hp @ 3,000 rpm	650 ft-lbs @ 1,500 rpm	6.7-liter displacement

*Automatic Transmission ** Automatic rated same as 5-spd

The torque converter on the Cummins is severely stressed when you're adding extra horsepower and torque. Banks and other manufacturers offer high-performance replacement converters that hold extra torque with increased durability.

Efficient exhausts and turbochargers from Banks can make earlier B-series engines more powerful. Don't forget to add more fuel. The later-model common-rail engines can also benefit from upgraded airflow products, as well as re-programming using tuners.

remained essentially unchanged during those years, with the exception of an intercooled version coming along in 1991, as well as a few turbo housing size changes. The changes are noted by the different Control Parts List (CPL) code. The CPL is included on the Cummins engine data plate attached to the engine on the driver's side, near the timing gear cover. The original turbocharger exhaust housing had an 18.5-cm² cross-sectional area. Early intercooled engines used a 21-cm² housing, but the 18.5-cm² housing was used again during 1993.

The Bosch VE Rotary injection pump didn't really offer any performance options. It could only provide enough fuel to make 200 to 250 hp at the wheels with tuning and injector changes. Some builders experimented with larger intercoolers and turbos, but without additional fuel, additional air mass through the engine could only provide modest (I'm being kind) power gains. The later (1994–1998.5) Bosch P7100 inline injection pump can be retrofitted to the early engine, but a new front gear case, pump gear, injection lines, brackets, etc., also need to be swapped.

The transmissions were satisfactory for the power levels available with the VE Rotary pump, although upgrades to the automatic are advisable. The Getrag 5-speed does not have a great reputation for durability under high power usage. Rebuilt units and parts are available from Standard Transmission and Gear in Fort Worth, Texas, and other vendors.

1994–1998: Second Generation

It wasn't until the 1994 model year and the addition of the P7100 inline injection pump that the B5.9-liter began to seriously interest aftermarket tuners. Since the new injection pump could be tweaked to deliver enough fuel to make it worth designing free flowing intakes, larger turbos, and better boost control, the second-gen B5.9L garnered support. These upgrades make enough power (essentially doubling it) to warrant transmission upgrades.

The New Venture 4500 5-speed transmission was stout, although fifth gear tended to pound on its retaining nut until it could slide out of position, because the main shaft was not fully splined under the gear. Upgrades are available from Standard Transmission and others. The automatic transmissions needed some help with the line pressure, valve body, and torque converter. Companies such as BD Power stepped up and developed upgrades. Gauges were commonly added to monitor engine conditions, such as EGT and boost.

In stock trim, the engine was rated between 160 hp at 2,500 rpm and 400 ft-lbs at 1,500 rpm in 1994, to 215 hp at 2,500 rpm and 440 ft-lbs at 1,500 rpm, depending on the emission control package and transmission. All Dodge versions of the B engine had catalytic converters beginning in January 1994, and California versions added EGR in January 1996.

Early on, many owners felt the 160 hp engine was underpowered.

Dodge and Cummins brought the B-series engine into the common-rail era with the 2003 model year. The Cummins 555 was introduced with Bosch high-pressure common-rail fuel injection for 305 hp and 555 ft-lbs of torque. The Cummins 600 was rated to 325 hp at 2,900 rpm and 600 ft-lbs of torque at 1,600 rpm. In the 2005, the H.O.'s torque rating was upped to 610 ft-lbs. (Photo courtesy of Cummins)

Mark Chapple, a Cummins engineer for 33 years, started TST Products and developed a Power Kit in 1995. This kit consists of a torque plate (Bosch called it a full load fuel stop plate) and a boost control elbow. The elbow is simple to install and replaces the stock boost line elbow and raises boost pressure approximately 50 percent from a stock 18 to 23 psi to 28 to 37 psi to burn the additional fuel that was allowed by the richer torque plate.

Other companies such as BD Power have offered larger injectors to hop up these 5.9L engines ever since they became popular. The Dodge versions of the Cummins B-series engine all had straight outside-diameter valvesprings known as "35 psi" springs, meaning that they were safe with that amount of exhaust backpressure created by an exhaust brake. Cummins also offered "60 psi" barrel-type springs designed for use with the stronger exhaust brakes.

1998.5–2002: ISB Upgrade

Midway through the 1998 model year, EPA emissions regulations were tightened, and Dodge and Cummins introduced an extensively redesigned B5.9L engine. It was updated with 24 valves (four valves per cylinder), an electronic

Continued on page 142

World's Fastest Pickup

The Banks Sidewinder Cummins B-series powered Dakota set the pickup class land speed record of 222.139 mph. The engineering team at Cummins built the base engine, code named "Salt Quake," for the Sidewinder on their own time. The Cummins started with a Holset HX40 turbo and a 15.1:1 compression ratio to make 393 hp at 3,800 rpm and 600 ft-lbs of torque over a broad RPM range. The electronics are Cummins and the fuel injection is state-of-the-art common rail. This stout engine has provided a durable, powerful base on which to build, impressing the dynamometer test engineers at every step. Most notable has been the apparent ease with which this engine makes power. It is deceptively quiet and doesn't sound like it's laboring even when subjected to a full load on the dyno.

Banks engineering then modified the engine significantly, including a Holset HY55 variable geometry turbo set to make 50 psi boost. The intake charge is kept under control by an efficient air-to-water intercooling system that uses twin Cummins marine air-to-water intercoolers fed by dual Stewart high-capacity electric water pumps. The baffled 40-gallon water tank is mounted in the bed. The truck runs a Banks air-to-air intercooler on the street, which offers more consistent performance over long drives.

The fuel system consists of a 22-gallon Fuel Safe fuel cell with an internal fuel trap with one-way valves to assure a continuous supply of fuel during the high G-forces. The number-2 diesel fuel flows from the fuel cell through –10AN lines to an adjacent Holley 110 GPM pump, which supplements the stock Cummins diesel lift pump in the engine compartment. The fuel then flows through a stock Cummins fuel filter/water separator assembly and then to the mechanical high-pressure fuel pump. A state of the art common rail fuel injection system helps the Cummins produce 700+ hp and 1,200+ ft-lbs of torque.

All that torque necessitates the clamping force of a custom-built 12-inch dual-disc clutch with a precision ground billet steel flywheel. The material used on the discs is an organic compound with a Kevlar weave for added strength and durability. While the maximum capacity of this clutch is right at the peak torque output of the engine, tire slippage is expected on the salt well before clutch slippage becomes a problem. The larger diameter of the dual-disc system provides an optimum compromise between controlling the power, and allowing for easy street driving when compared to off-the-shelf small diameter multi-disc racing clutch systems. While able to handle the torque requirements, these smaller systems can often prove very sensitive to slippage, as might be encountered in street driving, or in starting out with a trailer in tow! (Photos courtesy of Banks)

The Banks Sidewinder holds two Federation International De L'Automobile (FIA) international speed records set at the Bonneville Salt Flats at the SCTA-BNI World Finals in October 2002. The records were set in the FIA International Category B, Group 3, Class 17.

The truck set the Flying Start, Two-Way Average record for the kilometer at 349.863 kp/h and for the mile at 217.306 mph. The records firmly establish the Banks Sidewinder as the World's Fastest Pickup—regardless of engine type.

engine management system, and a computer-controlled Bosch VP44 fuel pump. The name changed to reflect the computerized controls, as Interact System, B series (ISB). It produced 235 hp at 2,700 rpm and 460 ft-lbs at 1,600 rpm when backed by a manual transmission; automatics were slightly downrated. The 2001 high output (H.O.) version produced 245 hp at 2,700 rpm and 505 ft-lbs at 1,600 rpm backed by a heavy-duty 6-speed manual transmission. The ISB engines did not have catalytic converters.

The new ISB, with its iron head and block, featured 17.2:1 compression and forged steel connecting rods, but did not seem to respond that well to power upgrades. The fuel injection pump and electronic controls seemed to be the limiting component. However, it was a decent performer in stock trim. Cummins offered versions for commercial trucks with 260 hp and 660 ft-lbs of torque.

TST Products and Edge Products soon developed electronic power-adding modules for this engine. These modules added 40 to 130 hp. Bosch injectors from the 275-hp recreational vehicle version of the engine added 33 to 50 hp to the various Dodge versions. Diesel Dynamics, now a division of Edge Products, began manufacturing upgraded injectors by a proprietary version of an Extrude-Hone process in 1999, could add 100 hp or more to the engine. Power junkies soon found that the higher power additions required the use of an electronic "boost fooler" to keep the Cummins computer from derating the engine by reduce fueling. Programmers such as the Smarty also became available.

The new layout set the stage for the common rail design, which would come in 2003. Its single-piece cylinder head and four-valve per cylinder configuration increased air-

Some diesel enthusiast put as much money and effort into the appearance of their rigs as they do making them fast, powerful, and reliable. When you've got both, you're a winner every time. (Photo courtesy of DHRA)

flow and allowed vertically mounted injectors, centered over the piston bowl for improved combustion, low-end torque, and fast response. Its "No-Adjust" Overhead Rocker System was designed to reach a minimum 100,000 miles without adjustment. And its standard 60-psi heavy-duty valvesprings were compatible with exhaust brakes.

The block was structurally redesigned for reduced noise (up to 4 dB less) and increased durability (Cummins claimed 15 percent longer life to overhaul). This redesigned block had longitudinal stiffening ribs and used straight thread O-ring metric (STORM) tapped holes for oil pressure fittings. It also integrated the water pump, oil pump, and cooler external housings to eliminate potential leak points. The crankshaft is full fillet-hardened and integrally balanced, with internal cross-drilling for lubrication.

The third-generation Cummins also introduced a new symmetrical combustion bowl to work with the vertical centered injectors and higher injection pressures to increase power (up to 20 percent more HP) and fuel efficiency while improving oil con-

trol. The Bosch VP44 electronic fuel pump provides higher injection pressures, electronically controlled timing, and fueling for precise and instantaneous control. The turbo is a Holset HX35 wastegated design for better low-RPM performance and high-engine speed boost.

Cummins proprietary design for the engine management system with Motorola microprocessor allowed advanced diagnostics and prognostics, in addition to a complete set of programming options for easy upgrading of the engine.

2003–2007: Common Rail Era

For the 2003 model year, the Cummins 555 ft-lb High Output was introduced, along with lower horsepower versions, all with Bosch high-pressure common-rail fuel injection. The H.O. was rated at 305 hp at 2,900 rpm and 555 ft-lbs of torque at 1,600 rpm. In 2004.5, the ratings were increased to 325 hp and 600 ft-lbs, and in 2005, the H.O. model's torque rating was upped to 610 ft-lbs. The 2004.5 engine finally gave California (and

Edge Products sells these custom-built Jammer injectors for the 5.9-liter Cummins engine. They features eight holes in the injector tip, an improvement over the stock seven. Edge claims these injectors are manufactured to flow within one percent of each other, while the stock injector's flow can vary by as much as 11 percent! (Photo courtesy of Edge Products)

other states using that emissions specification) buyers the full horsepower rating that was available in the other states, but also incorporated a catalytic converter to meet the new EPA regulations. California 235-hp versions used in 2003–2004.5 also had catalytic converters.

How did Cummins increase the power to make 555 and 600 ft-lbs of torque? They used all the diesel performance tuning tricks in the book:

- Enhanced fueling tactics (more fuel) using larger multiple injections.
- Exhaust system increased to four-inch diameter from turbo to tailpipe to reduce backpressure.
- Larger turbocharger compressor wheel and housing for increased airflow.
- Higher-flow intercooler and engine-mounted shroud for improved forced airflow and cooling.
- Strengthened block, better valves and seats, improved airflow.

Aftermarket suppliers quickly developed fueling modules, such as the Edge Products EZ box, the Edge Juice with Attitude (gauges), and the TST PowerMaxCR. The latter two are available with gauges built in, a boon to installers of such vital monitoring devices for diesels with power additions. Programmers also became available, such as the Smarty from MADS Electronics. Diesel Dynamics and others developed high-flow injectors. The high injection pressures afforded by the common-rail system responded well to even higher rail-pressure commands via electronics, increased injection durations, and larger injectors. Whereas extensive tuning and modifications were needed to take the older 12-valve engines with P7100 injection pumps to 600 or even 800 hp at the wheels, the new engines could approach 600 hp with simple power add-ons. At that point, the Bosch CP3 high-pressure injection pump becomes the limiting factor. Vendors such as Floor It are now modifying these pumps for more fueling.

2007.5–On: 6.7L

To meet the new emissions standards and keep up with the competition, Dodge introduced a new 6.7-liter Cummins engine. This tur-

TST manufactures this PowerMax tuner for common-rail Cummins diesels. It allows you to adjust the fuel timing, as well as the rail pressure, and even includes tunes for twin-turbo swaps. (Photo courtesy of TST)

bocharged, intercooled straight six makes 350 hp at 3,000 rpm and 650 ft-lbs of torque at 1,500 rpm, while reducing noise by 50 percent.

Extra performance comes by way of an electronically controlled VGT, which is available with an exhaust brake function straight from the factory, plus a six-speed automatic transmission. The new 6.7-liter gets its displacement from a 107-mm bore and 124-mm stroke, versus a 102-mm bore and 120-mm stroke for the 5.9-liter engine. The cylinder heads feature a high-swirl combustion system and contribute to the 17.2:1 compression ratio.

The Dodge Ram's Cummins is one of the most forceful, durable, and reliable engines available in a pickup. That's why you're bound to find them in the winner's circle at sled pull competitions, drag races, and towing race vehicles to and from events. (Photo courtesy of DHRA)

APPENDIX: SOURCE GUIDE

Association of Diesel Specialists
10 Laboratory Dr.
PO Box 13966
Research Triangle Park, NC
27709-3966
(919) 406-8804
www.diesel.org

ATS Diesel Performance, Inc.
5293 Ward Rd., Unit 11
Arvada, CO 80002
(800) 949-6002
www.atsdiesel.com

BD Diesel Performance
Box 231
Sumas, WA, 98295
(800) 887-5030
www.bd-power.com

Bosch
www.bosch.us

Robert Bosch LLC
2800 S. 25th Ave.
Broadview, IL 60155
www.boschautoparts.com

Bully Dog Technologies
3799 Arapaho
Addison, Texas 75001
(866) BullyDog
(888) 285-5936
www.bullydog.com

Cummins Inc.,
Box 3005,
Columbus, IN 47202-3005
www.cummins.com

DaimlerChrysler Corporation
www.daimlerchrysler.com

Diesel Dynamics
(800) 628-8111
www.dieseldynamics.com

Diesel Hot Rod Association, Inc.
920 W. Walnut St.
Albany, IN 47320
(765) 768-6400
www.dhraonline.com

Diesel Technology Forum
5291 Corporate Drive – Suite 102
Frederick, MD 21703
(301) 668-7230
www.dieselforum.org

Edge Products
Corporate Offices
1080 South Depot Drive
Ogden, Utah 84404
(888) 360-3343
www.edgeproducts.com

Ford Motor Company
www.ford.com

Gale Banks Engineering
546 Duggan Avenue
Azusa, California 91702
(800) 601-8072
www.bankspower.com

General Motors Corporation
www.gm.com

Hypermax Engineering, Inc
255 East Route 72
Gilberts, IL 60136
(847) 428-5655
www.gohypermax.com

Hypertech, Inc.,
3215 Appling Road,
Bartlett, TN 38133
(901) 382-8888
www.hypertech.com

MSD
(915) 857-5200
www.msdignition.com

National Hot Rod Diesel Association
14702 Smokey Point Blvd
Marysville, WA 98271
(360) 658-4353
www.nhrda.com

TST Products, Inc
7440 S International Dr
Columbus, IN 47201
(812) 342-6741
www.tstproducts.com

Turbo Diesel Register
www.turbodieselregister.com

Turbonetics, Inc.
2255 Agate Ct.
Simi Valley, CA 93065
(805) 581-0333
www.turboneticsinc.com

MORE GREAT TITLES AVAILABLE FROM CARTECH®

CHEVROLET
How To Rebuild the Small-Block Chevrolet* *(SA26)*
Chevrolet Small-Block Parts Interchange Manual *(SA55)*
How To Build Max Perf Chevy Small-Blocks on a Budget *(SA57)*
How To Build High-Perf Chevy LS1/LS6 Engines *(SA86)*
How to Build Big-Inch Chevy Small-Blocks *(SA87)*
How to Build High-Performance Chevy Small-Block Cams/Valvetrains SA105)
Rebuilding the Small-Block Chevy: Step-by-Step Videobook *(SA116)*
High-Performance Chevy Small-Block Cylinder Heads *(SA125P)*
High Performance C5 Corvette Builder's Guide *(SA127)*
How to Rebuild the Big-Block Chevrolet* *(SA142P)*
How to Build Max-Performance Chevy Big Block on a Budget *(SA198)*
How to Restore Your Camaro 1967–1969 *(SA178)*
How to Build Killer Big-Block Chevy Engines *(SA190)*
How to Build Max-Performance Chevy LT1/LT4 Engines *(SA206)*
Small-Block Chevy Performance: 1955-1996 *(SA110P)*
How to Build Small-Block Chevy Circle-Track Racing Engines *(SA121P)*
High-Performance C5 Corvette Builder's Guide *(SA127P)*
Chevrolet Big Block Parts Interchange Manual *(SA31P)*
Chevy TPI Fuel Injection Swapper's Guide *(SA53P)*

FORD
High-Performance Ford Engine Parts Interchange *(SA56)*
How To Build Max Performance Ford V-8s on a Budget *(SA69)*
How To Build Max Perf 4.6 Liter Ford Engines *(SA82)*
How to Build Big-Inch Ford Small-Blocks *(SA85)*
How to Rebuild the Small-Block Ford* *(SA102)*
How to Rebuild Big-Block Ford Engines* *(SA162)*
Full-Size Fords 1955–1970 *(SA176)*
How to Build Max-Performance Ford FE Engines *(SA183)*
How to Restore Your Mustang 1964 1/2–1973 *(SA165)*
How to Build Ford RestoMod Street Machines *(SA101P)*
Building 4.6/5.4L Ford Horsepower on the Dyno *(SA115P)*
How to Rebuild 4.6/5.4-Liter Ford Engines *(SA155P)*
Building High-Performance Fox-Body Mustangs on a Budget *(SA75P)*
How to Build Supercharged & Turbocharged Small-Block Fords *(SA95P)*

GENERAL MOTORS
GM Automatic Overdrive Transmission Builder's and Swapper's Guide *(SA140)*
How to Rebuild GM LS-Series Engines* *(SA147)*
How to Swap GM LS-Series Engines Into Almost Anything *(SA156)*
How to Supercharge & Turbocharge GM LS-Series Engines *(SA180)*
How to Build Big-Inch GM LS-Series Engines *(SA203)*
How to Rebuild & Modify GM Turbo 400 Transmissions *(SA186)*
How to Build GM Pro-Touring Street Machines *(SA81P)*

MOPAR
How to Rebuild the Big-Block Mopar *(SA197)*
How to Rebuild the Small-Block Mopar* *(SA143P)*
How to Build Max-Performance Hemi Engines *(SA164)*
How To Build Max-Performance Mopar Big Blocks *(SA171)*
Mopar B-Body Performance Upgrades 1962-1979 *(SA191)*
How to Build Big-Inch Mopar Small-Blocks *(SA104P)*
High-Performance New Hemi Builder's Guide 2003-Present *(SA132P)*

OLDSMOBILE/ PONTIAC/ BUICK
How to Build Max-Performance Oldsmobile V-8s *(SA172)*
How To Build Max-Perf Pontiac V8s SA78)
How to Rebuild Pontiac V-8s* *(SA200)*
How to Build Max-Performance Buick Engines *(SA146P)*

SPORT COMPACTS
Honda Engine Swaps *(SA93)*
Building Honda K-Series Engine Performance *(SA134)*
High-Performance Subaru Builder's Guide *(SA141)*
How to Build Max-Performance Mitsubishi 4G63t Engines *(SA148)*
How to Rebuild Honda B-Series Engines* *(SA154)*
The New Mini Performance Handbook *(SA182P)*
High Performance Dodge Neon Builder's Handbook *(SA100P)*
High-Performance Honda Builder's Handbook Volume 1 *(SA49P)*

*Workbench® Series books featuring step-by-step instruction with hundreds of color photos for stock rebuilds and automotive repair.

ENGINE
Engine Blueprinting *(SA21)*
Automotive Diagnostic Systems: Understanding OBD-I & OBD II *(SA174)*

INDUCTION & IGNITION
Super Tuning & Modifying Holley Carburetors *(SA08)*
Street Supercharging, A Complete Guide to *(SA17)*
How To Build High-Performance Ignition Systems *(SA79)*
How to Build and Modify Rochester Quadrajet Carburetors *(SA113)*
Turbo: Real World High-Performance Turbocharger Systems *(SA123)*
How to Rebuild & Modify Carter/Edelbrock Carbs *(SA130)*
Engine Management: Advanced Tuning *(SA135)*
Designing & Tuning High-Performance Fuel Injection Systems *(SA161)*
Demon Carburetion *(SA68P)*

DRIVING
How to Drift: The Art of Oversteer *(SA118)*
How to Drag Race *(SA136)*
How to Autocross *(SA158P)*
How to Hook and Launch *(SA195)*

HIGH-PERFORMANCE & RESTORATION HOW-TO
How To Install and Tune Nitrous Oxide Systems *(SA194)*
Custom Painting *(SA10)*
David Vizard's How to Build Horsepower *(SA24)*
How to Rebuild & Modify High-Performance Manual Transmissions* *(SA103)*
High-Performance Jeep Cherokee XJ Builder's Guide 1984–2001 *(SA109)*
How to Paint Your Car on a Budget *(SA117)*
High Performance Brake Systems *(SA126P)*
High Performance Diesel Builder's Guide *(SA129)*
4x4 Suspension Handbook *(SA137)*
How to Rebuild Any Automotive Engine* *(SA151)*
Automotive Welding: A Practical Guide* *(SA159)*
Automotive Wiring and Electrical Systems* *(SA160)*
Design & Install In Car Entertainment Systems *(SA163)*
Automotive Bodywork & Rust Repair* *(SA166)*
High-Performance Differentials, Axles, & Drivelines *(SA170)*
How to Make Your Muscle Car Handle *(SA175)*
Rebuilding Any Automotive Engine: Step-by-Step Videobook *(SA179)*
Builder's Guide to Hot Rod Chassis & Suspension *(SA185)*
How To Rebuild & Modify GM Turbo 400 Transmissions* *(SA186)*
How to Build Altered Wheelbase Cars *(SA189)*
How to Build Period Correct Hot Rods *(SA192)*
Automotive Sheet Metal Forming & Fabrication *(SA196)*
Performance Automotive Engine Math *(SA204)*
How to Design, Build & Equip Your Automotive Workshop on a Budget *(SA207)*
Automotive Electrical Performance Projects *(SA209)*
How to Port Cylinder Heads *(SA215)*
Muscle Car Interior Restoration Guide *(SA167)*
High Performance Jeep Wrangler TJ Builder's Guide: 1997-2006 *(SA120P)*
Dyno Testing & Tuning *(SA138P)*
How to Rebuild Any Automotive Engine *(SA151P)*
Muscle Car Interior Restoration Guide *(SA167P)*
How to Build Horsepower - Volume 2 *(SA52P)*
Bolt-Together Street Rods *(SA72P)*

HISTORIES & PERSONALITIES
Fuelies: Fuel Injected Corvettes 1957–1965 *(CT452)*
Yenko *(CT485)*
Lost Hot Rods *(CT487)*
Grumpy's Toys *(CT489)*
Rusted Muscle — A collection of junkyard muscle cars. *(CT492)*
America's Coolest Station Wagons *(CT493)*
Super Stock — A paperback version of a classic best seller. *(CT495)*
Rusty Pickups: American Workhorses Put to Pasture *(CT496)*
Jerry Heasley's Rare Finds — Great collection of Heasley's best finds. *(CT497)*
Street Sleepers: The Art of the Deceptively Fast Car *(CT498)*
Ed 'Big Daddy' Roth — Paperback reprint of a classic best seller. *(CT500)*
Rat Rods: Rodding's Imperfect Stepchildren *(CT486)*
East vs. West: Rods, Customs Rails *(CT501)*
Car Spy: Secret Cars Exposed by the Industry's Most Notorious Photographer *CT502)*

CarTech®, Inc. 39966 Grand Ave., North Branch, MN 55056. Ph: 800-551-4754 or 651-277-1200 • Fax: 651-277-1203
Brooklands Books Ltd., PO Box 146 Cobham, Surrey KT11 1LG, England. Ph: 01932 865051 • Fax 01932 868803
Brooklands Books Aus., 3/37-39 Green Street, Banksmeadow, NSW 2019, Australia. Ph: 2 9695 7055 • Fax 2 9695 7355

Visit us online at
www.cartechbooks.com for more info!

Additional books that may interest you...

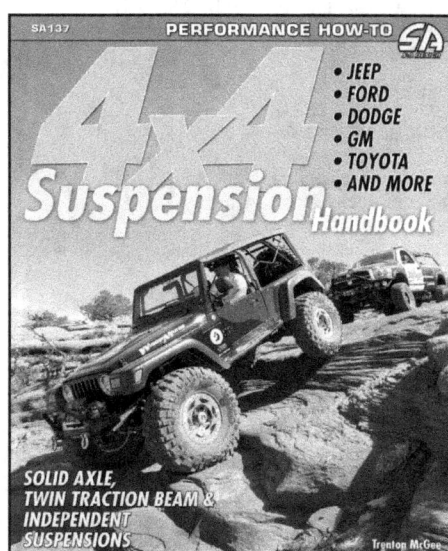

4x4 SUSPENSION HANDBOOK *by Trenton McGee* The popularity of off-roading and rock crawling is at an all-time high, and many people are upgrading their suspension systems for increased off-road prowess as well as for aesthetic and show-quality purposes. 4x4 and off-road suspension systems can be complicated, so it's important to understand them when making modifications and upgrades. This book covers front and rear solid axle, twin-traction beam, and independent suspension systems, as well as coil springs, leaf springs, shocks, and more on the types of suspensions available from all the major manufacturers including Jeep, Toyota, Ford, Chevy, and Dodge. Softbound, 8.5 x 11 inches, 144 pages, 260 color photos. ***Item # SA137***

ENGINE MANAGEMENT: ADVANCED TUNING *by Greg Banish* As tools for tuning modern engines have become more powerful and sophisticated in recent years, the need for in-depth knowledge of engine management systems and tuning techniques has grown. This book takes engine-tuning techniques to the next level, explaining how the EFI system determines engine operation and how the calibrator can change the controlling parameters to optimize actual engine performance. It is the most advanced book on the market, a must-have for tuners and calibrators and a valuable resource for anyone who wants to make horsepower with a fuel-injected, electronically controlled engine. Softbound, 8.5 x 11 inches, 128 pages, 250 color photos. ***Item # SA135***

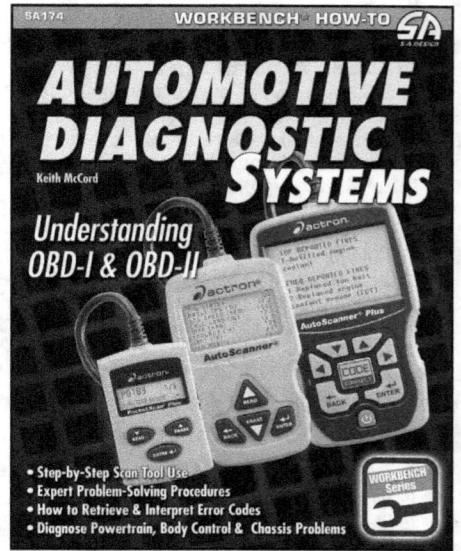

AUTOMOTIVE DIAGNOSTIC SYSTEMS: Understanding OBD I & OBD II *by Keith McCord* Currently, OBD II (OnBoard Diagnostic II) is the standard of the industry, and this book provides a thorough explanation of this system. It details its main features, capabilities, and characteristics. It shows how to access the port connector on the car, the serial data protocols, and what the serial data means. To understand the diagnostic codes, the numbering system is defined and the table of common DTCs is shown. But most importantly, McCord provides a thorough process for troubleshooting problems, tracing a problem to its root, explaining why DTCs may not lead to the source of the underlying problem, and ultimately resolving the problem. Softbound, 8.5 x 11 inches, 144 pages, 172 color photos. ***Item # SA174***

HOW TO DESIGN, BUILD & EQUIP YOUR AUTOMOTIVE WORKSHOP ON A BUDGET *by Jeffrey Zurschmeide* Most enthusiasts have a limited amount of car space and an even more limited budget. This book is designed to help the practical hobbyist mechanic make the most of any available space, balancing looks and functionality, while staying within almost any budget. Includes practical tips for common situations that mechanics encounter in a standard garage. Step-by-step instructions for the most essential and practical procedures, including basic electrical wiring, plumbing, workbenches, storage, organization, tool selection, and safety. Author Jeffrey Zurschmeide provides all the necessary information as you consider various tools, designs, installations, and products available for your automotive workspace. Softbound, 8.5 x 11 inches, 144 pages, 350 color photos. ***Item # SA207***

CHECK OUT CARTECH'S NEW, IMPROVED WEB SITE!

- Find helpful tech tips & articles
- Get bonus material from our books
- Browse expanded e-book selection
- Join the discussion on our blog
- Look inside books before you buy
- Rate & review your CarTech collection
- Easy, user-friendly navigation
- Sign up to get e-mails with special offers
- Lightning fast, spot-on search results
- Secure online ordering
- 24/7 access

- Check out our Featured Weekly Ride
- Reader's Rides – Show off your car!

www.cartechbooks.com

www.cartechbooks.com or 1-800-551-4754

www.ingramcontent.com/pod-product-compliance
Lightning Source LLC
Chambersburg PA
CBHW051412070526

44584CB00023B/3396